D0116859

The
Good
Egg

The
Good
Egg

More than 200 Fresh Approaches from Soup to Dessert

Marie Simmons

Houghton Mifflin Company

Boston New York

For information about permission to reproduce selections from
this book, write to Permissions, Houghton Mifflin Company,
215 Park Avenue South, New York, New York 10003.

Visit our Web site: www.hmco.com/trade.

Library of Congress Cataloging-in-Publication Data
Simmons, Marie
The good egg: more than 200 fresh approaches from soup to dessert /
Marie Simmons.
p.cm.
ISBN 0-395-90991-0
1. Cookery (Eggs) I. Title
TX745.S543 2000
641.6'75—dc21   00-026901

Book design by Lisa Diercks
Typeset in Perpetua
Cover photograph by Jim Scherer

Printed in the United States of America
RRD 10 9 8 7 6 5 4 3 2

Oh who that ever lived and loved
Can look upon an egg unmoved?
The egg it is the source of all.
'Tis everyone's ancestral hall.
The bravest chief that ever fought,
The lowest thief that e'er was caught,
The harlot's lip, the maiden's leg,
They each and all came from an egg.

The rocks that once by ocean's surge
Beheld the first of eggs emerge—
Obscure, defenseless, small and cold—
They little knew what egg could hold.
The gifts the reverent Magi gave,
Pandora's box, Aladdin's cave,
Wars, loves, and kingdoms, heaven and hell
All lay within that tiny shell.

Oh, join me gentlemen, I beg,
In honoring our friend, the egg.

—CLARENCE DAY, 1874–1935

"If you aren't up to a little magic occasionally, you shouldn't waste time trying to cook."

—COLETTE

Acknowledgments

So many people have helped me with this project that I barely know where to begin —I guess at the beginning. It was Shirley King and Susan Hermann Loomis, two veteran cookbook writers and colleagues, who convinced me that I should write this book. I am grateful to Judith Weber for her encouragement and for coming up with the title. I thank Rux Martin and Barry Estabrook at Houghton Mifflin for believing this would be a book long before it became a reality.

Many friends and colleagues kept me going throughout the long process. Although they weren't aware of it, Flo Braker and Shirley Corriher, two of my favorite teachers and cookbook authors, were constantly at my side as I read and reread their books, making sure that my meringues, soufflés, genoises and other desserts were as expert as theirs. Shirley and Harold McGee held my hand through the chapter on sauces and my struggle to understand the science of emulsion.

I found inspiration in the e-mails that my friend Ellye Bloom kept sending my way, filled with egg quotes, recipes and keen observations; the Peruvian egg stories from Nadia Merzliakov; translations of unusual Italian egg dishes from Michele Scicolone; favorite Thai recipes from Kasma Loha Unchit; and old family recipes from Mom and Aunt Tess, my good friend Tim Biancalana and Mom's neighbor Ann Hellyer.

A very special thanks to Linda Braun of the American Egg Board. Linda repeatedly went the extra mile for any information I needed, and for that I will always be indebted. Thanks as well to Howard Helmer for his wonderful egg stories and to Dr. Jill Snowdon and Dr. Don McNamara at the Egg Nutrition Council.

Thank you, Anna Teresa Callen, Alice Medrich, Kitty Morse, Jean Anderson and Paula Wolfert, for sharing your expertise and recipes so generously. Thank you to all our new friends in Oakland, California, and throughout the San Francisco Bay Area for putting up with my all-egg-recipe-testing dinner parties. Especially to my Oakland neighbor Jane Ellison, who didn't frown when I left quiche, custards and roulades on her doorstep or dropped off dozens of stuffed eggs just as her dinner guests were about to arrive.

I thank Peter and Debbie Rugh for being as warm, gracious and polite about my failures as they were exuberant about my successes. I thank dear friends Linda Carucci and Paula Hamilton for their help, love and laughter when I needed it most; Maria Lorraine Binchet for research assistance; Alan Ritch and Margaret Gordon at the University of California at Santa Cruz and Loyce Stulz at Indiana University for their impeccable research; and Grace Robinson for hand-delivering a hard-to-find out-of-print book on eggs and symbolism that I was determined to read.

Thank you, Mindy Shreil, for being there when the testing and retesting became over-whelming. Thanks to Lori Galvin-Frost for keeping things flowing smoothly at Houghton Mifflin, to designer Lisa Diercks and to Deborah DeLosa for creative publicity efforts.

This book would not be what it is without the help of David Nussbaum, who was my savior in the last intense hours.

Last, thank you, John. I am relieved to look up from my computer screen and from stacks of books and piles of papers and pots and pans and see that you are still here.

Contents

The Egg Man

 The egg man, whose name was Mr. Bell, delivered fresh-laid eggs to our house every Saturday afternoon. Two dozen, or more, if it was holiday time, kept us supplied for a week. I liked it when the egg man came, because he was friendly and loquacious and had the silly habit of asking and answering his own questions.

"Hello, how are you?" he would ask, and before we could say a word, he'd answer, "Fine, fine."

Then he would continue, "Nice day, isn't it? Yes, yes." And on and on. I found the one-way conversation fascinating.

My mother paid him 35 cents a dozen for those eggs—the freshest money could buy.

Introduction

A conversation with a couple of colleagues a few years ago led me to write this book. We were sharing food memories, and I found myself describing my favorite childhood breakfast: a soft-cooked egg.

On Saturday mornings, when there was no school bus to catch, my mother would cook an egg and present it to me in a colorful Mexican eggcup, a gift to me from my Aunt Tess. Alongside, crispy strips of buttered toast were lined up like little soldiers. With my tiny child's spoon, I'd carefully tap, tap, tap on the top of the shell until the crown shattered.

I'd peel away the flakes of shell carefully (the outside of the egg was very hot), finally exposing the shimmering white, then, with the spoon, break through to the molten yolk within. At last, putting down the spoon, I'd reach for the toast fingers and start dipping. As I savored the rich yolk and salty butter dripping from the toast, Mom let me dawdle and daydream, a rare luxury reserved for weekend mornings.

Recounting the details of this memory to my colleagues unleashed more egg memories: puffy cheddar cheese soufflés for dinner on meatless Friday nights; tender omelettes made by Dad as a Sunday-morning ritual; egg whites magically transformed into angel food cake served with berries and custard sauce (made from the yolks), traditionally prepared for our annual Fourth of July celebration; and Mom's fried green pepper and scrambled egg sandwiches wrapped in waxed paper and taken on the road, before the days of fast food.

As children, each of us had been encouraged to help out in the kitchen. From learning to separate eggs without breaking the yolks to turning the crank of the handheld egg-beater to making eggnog, scrambling eggs and peeling hard-cooked eggs — all the tasks were centered on our favorite food: the egg.

Our recollections eventually led — as those of avid cooks are wont to do — to a passionate discussion of the wonder of the egg and of the many recipes in which it plays a central role. Enough recipes, in fact, to fill a book.

I've added fresh twists to my favorite dishes, baking eggs in tomato-cilantro salsa, cooking them sunny-side up on crisp potatoes seasoned with fresh rosemary, poaching them and perching them on a creamy pillow of white corn polenta, scrambling them with fresh chanterelle mushrooms or using them to thicken a lamb stew in the Greek style with lemon juice. The egg has inspired me to create innumerable takeoffs on classics. I've wrapped omelettes around various fillings, including broccoli rabe sautéed with olive oil and garlic; avocado, bacon and Brie; even strawberries and ricotta cheese. Deviled eggs, too, proved the perfect canvas for my invention, stuffed with Italian tuna and capers or with salmon and potato or with cream cheese and chutney. And as for the favorite custard of my childhood, it's been reborn as a crème brûlée, delicately infused with Earl Grey tea.

Certainly the egg dishes I've eaten while traveling the globe have confirmed that the egg is universally revered. I've included some of the most memorable ones, such as a delightfully soft egg folded into an envelope of flaky filo dough, a favorite street food in Tunisia; eggs scrambled with vegetables and exotic spices from Morocco; and a Spanish layered omelette served with red pepper sauce that I enjoyed in a sunny square in Seville.

Who could imagine a world without pudding, pot de crème or flan? Without garlicky aïoli to stir into soup or spread on a sandwich? Without the pleasures of a soft-cooked egg in the morning? Eggs make a custard set, a sauce thicken, a cake rise and a soufflé puff. They add tenderness to cookies and tart shells and richness to soups and stews. I'm proud to say I couldn't do without them.

Taking a fresh look at the egg involved looking beyond the memories and the food to the hows and whys of egg cookery to understand how an egg and oil combine to create mayonnaise, why some omelettes turn hard while others cook up soft as satin and dozens of other pesky questions in between.

It also meant facing up to the fact that over the past several decades, the egg had fallen out of favor with health experts. During the 1970s and 1980s, scientific research into the effects of cholesterol in the body cast the egg under a cloud of suspicion and fear as a significant contributor to heart disease. To my astonishment, millions of Americans stopped eating eggs altogether or radically reduced their consumption of them. (Yet at the same time, I noticed, sales of "superpremium" ice creams soared.) The little oval that for thou-

Freshness: How to Get It, How to Keep It

 Can you actually taste the freshness of a farm-fresh egg? I can. A truly fresh egg—laid within the last day or two and kept refrigerated—has a clearly superior flavor. So whenever possible, I look for such eggs at my local farmers' market.

But if you follow the tips below, you can also find good-tasting, high-quality eggs in busy supermarkets. Proper refrigeration and handling are the keys to maintaining freshness, and a supermarket egg may well be "fresher" than a more recently laid egg that has not been kept cool. At room temperature, an egg deteriorates quickly: moisture and carbon monoxide escape through the thousands of tiny pores in the shell; the air cell in the egg expands and the egg white starts to thin. In fact, an egg at room temperature will "age" more in a single day than one that's been refrigerated for a week.

♦ Purchase eggs only from a busy market where there is a rapid turnover.

♦ Buy eggs only from refrigerated cases.

♦ Check the eggs in the carton, and don't buy any with cracked or soiled shells.

♦ Bring eggs home quickly (or keep them in a cooler in the car in warm weather). If an egg breaks on the way, discard it. Refrigerate eggs immediately once you're home.

♦ To maintain the proper temperature, leave the eggs in the carton and store them on an inside shelf of the refrigerator, not in those little egg slots on the door. The carton also prevents moisture loss and absorption of odors from other foods in the refrigerator.

sands of years had been hailed as the perfect food—and revered as a symbol of life—was cast in the role of killer!

Thankfully, as the new millennium unfolds, the clouds are beginning to lighten and the Big Scare is over. The latest dietary research shows what many of us egg lovers have always believed: for a healthy person, eating eggs in moderate amounts as part of a balanced diet —even every day—is perfectly fine. Scientists now agree that eating eggs and other foods that contain cholesterol does not necessarily raise the level of cholesterol in the blood or increase the risk of heart disease. (See the opposite page for more details.)

Nutritionists, too, are reaffirming what our mothers told us: the egg is good food. In fact, it's an incredible storehouse of nutrients. It remains the best source of complete protein of any food in our diet, delivering all the essential amino acids—the building blocks of protein—in the most efficient amounts and ratios to sustain growth and good health. In addition, eggs provide a host of vitamins and minerals, notably vitamin A and several important B vitamins. In fact, egg yolks are one of the few food sources for vitamin D, so critical for maintaining healthy bones and teeth.

But because of the egg phobia that has gripped America for the past few decades, it's my guess that today there are quite possibly one (even two) new generations that know nothing about cooking, eating and truly enjoying an egg. *The Good Egg*, I hope, can help them learn some of the lessons they missed. Eggs are inexpensive and plentiful and, in an age when there seems to be less and less time to cook, a more practical food than ever. So let's get cracking!

The Cholesterol Controversy

During the 1970s and 1980s—for perhaps the first time in the 5,000 years that people have kept chickens—the egg seemed to be headed for the endangered (even dangerous) food list. Medical research had linked high levels of cholesterol in the blood to increased risk of heart disease. And since egg yolks are relatively high in cholesterol, it was widely held that individuals who consumed eggs regularly would suffer increases in their blood cholesterol levels.

That assumption has now been shown to be erroneous: there is no direct link between the amount of cholesterol in a particular food and the level of cholesterol in the blood. Many studies have found that the vast majority of people who are not genetically predisposed to coronary disease can eat eggs every day with no increased risk to their health. At the same time, research has shown that blood cholesterol levels are more affected by the amount of fats, especially saturated fats, in the diet. And from that perspective, eggs look a whole lot better. One large egg has less than 2 grams of saturated fat, while a cup of whole milk has 5 grams and a tablespoon of butter a cautionary 7 grams.

Eggs are a wonderfully tasty, inexpensive and marvelously nutritious food, and in a balanced diet that includes plenty of fresh fruits, vegetables and grains and a moderate amount of meats and other fatty foods, they are, and should continue to be, a delicious staple in our kitchens.

Choices at the Egg Case

It used to be that consumers had a selection of only medium, large or jumbo eggs and brown or white eggs. But today the egg cases of our food markets hold a range of choices.

Fertile eggs are produced by hens who have mated with a rooster and, if incubated, could develop into chicks. Some ethnic groups consider fertile eggs a delicacy, but there are no known advantages to consuming them. They may contain a small amount of male hormone, although scientists believe it is more likely that the hormone dissipates once the egg is laid.

Free-range eggs are produced by hens raised outdoors or with daily access to the outdoors. Eggs from hens that roam and scratch for food and so have a varied diet generally have deep yellow yolks and a more distinct eggy flavor than eggs from large hatcheries, although their nutritional content is the same. But be aware that the term can be used misleadingly. Some egg farms with large indoor facilities where hens can roam indoors refer to themselves as "free-range." Free-range eggs are generally somewhat more expensive than eggs from a large commercial hatchery, but to me, the taste is worth it.

Nutrient-enhanced eggs, a recent entry in the supermarket case, come from hens on special diets. By giving their birds nutrient-rich feeds, some egg farmers have been successful at decreasing the saturated-fat content and increasing the unsaturated-fat content of the eggs. Other feed choices have resulted in eggs with added omega-3 fatty acids, the ones found in fish, which confer the same heart-protecting benefits. Still other eggs have increased levels of vitamins and/or minerals. These specialty eggs are found under several brand names and, depending on feed costs, at various prices in the stores. Check labels for nutrient facts.

Organic eggs come from hens that have been fed rations with ingredients that were grown organically, following strict agricultural limits on pesticides, fungicides, herbicides and commercial fertilizers and antibiotics. Owing to higher production costs and lower volume per farm, organic eggs are more expensive than eggs from hens fed conventional feed, but they taste better and their health benefits are well worth the small extra cost.

Vegetarian eggs are produced by hens on chicken feed containing only vegetable foods and no meat or seafood byproducts. Like free-range eggs, these tend to have an eggier flavor.

CHAPTER 1   *Artfully Scrambled and Fried*

"Scrambled eggs have been made, and massacred, for as long as people knew about pots and pans, no doubt."
—M.F.K. FISHER

Scrambled eggs are simple to "massacre," as M.F.K. Fisher correctly observed, but it's just as easy to make them right—moist and tender, full of flavor and with all kinds of delicious embellishments. All it takes is a good pan and a bit of know-how.

I got my perfect pan when I was just a newlywed and my husband brought home a small heavy black cast-iron skillet. This, he informed me, was to be reserved for scrambled eggs. And, he added, it should never be touched by soap or water: after each use, it must be wiped clean with a towel and "seasoned" with a small amount of vegetable oil. Here, I thought, is a man who takes his scrambled eggs seriously—and from then on, so did I.

Over the past three decades, I have carefully cooked thousands of eggs into creamy scrambles in that pan, perfecting my basic technique and concocting countless tasty variations. Though I confess that I have broken the rules once or twice—dipping the pan in hot soapy water when absolutely necessary—I have always wiped, heated and oiled it afterwards to maintain its beautiful dark patina.

My basic scrambled eggs are as simple as can be: I crack the eggs into a bowl, add a small pinch of salt (too much can toughen the whites) and beat them lightly with a fork for just a few moments, until the broken yolks are marbled with streaks of white. I heat the pan slowly, add a pat of butter and wait until it starts to sizzle. Then I pour in the eggs and stir them slowly and steadily with a heatproof rubber spatula or a round or flat-edged wooden spoon as large curds form. In only a minute or so, when the curds are evenly cooked but still moist, the eggs are ready to serve. That's it!

Unadorned scrambled eggs are wonderful, but I love scrambled eggs best as a canvas for flavorful combinations and culinary inspirations. With a few well-chosen additions, you can scramble up a special dish for brunch, lunch or even dinner. You don't need a pan seasoned by decades of use—and married bliss—to make scrambled eggs my way; a heavy nonstick pan will do just as well.

Perfect fried eggs, like scrambles, are quick and easy, provided you have a good pan and pay attention to what's cooking in it. Almost everyone loves the familiar sound of eggs sputtering in butter (or bacon fat) in a big skillet on the stove. But eggs fried that way are usually tough and greasy. My own fried-egg method is leaner and quieter. I use a heavy pan, a small amount of butter, oil or cooking spray and, most important, gentle cooking over low to medium heat. Gentle heat is the secret: I keep the pan just hot enough to set the egg whites, so that they don't run all over the pan, but low enough so that they don't cook too fast or toughen and the yolks thicken but stay evenly soft, without any hard spots. And with low heat, my eggs absorb less fat, making them lighter and more palatable.

I love the simplicity of a plain fried egg: the sunny yolk, its silken richness next to the white. But there are lots of lovely enhancements, as you will find in the following recipes. Nap fried eggs with sauces, set them on top of sautéed vegetables or stack them in a savory tower of eggplant, tomato and mozzarella slices.

Scrambled Perfection: The Basics

 ♦ **Choose the right pan:** One that's heavy, preferably non-stick, or a well-seasoned cast-iron pan, according to the number of eggs you are cooking. For 2 eggs, use a 6-inch pan; for 4 eggs, an 8-inch pan; for 6 to 8 eggs, a 10-inch pan.

♦ **Break the eggs into a bowl** instead of directly into the pan. That way, if a piece of shell falls into the egg, you can remove it more easily. The eggs are also easier to beat to the right consistency in a bowl.

♦ **Season to taste:** Before you mix the eggs, add a sprinkling of any of the following: kosher salt and coarsely ground black pepper; freshly grated Parmigiano-Reggiano, Asiago or other hard grating cheese; fresh thyme (lemon thyme is lovely) or rosemary leaves stripped from the stems or snipped fresh chives, fresh dill or sliced scallion greens. You can also add a bit of cream or milk for greater richness or a little water, which will create steam and make the eggs lighter and fluffier. Use no more than 1 tablespoon liquid per egg.

♦ **Beat the eggs briefly** to the desired consistency—streaky or uniformly mixed—but for no more than 10 seconds so they remain thick, not liquefied. Use a wire whisk or fork. Don't use a silver fork, because the eggs will tarnish it.

♦ **Cook over low to medium-low heat:** Heat the dry pan over low to medium-low heat, then add 1 scant teaspoon butter per egg. When the butter starts to sizzle, pour in the eggs all at once. Stir slowly and constantly with a round wooden spoon for large curds, or gently scrape the eggs with the flat edge of a wooden or heatproof rubber spatula to create soft, fluffy curds. For small, moist curds, stir rapidly with a fork. Tilt the pan as necessary to distribute the runny uncooked egg into the set curds.

♦ **Serve immediately:** Residual heat in the pan can dry and toughen the eggs. As soon as they are done, remove the pan from the heat and spoon the eggs onto warm plates or a serving platter.

French-Style Scrambled Eggs

These French-style scrambled eggs are made in the top of a double boiler.

2 tablespoons unsalted butter

4 large eggs

Kosher salt and freshly ground black pepper

Warm buttered toast

1. Place 1 inch of water in the bottom of a double boiler and heat until boiling; reduce the heat to very low. When the water is simmering, place the top of the double boiler over the water. Add 1 tablespoon of the butter and heat until melted.

2. Meanwhile, whisk the eggs in a medium bowl just until combined. Add the remaining 1 tablespoon butter, cut into small pieces, salt to taste and a grinding of pepper. Pour into the double boiler.

3. Cook, stirring constantly with a wooden spoon or heatproof rubber spatula, until the eggs are thickened into soft curds, 10 to 15 minutes.

4. To serve, place a slice of toast on the side of each of two plates and spoon the eggs into the center.

Makes 2 servings

Eggs Scrambled with Parmesan and Rosemary

For this dish, the cheese is chopped into small pieces, not grated. Serve piled on thin slices of toasted Italian bread.

4–6 **large eggs**

 ½ **cup chopped (¼-to-½-inch pieces) Parmigiano-Reggiano cheese**

 2 **tablespoons unsalted butter**

 4 **large slices (or more) Italian or other crusty bread, toasted and buttered**

 ½ **teaspoon chopped fresh rosemary**

  Freshly ground black pepper

1. Whisk the eggs and cheese in a medium bowl until blended.

2. Melt the butter in a medium nonstick skillet over medium heat. When the butter sizzles, reduce the heat to low, add the egg mixture all at once and cook, stirring gently, until soft-set but still creamy, about 2 minutes.

3. Spoon the eggs onto the toast. Sprinkle with the rosemary and a grinding of pepper. Serve at once.

Makes 2 to 3 servings

For a heartier meal, serve grilled sausages on the side.

Parmigiano-Reggiano: How to Recognize the Best

 Considered by experts to be the best Parmesan cheese, Parmigiano-Reggiano is a cow's milk cheese made only in areas of Emilia and Mantua in Italy. It is a hard cheese, aged 18 months to 3 years, and is delicious grated or served in curls or chunks. It melts in your mouth and has a rich nutty flavor that isn't sharp or strong. Save the rind (which is simply the outside of the cheese that has been hardened by exposure to air) and add to soups, where it will cook up soft and chewy. Beware impostors—there are many—and if in doubt, ask to see the whole wheel of cheese. If it's the real thing, it will have the words "Parmigiano-Reggiano" stenciled on the outside.

Favorite Summertime Scramble with Tomato and Basil

Often the most satisfying dishes are those made with freshly harvested local ingredients. Plum tomatoes and basil from the farmers' market make the flavors in this favorite summertime combination sing.

2 tablespoons extra-virgin olive oil

1 garlic clove, minced

2 plum tomatoes, cored and diced (about 1 cup)

Kosher salt and freshly ground black pepper

4–5 large eggs

2 tablespoons freshly grated Parmigiano-Reggiano cheese

2 tablespoons torn fresh basil leaves

Warm buttered toast

1. Heat the oil and garlic in a large nonstick skillet over medium-low heat just until the garlic begins to sizzle. Add the tomatoes and sprinkle with salt to taste and a grinding of pepper.

2. Whisk the eggs in a medium bowl. Whisk in the cheese. Add to the skillet, reduce the heat to low and cook, stirring gently, until the eggs are soft-set but still creamy, about 2 minutes. Sprinkle with the basil and serve with the toast.

Makes 2 servings

Serve for breakfast, lunch or a light supper.

Eggs Scrambled with Wild Mushrooms and Fresh Herbs

If chanterelles are not available, try a mixture of oyster, shiitake and white button mushrooms.

2 tablespoons unsalted butter

8 ounces chanterelle mushrooms, rinsed, dried, trimmed and cut into ½-inch pieces

½ cup chopped fresh parsley

1 tablespoon minced fresh thyme or a mixture of thyme, rosemary and marjoram

1 garlic clove, minced

Kosher salt and freshly ground black pepper

6 large eggs

Buttered toasted French bread

1. Melt the butter in a large nonstick skillet over medium-low heat. When the foam subsides, add the mushrooms and sauté, stirring, until just beginning to soften, about 3 minutes. Add the parsley, thyme or herb mixture and garlic and sauté for 1 minute. Sprinkle with salt to taste and a grinding of pepper.

2. Whisk the eggs in a large bowl. Add the eggs to the skillet, reduce the heat to low and cook, stirring gently, until the eggs are soft-set but still creamy, about 3 minutes. Serve immediately with the toast.

Makes 2 to 3 servings

Scrambled Eggs with Ricotta Cheese

My friend Linda Carucci shared this recipe, which her grandmother, Filomena Maulucci Guglietta, used to make with the ricotta from the family's commercial dairy in Bloomfield, Connecticut. "The ricotta was warm, soft and custardy and had a delicious flavor I can recall to this day," says Linda. Even with ordinary ricotta, however, this dish is wonderful. Be careful not to overcook the eggs, or they will "weep"—the result should be a soft, creamy cloud of eggs.

6 large eggs

1 cup whole-milk ricotta cheese, stirred to blend

1 tablespoon unsalted butter

   Kosher salt and freshly ground black pepper

1 tablespoon torn fresh basil leaves

   Generously buttered toasted Italian bread

2 tomatoes, cored and thinly sliced (optional, in season)

1. Combine the eggs and ricotta in a large bowl and whisk until blended.

2. Melt the butter in a large nonstick skillet over medium-low heat. When the foam subsides, add the egg mixture. Cook, stirring constantly, until the eggs are soft-set but still creamy, about 3 minutes. Do not allow the eggs to develop a curdlike consistency—that means they are overcooked.

3. Sprinkle with salt to taste and a grinding of pepper. Sprinkle with the basil leaves and serve at once, with the toast and tomatoes, if using.

Makes 2 to 4 servings

VARIATION

Sauté 1 cup chopped tomatoes in the butter until the juices evaporate, then add the egg mixture in step 1. Proceed as directed, omitting the sliced tomatoes.

Creamy Scrambled Eggs with Curry and Cardamom

Whisking eggs with a bit of heavy cream creates soft, fluffy scrambled eggs. The curry and cardamom flavor is hauntingly delicate.

4 **large eggs**

2 **tablespoons heavy cream**

Pinch of kosher salt

½ **teaspoon curry powder**

¼ **teaspoon ground cardamom**

1 **tablespoon unsalted butter**

1–2 **tomatoes, cored and thinly sliced, for garnish**

Chopped fresh cilantro for garnish

Warm buttered toast

1. Whisk the eggs, cream and salt in a medium bowl until just blended.

2. Sprinkle the curry powder and cardamom into a large nonstick skillet over medium-low heat. After about 20 seconds, add the butter. When the butter begins to sizzle, add the eggs all at once. Cook the eggs, stirring slowly with a flat wooden spatula or heat-proof rubber spatula, just until the eggs are set, about 2 minutes.

3. Transfer to plates and garnish with the tomato and a sprinkling of cilantro. Serve immediately with the toast.

Makes 2 servings

Cheddar Scrambled Eggs
in Tortillas with Tomato-Avocado Salsa

This is a great dish for breakfast, lunch or a casual dinner. You can serve it in one of two different ways. Either let everybody assemble his or her own tortillas, helping themselves from a warm platter of the eggs, a serving basket with the tortillas wrapped in a napkin and a bowl of the salsa, or put the tortillas together yourself and serve them lined up on a large serving platter or on individual dinner plates.

8 10-inch flour tortillas

Tomato-Avocado Salsa

2 cups diced plum tomatoes (about 6)

½ pitted and peeled avocado, diced

½ cup chopped red or yellow onion

¼ cup minced fresh cilantro

2 tablespoons fresh lemon or lime juice

2 tablespoons extra-virgin olive oil

1 jalapeño, seeded and finely chopped (optional)

Kosher salt

1. Preheat the oven to 350°F. Wrap the tortillas in foil and place in the oven until warm, about 10 minutes.

2. **Meanwhile, make the salsa:** In a medium bowl, combine the tomatoes, avocado, onion, cilantro, lemon or lime juice, oil, jalapeño (if using) and salt to taste. Set aside.

Although there are three different parts to this dish, none of them is difficult to prepare. The tortillas can warm in the oven while you put together the salsa. Once that's done, just scramble the eggs.

6–8 **large eggs**

¼ **cup water**

1 **teaspoon kosher salt**
Freshly ground black pepper

1 **tablespoon extra-virgin olive**
oil

½ **cup grated cheddar or**
Monterey Jack cheese

6 **large soft lettuce leaves,**
washed, dried and cut
crosswise into thin slices
(about 4 cups)

½ **cup sour cream or plain**
yogurt (optional)

3. Break the eggs into a large bowl. Add the water, salt and a grinding of pepper. Whisk until blended. Heat the oil in a large nonstick skillet over medium-low heat. Add the eggs and cook, stirring gently, until soft-set, 3 to 5 minutes. Sprinkle the eggs with the cheese, cover and remove from the heat.

4. Place a handful of the lettuce on each warm tortilla. Add a spoonful of the eggs in a strip down the center, top with about ⅓ cup of the salsa and add a spoonful of the sour cream or yogurt, if using. One at a time, roll up the tortillas and place seam side down on a platter. Cover with foil to keep warm while you assemble the remaining tortillas. Or, if you prefer, simply set out a basket of the warm tortillas, a platter of the eggs and the lettuce, salsa and sour cream or yogurt, if desired, in serving bowls and let each person assemble his or her own tortilla.

Makes 4 servings

Eggs Scrambled with Salt Cod and Crispy Potatoes

The idea for this dish came from a Brazilian friend. Salt cod, once a staple aboard ships, can be hard to find in some areas and is sometimes expensive. Look for it in Italian or Latino specialty stores or in well-stocked supermarkets. Select salt cod that is meaty and fairly white. Plan ahead: the cod must be soaked in a bowl of water in the refrigerator for at least 24 hours.

8	ounces salt cod
2	tablespoons extra-virgin olive oil
2	large all-purpose potatoes, peeled and diced (about 3 cups)
½	cup diced onion
1	teaspoon minced fresh rosemary
	Freshly ground black pepper
4–6	large eggs
	Pinch of kosher salt

1. Cut the salt cod into 2-inch chunks, place in a bowl and add cold water to cover. Soak in the refrigerator for 24 hours or more, changing the water at least four times. Drain.

2. Fill a medium saucepan half-full with water and bring to a boil. Add the cod, reduce the heat to medium-low and poach for 15 minutes. Drain the cod well and pat dry with paper towels. Remove any bones and tear the cod into small pieces.

3. Heat the oil in a large nonstick skillet over medium-high heat until hot enough to sizzle a cube of potato. Add the potatoes and sauté, turning frequently, for about 10 minutes. Add the onion and cook until the potatoes are golden brown and the onion is tender, about 5 minutes more. Stir in the cod, rosemary and a grinding of pepper.

4. Whisk the eggs with the salt in a medium bowl. Reduce the heat to low, pour the eggs over the potato mixture and cook, stirring gently, until the eggs are soft-set but still creamy, about 2 minutes. Serve immediately.

Makes 4 servings

This is a perfect dish to serve for brunch with a crisp green salad and an equally crisp white wine.

Eggs Scrambled with Buckwheat Groats, Mushrooms and Onions

Groats, hulled buckwheat kernels (known as kasha when they are roasted), can be found in most health-food stores and in the organic section of some supermarkets. They have a decidedly nutty taste, not unlike wheat berries, but cook up almost as quickly as rice. A coarse or medium grind is best for this recipe. The heat from the jalapeño adds a nice kick to an otherwise mild dish.

3 **tablespoons unsalted butter**

2 **cups sliced white button or cremini mushrooms**

½ **cup chopped onion**

1 **garlic clove, minced (optional)**

   Kosher salt and freshly ground black pepper

2 **cups cooked buckwheat groats, at room temperature (see box)**

4–6 **large eggs**

1 **tablespoon minced jalapeño**

1. Melt 2 tablespoons of the butter in a large nonstick skillet over medium heat. When the foam subsides, add the mushrooms, onion and garlic, if using, and cook, stirring, until the onion is tender and the mushrooms are lightly browned. Sprinkle with salt to taste and a grinding of pepper. Stir in the buckwheat groats and cook until heated through, about 1 minute. Reduce the heat to low.

2. Whisk the eggs with the jalapeño and a pinch of salt in a large bowl. Using a spatula, push the buckwheat mixture to the edges of the skillet. Place the remaining 1 tablespoon butter in the center of the skillet and, when it is melted, pour in the eggs. Cook until the eggs begin to set on the bottom, about 2 minutes. Cook, stirring gently, until soft-set but still creamy, about 2 minutes more. Carefully stir the eggs into the buckwheat mixture, trying not to break them up too much. Serve immediately.

Makes 2 to 3 servings

TO COOK BUCKWHEAT GROATS: *Stir 1 cup buckwheat groats into 2 cups boiling salted water. Cook, uncovered, stirring occasionally, for about 15 minutes, or until tender. Drain. You will have 3 cups groats. You need 2 cups for this recipe.*

Scrambled Eggs with Olives, Onions and Cilantro

This Moroccan stew incorporates scrambled eggs and is delicious served as a brunch or supper dish with crusty bread to sop up the juices. The recipe is adapted from Moroccan-born writer Kitty Morse from her book *Cooking at the Kasbah* (Chronicle Books, 1998).

20 green olives, pitted

1 28-ounce can plum tomatoes, with their juice

2 tablespoons extra-virgin olive oil

2 onions, finely chopped

½ teaspoon sugar

2 garlic cloves, minced

1 bay leaf

8 large eggs

¼ cup minced fresh cilantro, plus whole leaves for garnish

2 teaspoons ground cumin

½ teaspoon kosher salt

Freshly ground black pepper

1. Fill a small saucepan half-full with water and bring to a boil. Add the olives and boil for 1 minute. Drain and set aside.

2. Set a strainer over a large bowl and drain the tomatoes in it. Remove the tomatoes from the strainer, leaving it set over the bowl. Halve the tomatoes, scoop out the seeds and pulp and return the seeds and pulp to the strainer. Set the tomato flesh aside. With a wooden spoon, press down on the seeds and pulp to extract as much juice as possible. Discard the seeds and pulp. Add the tomatoes to the strained juices and set aside.

3. Heat the oil in a large nonstick skillet over medium-low heat. Add the onions, olives and sugar. Cook, stirring, until the onions are golden but not browned, about 10 minutes. Add the tomatoes and their juices, the garlic and bay leaf and cook, breaking up the tomatoes with a spoon, until most of the liquid has evaporated and the sauce has thickened, about 20 minutes. Remove and discard the bay leaf.

4. In a large bowl, whisk the eggs with the minced cilantro, cumin, salt and a grinding of pepper. Pour the egg mixture into the skillet, increase the heat to medium and cook, stirring gently, until the eggs are set. Transfer to a serving bowl and garnish with cilantro leaves.

Serve with crusty bread.

Makes 4 servings

Scrambled Eggs as Meditation

My regular scrambled eggs take just a few minutes to prepare, but in *With Bold Knife and Fork*, M.F.K. Fisher boasts that hers "take about a half hour to prepare, and they are worth waiting for."

Now, inspired by Ms. Fisher, I occasionally do cook scrambled eggs very slowly in a double boiler, a method that is quite extravagant when you consider the time spent stirring. What intrigues me about the technique is that she cooks her eggs not in a double boiler but in a warm skillet. First she melts some sweet butter in a heavy pan, then adds some cream and breaks the eggs into this "gentle puddle." She stirs the eggs very carefully and slowly with a spoon, "gradually pulling in the sides as they cook." She must keep the heat *very* low, because after half an hour, she claims, the finished eggs are "lightly blended and set . . . in large soft curds."

She calls her technique a "dreamy process," and I agree. I'm a believer in the Chinese proverb that says, "Working with the hands frees the mind for other things," and her recipe is a perfect example of cooking as meditation. The recipe, she says, "will not succeed if the cook is either hurried or harried." This unhurried state of mind is beneficial for both the cook and the eggs.

Scrambled Eggs Mu Shu Pork–Style

My favorite version of mu shu pork, as served in my local Chinese restaurant, is a delicate mélange of slivered marinated pork, Chinese mushrooms and other vegetables surrounded by tender clumps of scrambled egg. It's served without the traditional pancakes. Traditionally, mu shu pork is made with bamboo shoots, but since I'm not a fan of the canned type, which is usually all that's available, I've used fresh spinach leaves instead. Serve on a bed of hot steamed rice.

2 tablespoons cloud ears (also known as black mushrooms)

¼ cup golden needle mushrooms (about 20)

5 teaspoons soy sauce, plus more to taste

1 tablespoon water

2 teaspoons cornstarch

2 teaspoons dry sherry or white wine

1 8-ounce piece pork tenderloin (about ½ tenderloin), cut into ⅛-inch-thick diagonal slices

4 large eggs

Kosher salt

2 tablespoons chicken broth, vegetable broth or water

1 teaspoon sugar

1. Place the cloud ears and golden needle mushrooms in two separate medium bowls; cover with boiling water. Let stand for at least 30 minutes, or until softened.

2. Meanwhile, combine 2 teaspoons of the soy sauce, the water, cornstarch and sherry or white wine in a pie plate and stir to blend. Add the slices of pork and turn to coat. Cover and let stand while the mushrooms are soaking.

3. Once the mushrooms have been rehydrated (the cloud ears will become large and floppy and the golden needles soft and pliable), drain them. Cut out and discard the hard core from the center of the cloud ears and the hard tips from the golden needles. Pat dry with a paper towel and set aside.

4. Whisk the eggs with ½ teaspoon salt in a medium bowl; set aside. In a small bowl, stir together the broth or water, the remaining 1 tablespoon soy sauce and the sugar; set aside.

3 tablespoons vegetable oil

1 tablespoon finely chopped
   ginger

1 bag (6 ounces) baby spinach
   (about 2 cups packed)

5. Heat a large skillet or a wok over medium-high heat until hot enough to evaporate a drop of water upon contact. Add 1 tablespoon of the oil and reduce the heat to medium-low. Add the eggs all at once and let cook into a large flat omelette, lifting the edges as they set and tilting the pan so that the runny center can run under the edges. When the eggs are almost set, break the pancake into pieces with the spatula and transfer to a plate. Do not overcook; the eggs should still be very soft.

6. Add 1 tablespoon of the oil and the ginger to the pan; stir-fry for 30 seconds. Add the cloud ears and golden needles and stir-fry just to coat with oil; transfer to the dish with the eggs.

7. Add the remaining 1 tablespoon oil to the pan. When it is very hot, add the slices of pork in batches, separating the slices with a chopstick or spatula, and stir-fry just until no longer pink. Add the broth mixture and stir-fry just to coat the pork. Add the reserved eggs and mushrooms and the spinach, increase the heat to high and stir-fry just until the spinach wilts, about 45 seconds. Sprinkle with salt and soy sauce to taste and serve immediately.

Makes 4 servings

Tree ears (also called wood ears and cloud ears) and lily buds (also called golden needles and dried tiger lilies) are sold in plastic bags at markets that carry Chinese ingredients. Both need to be soaked before using. Dried tree ears and lily buds will keep indefinitely, tightly sealed.

Scrambled Eggs Piperade

Piperade is a tomato, red pepper, onion and egg specialty from the Basque region of northern Spain, in the Pyrenees along the French border. Like the rest of the food of the Basque people, this dish is hearty and flavorful. It has many variations. Sometimes the tomato mixture is cooked into a sauce and served over scrambled eggs. Sometimes it is made with ham, sometimes with bacon. In this version, beaten eggs are stirred directly into the sauce. The trick is to resist the desire to overcook the eggs. They should remain fluid and creamy, which they will if you slowly stir them with a fork over low heat as they cook. Serve with toast or oven-roasted cubed potatoes.

¼ cup bacon fat

4 onions, halved lengthwise and cut lengthwise into thin slices (about 3 cups)

2 green bell peppers, cored, seeded and cut into ¼-inch-wide strips

1 red bell pepper, cored, seeded and cut into ¼-inch-wide strips

3 ripe tomatoes, cored and cut into ¼-inch dice (about 3 cups)

1 garlic clove, minced (optional)

½ cup diced ham (optional)

1 teaspoon kosher salt
Freshly ground black pepper

6–8 large eggs

1. Heat the bacon fat in a large nonstick skillet over medium-low heat. Add the onions and bell peppers and cook, stirring, until very tender but not browned, about 10 minutes.

2. Add the tomatoes and garlic, if using, increase the heat to medium and cook, stirring, until the liquid evaporates, about 10 minutes. Add the ham (if using), the salt and a grinding of pepper.

3. Whisk the eggs in a large bowl. Add the eggs all at once to the skillet, reduce the heat to low and cook, gently stirring the eggs into the vegetables with a fork, until the eggs are soft-set but still creamy, about 3 minutes. Serve immediately.

Makes 4 servings

VARIATION

Keep the cooked vegetable mixture warm over low heat. In another large nonstick skillet, melt 2 tablespoons butter. Cook the eggs, stirring gently, until soft-set but still creamy, about 3 minutes. Spoon the eggs onto a platter and top with the vegetable mixture.

Brown Eggs or White?

 Brown eggs come from chicken breeds with reddish brown feathers, such as Rhode Island Red, New Hampshire and Plymouth Rock, breeds that are favored by New Englanders. The vast majority of eggs in the United States are white and come from breeds with white feathers and earlobes, such as the most common American chicken, the "single comb" White Leghorn. Named for the town of Livorno, Italy ("Leghorn" in English), this breed reaches maturity early, utilizes its feed efficiently, has a small body size, adapts well to different climates and produces a relatively large number of eggs.

A fairly rare breed called Araucana lays eggs in varying pastel shades of blue and green.

The bottom line: the color of the eggshell is purely a function of the breed of the chicken; it has no bearing on the taste or the nutritional content of the egg.

Fabulous Fried

Sunny-Side Up, Over Easy or "In the Shade"

 ♦ **Choose the right size pan:** Select a heavy pan, prefer-ably nonstick, with sloping sides, which make it easier to reach in with a wide spatula. For 1 egg, use a 6-inch pan; for 2 eggs, use an 8-inch pan; for 3 or 4 eggs, use a 10-inch pan. For more than 4 eggs, fry in batches.

♦ **Use a small amount of cooking fat:** 1 teaspoon of butter or oil for each egg is usually enough. I prefer to fry eggs in butter, but when I am serving them with an olive oil–based garnish, I use olive oil as the frying medium, to match the flavors. To reduce the saturated fat, you can fry with nonstick cooking spray, vegetable oil or a mixture of half vegetable oil and half butter.

♦ **Heat the pan slowly:** Typically, I heat the pan over medium-low heat just enough so that I can feel the warmth (not searing heat!) of the pan when I hold my hand about 1 inch from its surface. Then I add the butter or oil and reduce the heat to low. (If using cooking spray, coat the cold pan and then begin to heat.) Butter is hot enough when it begins to sizzle; oil is hot enough when a drop of egg or a bread crumb sizzles gently when added.

♦ **Add the eggs carefully:** Breaking an egg on the side of the pan and flopping it into a hot skillet can risk broken yolks, shell fragments and burned fingers. I like to crack each egg into a small bowl or cup so I can remove any bits of eggshell or blood spots. (Use the tip of a knife or a tea-spoon-sized piece of the broken shell.) Also, if the yolk breaks when placed in the cup, the egg can be saved for another purpose. Pour each egg from the cup into a clear spot in the hot pan.

♦ **Fry the eggs over low to medium-low heat.**

Sunny-Side Up
Cook the eggs until the white begins to set, about 1 minute. For a very delicate white and a thick, creamy yolk, cover the pan and cook the eggs over low heat for about 5 minutes. Alternatively, cook the eggs entirely uncovered, adjusting the heat between medium and medium-low, for 4 to 5 minutes total time. This method produces a creamy yolk that is gently set on the bottom and a white that is lightly browned on the bottom.

Over Easy or Over Light
In this method of frying, the film of white that covers the yolk is set with direct heat. Cook the eggs as for sunny-side up, but flip each egg over during the last 15 to 20 seconds of cooking. The challenge here is to turn the egg over and then out of the pan without breaking the yolk in the process. It's easiest to use a wide spatula. As in everything, practice makes perfect.

Sunny Side in the Shade
This is my name for a method that lightly cooks the thin layer of white covering the yolk but doesn't involve flipping. Fry the eggs following the procedure for sunny-side up, covering the pan after the whites are set. During the last 2 minutes of cooking, lift the lid and quickly sprinkle the eggs with 2 to 3 teaspoons of water. Immediately cover the pan and continue cooking. The steam will "baste" the eggs and set the film of white around the yolk, putting the sunny side "in the shade."

Fried Eggs with Fresh Tomato Salsa

Although eggs with butter are classic, my Italian-American heritage sometimes makes me yearn for eggs with olive oil.

Tomato Salsa

- 1 **cup diced ripe plum tomatoes**
- 2 **tablespoons chopped fresh basil**
- 1 **tablespoon minced sweet onion**
- ¼ **teaspoon minced garlic**

- 2 **tablespoons extra-virgin olive oil**
- 4 **large eggs**
  Kosher salt and freshly ground black pepper
  Toasted Italian bread

1. **Make the salsa:** Combine the tomatoes, basil, onion and garlic in a small bowl. Set aside.

2. Heat the oil in a large nonstick skillet over medium-low heat. When the oil is hot, break the eggs one a time into a cup and slip into the skillet. Reduce the heat to low and cook until the whites begin to set, about 1 minute. Cover and cook until the yolks are cooked to the desired doneness, about 5 minutes more. Transfer the eggs to two warm plates.

3. Immediately add the tomato mixture to the skillet and cook, stirring, over medium heat until just heated through, about 2 minutes. Sprinkle with salt to taste and a grinding of pepper and spoon the salsa over the eggs. Serve at once with the toast.

Makes 2 servings

Fried Eggs with Malt Vinegar and Butter Sauce

A simple way to make fried eggs just a little bit special is to deglaze the skillet with vinegar after you fry them and swirl in a little butter. The result is a creamy, tangy sauce to drizzle over the eggs. I like to use malt vinegar, but any flavorful vinegar will do.

5 tablespoons cold unsalted butter, cut into ¼-inch pieces

4 large eggs

½ cup malt vinegar or other flavorful aged vinegar

Kosher salt and freshly ground black pepper

4 slices sourdough bread, toasted and buttered

1. Warm two plates in the oven set to the lowest setting.

2. Meanwhile, melt 2 tablespoons of the butter in a large nonstick skillet over medium-low heat. When the butter sizzles, break the eggs one at a time into a cup and slip into the skillet. Reduce the heat to low and fry until the whites begin to set, about 1 minute. Cover and cook until the yolks are cooked to the desired doneness, about 5 minutes more. Transfer the eggs to the warm plates.

3. Immediately add the vinegar to the skillet, increase the heat to high and boil until reduced to 2 tablespoons, about 2 minutes. Remove from the heat. Add the remaining 3 tablespoons butter, ½ tablespoon at a time, swirling the pan to melt the butter into a sauce. (Do not return to the heat.) Drizzle the sauce over the eggs, sprinkle with salt to taste and a grinding of pepper and serve at once with the toast.

Makes 2 servings

This makes a nice brunch dish, but if you are making the recipe for 4 people, prepare the eggs and sauce in two batches, because even the largest skillet won't accommodate 8 fried eggs.

Eggs with Beurre Noir, Capers and Parsley

Beurre noir (literally "black butter" in French) is simply butter cooked until it is dark brown and nutty-flavored. It makes a sensational sauce for fried eggs.

4 tablespoons (½ stick) unsalted butter

4 large eggs

1 tablespoon fresh lemon juice

2 teaspoons finely chopped fresh flat-leaf parsley

1 tablespoon small capers, rinsed and drained

2–4 slices firm white bread, toasted and buttered

1. Warm two plates in the oven set at the lowest setting.

2. Melt 1 tablespoon of the butter in a large nonstick skillet over medium-low heat. When the butter sizzles, break the eggs one at a time into a cup and slip into the skillet. Reduce the heat to low and fry until the whites begin to set, about 1 minute. Cover and cook until the yolks are cooked to the desired doneness, about 5 minutes more. Transfer the eggs to the warm plates.

3. Add the remaining 3 tablespoons butter to the skillet and heat over medium heat just until the butter browns, about 2 minutes. Add the lemon juice and swirl to blend. Pour the sauce over the eggs, sprinkle with the parsley and capers and serve with the toast.

Makes 2 servings

Fried Eggs with Italian Frying Peppers

Growing up, I often awoke on Sunday mornings to the smell of frying peppers, for my mother's breakfast specialty was what we called peppers and eggs. You can use bell peppers in this dish, but I like the long, pale green Italian frying peppers.

¼ cup extra-virgin olive oil

1 garlic clove, bruised with the side of a knife

1 pound Italian frying peppers, halved, cored and seeded

1 tablespoon red wine vinegar

Kosher salt and freshly ground black pepper

4 large eggs

Italian bread, toasted if desired

1. Heat 2 tablespoons of the oil in a large nonstick skillet over medium-low heat. Add the garlic and cook until lightly browned, 2 to 3 minutes. Remove from the oil and discard. Add the peppers, cover and cook until softened, about 10 minutes. Uncover and cook, stirring, until the peppers are browned in a few places, about 5 minutes. Sprinkle with the vinegar and stir to coat. Add salt to taste and a grinding of pepper, transfer to a medium bowl and cover to keep warm.

2. Add the remaining 2 tablespoons oil to the skillet and heat until hot. Break the eggs one at a time into a cup and slip into the skillet. Reduce the heat to low and fry until the whites begin to set, about 1 minute. Cover and cook until the yolks are cooked to the desired doneness, about 5 minutes more. Transfer the eggs to two plates, place the peppers on the side and pour any juices from the peppers over the eggs. Serve at once with the bread.

Makes 2 servings

Spanish-Style Fried Eggs and Potatoes

A friend who lived in Spain described this wonderful dish of diced potatoes fried in extra-virgin olive oil until crisp and topped with slowly cooked eggs. It is a favorite Spanish supper dish, inexpensive and very satisfying. I like it for breakfast.

¼ cup extra-virgin olive oil

2 pounds potatoes, peeled and cut into ¼-to-½-inch dice (about 5 cups)

1 garlic clove, minced (optional)

Kosher salt and freshly ground black pepper

4 large eggs

1. Heat the oil in a large nonstick skillet over medium heat until hot enough to sizzle a piece of potato dropped into the pan. Add the potatoes, spread in an even layer and reduce the heat to medium-low. Fry the potatoes, turning them every few minutes with a wide spatula, until browned and crisp, 15 to 20 minutes. Stir in the garlic, if using. Sprinkle with salt to taste and a grinding of pepper.

2. Break the eggs one at a time into a cup and slip into the skillet on top of the potatoes, spacing them evenly. Cover and cook, without lifting the lid, until the whites are set, about 5 minutes. Serve immediately.

Makes 2 to 4 servings

Serve this dish with a tomato salsa, either freshly made (page 26) or store-bought, or a cooked tomato sauce (page 263).

Eggs and Sourdough Bread Fried in Olive Oil

Now that I live in the San Francisco Bay Area, I have developed an appreciation for the flavor of sourdough. It's not a bread to serve with all dishes (it does not go well with Italian food, for instance), but it is a spectacular match for eggs, especially these fried eggs seasoned with crushed red pepper and a dash of vinegar. At first glance, you might be tempted to serve this dish for breakfast, but I find the flavors a bit too sophisticated for my lazy morning palate. I prefer it for lunch or as a light supper, with a big green salad of naturally sweet romaine lettuce and little or no dressing.

4 **large slices sourdough bread**

1 **garlic clove, halved**

¼ **cup extra-virgin olive oil**

4 **large eggs**

   Pinch of crushed red pepper flakes

   Red wine vinegar

1. Rub the bread with the cut sides of the garlic. Finely chop the garlic and set aside.

2. Heat the oil in a large nonstick skillet over medium heat. Add the bread and cook until golden on both sides, about 2 minutes per side. Transfer the bread to two plates.

3. Break the eggs one at a time into a cup and slip into the skillet. Cook over medium-low heat, spooning the oil over the yolks, until the whites are set and the yolks have thickened, 3 to 4 minutes. Sprinkle each egg with a few crushed red pepper flakes. Transfer the eggs to the plates, placing 1 egg on each slice of bread. Add the garlic to the skillet and cook until sizzling, about 30 seconds. Spoon a little garlic and oil over each egg and sprinkle with a few drops of vinegar. Serve at once.

Makes 2 servings

If sourdough bread isn't available, try a good sour rye.

Fried Eggs and Plum Tomatoes with Parmesan and Bruschetta

Slowly cooked tomatoes, even out-of-season ones, have a deep, concentrated tomato flavor. This stovetop method, which comes from cookbook author and friend Susan Herrmann Loomis, makes a most satisfying meal, especially when served with a green salad and a loaf of crusty bread.

⅓ cup extra-virgin olive oil, plus more as needed

8 large plum tomatoes (about 1½ pounds), cored and halved lengthwise

½ teaspoon dried thyme

Kosher salt and freshly ground black pepper

1 garlic clove, minced

4 large eggs

2 tablespoons grated Parmigiano-Reggiano, Gruyère or Piedmont Toma cheese

4–8 thin diagonal slices French or Italian bread, toasted and drizzled with extra-virgin olive oil

1. Heat the ⅓ cup olive oil in a large nonstick skillet over medium heat. Add the tomatoes, skin side down, in a single layer, and adjust the heat to maintain a steady sizzle. Sprinkle the tomatoes with the thyme, salt to taste and a grinding of pepper and cook, without stirring, until the skins are blackened and blistered, 10 to 15 minutes. Carefully turn the tomatoes skin side up and sprinkle with salt to taste and a grinding of pepper. Cook, again without stirring, adjusting the heat as necessary to maintain a steady sizzle, until the cut sides of the tomatoes are browned, about 10 minutes. Sprinkle with the garlic and cook for 2 minutes more.

2. Preheat the broiler. Using a slotted spoon, transfer the tomatoes to a 10-inch round baking dish. Break the eggs one at a time into a cup and slip into the skillet. Reduce the heat to low and fry until the whites are set, about 2 minutes. Loosen the eggs from the skillet and, with a spatula, ease them into the baking dish, on top of the tomatoes. Sprinkle with the cheese. Broil until the eggs are cooked to the desired doneness, 1 to 2 minutes.

3. Place the toast on plates and top with the tomatoes, eggs and juices. Serve at once.

Makes 2 main-course servings

Fried Eggs Rancheros

Huevos rancheros is a classic Mexican dish of fried eggs served on warm tortillas, with a chile-laced tomato sauce. There are many versions. I have eaten the dish as a large casserole, smothered in cheese. I have also enjoyed a simpler rendition of individual servings with a roasted tomato and chile sauce. Another variation features both red and green chile sauces. You can use blue corn, yellow corn or flour tortillas.

**Roasted Tomato Sauce
with Chipotle Chiles**

- 3 **pounds plum tomatoes, cored and halved lengthwise**
- ½ **onion, thinly sliced**
- 3 **garlic cloves, bruised with the side of a knife**
- ¼ **cup extra-virgin olive oil**
  Kosher salt and freshly ground black pepper
- 1 **teaspoon ground cumin**
- 1–2 **teaspoons finely chopped canned chipotle chiles in adobo sauce (page 103)**
- ½ **cup chopped fresh cilantro**

1. **Make the sauce:** Preheat the oven to 400°F. Arrange the tomatoes, cut side up, on a heavy baking sheet (with sides) or in a large roasting pan. Scatter the onion and garlic over the top and drizzle with the olive oil. Sprinkle lightly with salt and a grinding of pepper.

2. Roast the tomatoes for 20 minutes. Turn the tomatoes over, sprinkle with salt to taste and spoon the juices and oil over them. Roast for 20 to 30 minutes more, or until the skins are slightly blackened. Let the tomatoes cool slightly.

3. Set a food mill over a large saucepan and transfer the tomato mixture and juices to the food mill. Press through the mill and discard the solids. (If you don't have a food mill, puree in a food processor and press through a strainer with a rubber spatula; discard the solids.) You should have 2 to 2½ cups sauce. Bring to a boil and reduce the sauce, if necessary, to about 2 cups.

4. Meanwhile, sprinkle the cumin into a small dry skillet set over low heat and heat just until the cumin is warmed and fragrant, about 10 seconds. Add the cumin to the simmering sauce and stir in 1 teaspoon of the chipotles. Taste and add more chiles if you want the sauce to be fiery. Add salt to taste, if necessary. Keep warm over very low heat.

4 large flour or corn tortillas

2 tablespoons vegetable oil

2 tablespoons extra-virgin olive oil

4–8 large eggs

½ cup crumbled Mexican queso fresco or very mild ricotta salata or feta cheese

1 avocado, peeled, pitted and cut into thin wedges for garnish

4 lime wedges for garnish
Fresh cilantro leaves for garnish

5. Heat a large nonstick skillet over high heat until hot enough to sizzle a drop of water. Brush the tortillas lightly on both sides with the vegetable oil. One at a time, quickly sear each tortilla on both sides until a few golden spots appear, about 5 seconds per side. Transfer to a large square of foil. When all the tortillas have been seared, wrap them in the foil and keep warm in the oven set to the lowest temperature.

6. Just before serving, add the olive oil to the skillet and heat over medium-low heat. Break 4 eggs one at a time into a cup and slip into the skillet. Reduce the heat to low and fry until the whites begin to set, about 1 minute. Cover and cook until the yolks are cooked to the desired doneness, about 5 minutes. If using 8 eggs, transfer the fried eggs to an ovenproof platter, cover with foil and place in oven to keep warm while you fry the remaining eggs.

7. Unwrap the tortillas and place one on each plate. Top each tortilla with 1 or 2 fried eggs. Stir the chopped cilantro into the sauce and spoon generously over the eggs. Top with the cheese. Garnish the plates with the avocado, lime wedges and cilantro leaves and serve.

Makes 4 servings

Fried Eggs with Eggplant and Tomato

One of my favorite dishes is a layered salad of sliced tomato and fried eggplant, served with a basil vinaigrette. For this dish, I adapted the theme, making a warm salad "tower" of sautéed tomato and eggplant slices, seasoned with garlic and fresh basil and topped with a fried egg.

6 tablespoons extra-virgin olive oil

4 ½-inch-thick slices ripe tomato

Kosher salt and freshly ground black pepper

1 garlic clove, minced

4 ½-inch-thick slices peeled eggplant

4 large eggs

1. Heat 2 tablespoons of the oil in a large nonstick skillet over high heat. Add the tomato slices and fry for about 1 minute per side, or until heated through. Transfer the tomato slices to a plate and sprinkle with salt to taste and a grinding of pepper. Add the garlic to the skillet and heat just until it sizzles, about 30 seconds. Pour the garlic oil over the tomatoes. Cover with foil to keep warm.

2. Wipe the skillet clean. Add 2 tablespoons of the oil to the skillet and heat over high heat until hot enough to sizzle a slice of eggplant. Add the eggplant slices and fry until lightly browned, about 3 minutes per side. Transfer to paper towels to drain.

3. Wipe the skillet clean. Add the remaining 2 tablespoons oil to the skillet and heat over medium-low heat until hot. Break the eggs one at a time into a cup and slip into the skillet. Reduce the heat to low and fry until the whites begin to set, about 1 minute. Cover and cook until the yolks are cooked to the desired doneness, about 5 minutes more. Remove from the heat.

¼ cup slivered fresh basil leaves

1–2 teaspoons red wine vinegar

4. Place a tomato slice in the center of each of four plates. (Reserve the tomato juices on the plate.) Sprinkle with a little of the basil. Top each with a slice of eggplant, sprinkle with a little more basil and top with an egg (set the skillet aside). Sprinkle with the remaining basil.

5. Add 1 teaspoon of the vinegar to the juices on the plate and stir to blend. Taste and add more vinegar, if desired. Pour into the skillet and reheat over low heat. Drizzle the hot dressing over the egg "towers." Serve at once.

Makes 4 servings

Serve with other warm or room-temperature salads as part of a late-summer lunch or supper. This dish goes well with corn on the cob and a warm salad of garden-fresh green beans tossed with mint and extra-virgin olive oil.

CHAPTER 2   *Omelettes and Frittatas*
WELL-ROUNDED   LITTLE   MEALS

". . . there is only one infallible recipe for the perfect omelette: your own."
—ELIZABETH DAVID

I've devoted this chapter to one of the most universally loved egg dishes, the omelette, and its cousin, the frittata. What we refer to as an omelette is a specialty of many cuisines around the world, known by many names. These international versions may vary greatly in appearance, shape and size—not to mention flavor—but they are all, in their essence, the same: beaten eggs cooked in a skillet into a flat disk. The disks may be thin as a knife blade—*lemelle* in Old French, from which came the word "omelette"—or thick as a cake, like the traditional Spanish omelette known as a *tortilla*. The disk may be folded over, as is the French omelette we're most familiar with, or left open and flat, as Italian, Spanish and Asian varieties are. And the eggs may be seasoned or embellished with all manner of savory or sweet ingredients: bits of meat, vegetables, cheeses, herbs, fruits or jam. Sometimes these are stirred into the beaten eggs, sometimes they are tucked inside the cooked eggs, and sometimes the eggs are poured over the other ingredients already in the pan. But however they're constructed or flavored, omelettes are fundamentally simple and fantastically versatile, a medium capable of infinite variation, delightful for breakfast, lunch or dinner, as a snack or even dessert.

In this chapter, I present some of my favorite versions of omelettes, drawn from several traditions. Many of the recipes are for individual French-style omelettes, in which a small number of eggs (usually 2 to 4) are quickly cooked and folded over a filling. If you follow the steps in my master recipe on page 42, you'll turn out perfectly formed, delicately textured omelettes in minutes.

Frittatas, as rounds of skillet-cooked beaten eggs are called in Italy, are made with a larger number of eggs (usually 8 or more), incorporating a variety of savory ingredients. Though many people think of frittatas as "baked omelettes," I usually prefer to cook them slowly on top of the stove until set, then turn the disk over in the pan briefly or quickly brown it under the broiler for a perfect finish. (See details on page 60.) Frittatas are simpler to make than French omelettes—there's no fancy pan handling—and especially convenient when you have a number of people to feed. Served hot, cut into large wedges, frittatas make a marvelous breakfast with toast and bacon or a fine dinner with roasted potatoes and a green salad. But they can be made ahead of time as well and are delicious served at room temperature. Cut them into small squares for an easy hors d'oeuvre, or slap a wedge between two pieces of bread for a great sandwich.

I have also included a few dishes from the world's cuisines that are well known by other names but are omelettes at heart. Among these are the classic potato-and-egg Tortilla Española, a posh version of frontier America's Hangtown Fry and the Chinese-American fried omelette called Egg Fu Yung.

Masterful French Omelettes

Everyone should have an infallible omelette recipe of his or her own. Here's mine.

Before you begin, you'll need a good pan. My favorite is a heavy 9-inch nonstick skillet with low, sloping sides and a comfortable handle that doesn't get hot. I use this for the single-serving omelette — from 2 to 3 eggs — in the following recipe. You can double this recipe to make a 2-serving omelette and cook it in the same pan, but it will be a thicker, sturdier omelette. I never make an omelette with more than 6 eggs or use a pan larger than 10 inches. If I have more than a couple of people to feed, I make several omelettes one after another — they're fast!

I almost always put a filling in my omelettes, either savory or sweet. The filling should be fully prepared, either warm or at room temperature, before you start to cook the eggs. You need only ¼ to ⅓ cup for each omelette.

I like to cook my eggs so they are soft-set — just barely moist on top — before adding the filling. And I don't let the eggs brown at all. You can cook the eggs to your taste — drier, if you like them that way, or still quite runny inside, which the French call *baveuse*. You can leave the omelette on high heat for a few moments if you want the outside to have a tinge of brown, but don't overcook the eggs, or they will be tough.

The Basic Omelette

A plain omelette made with two or three large eggs is the fastest meal on earth. I sometimes add a few tablespoons of water to my basic recipe to make the omelette a little fluffier. Traditionally, a French omelette is topped with a dab of softened butter before serving.

2–3 **large eggs**

  2 **tablespoons cold water**

     **Kosher salt and freshly
     ground black pepper**

  1 **tablespoon unsalted butter,
     plus (optional) 1 teaspoon
     unsalted butter at room
     temperature**

  1 **tablespoon finely chopped
     fresh parsley, tarragon,
     chives, lemon thyme and/or
     savory (optional)**

4–5 **tablespoons warm or
     room-temperature filling
     (pages 43–52; optional)**

1. Combine the eggs, water, salt to taste and a grinding of pepper in a medium bowl and gently whisk or beat with a fork just until blended.

2. Heat a medium nonstick skillet with low, sloping sides over medium heat for 2 minutes. Add the 1 tablespoon butter—it should sizzle—and swirl to coat the pan. When the butter stops sizzling, pour the egg mixture into the center of the pan, reduce the heat to low and cook until the bottom is set, about 10 seconds. Using a heatproof flat-edged rubber spatula or wooden spoon, pull the set eggs at the edges of the pan toward the center, allowing the unset eggs to run from the center to the sides. Adjust the heat if necessary so the bottom does not brown. Continue cooking until the eggs are soft-set—just a thin layer of unset moist egg should be visible on the top of the omelette—adjusting the heat if necessary so the bottom does not brown. The total cooking time should be less than 2 minutes.

3. If adding herbs and/or filling, do so now: slide the pan off the heat and sprinkle the herbs evenly over the surface of the omelette or spoon the filling over the third of the omelette surface closest to the handle. Using the spatula, fold the third of the omelette nearest the handle over the center third. Then, holding the pan by the handle, tilt it so that the omelette rolls out of the pan and onto a plate seam side down. Serve at once, topped with the 1 teaspoon butter, if using.

Makes 1 serving

Broccoli Rabe Omelette

An omelette made with a filling of tender greens is a nutritious and convenient meal. Any green, such as dandelions, escarole, spinach or Swiss chard, can be used in place of broccoli rabe—either freshly cooked, as here, or left over.

4 ounces broccoli rabe, rinsed, thick stems trimmed, and cut into 2-inch lengths

2 tablespoons extra-virgin olive oil

½ garlic clove, minced

¼ cup diced tomato (optional)

1½ teaspoons thinly sliced fresh basil leaves (optional)

Pinch of kosher salt

Freshly ground black pepper

1½ teaspoons freshly grated Parmigiano-Reggiano cheese (optional)

1. Cook the broccoli rabe in 4 cups of boiling salted water until tender, about 5 minutes. Drain well. Pat dry with paper towels.

2. Combine 1 tablespoon of the oil and the garlic in a medium skillet with low, sloping sides and heat over low heat until the garlic sizzles. Add the broccoli rabe, increase the heat to medium and sauté until heated through, about 1 minute. Stir in the tomato and basil, if using, salt and a grinding of pepper. Remove from the heat.

3. Place a strainer over a bowl and spoon the broccoli rabe mixture into the strainer. Cover with a piece of foil to keep warm.

4. Prepare the omelette as directed in the basic recipe (page 42) using the remaining 1 tablespoon oil in place of the butter. Spoon the broccoli rabe mixture onto the third of the omelette closest to the handle of the skillet. Finish the omelette as directed. Sprinkle with the cheese, if using, instead of the optional butter in the basic recipe and serve immediately.

Makes 1 serving

Bacon, Apple and Stilton Omelette

2 slices bacon

1 tablespoon unsalted butter

½ apple, peeled, cored and
thinly sliced

Pinch of sugar

2 tablespoons crumbled
Stilton cheese

1. Cook the bacon in a medium nonstick skillet with low, sloping sides until crisp; drain on paper towels.

2. Cut into ½-inch pieces and set aside. Discard the bacon fat and wipe out the pan. Melt ½ tablespoon of the butter in the pan. Add the apple, sprinkle with the sugar and sauté, stirring, until golden and tender, about 3 minutes. Transfer the apple to a small bowl and set aside.

3. Melt the remaining ½ tablespoon butter in the skillet. Prepare the omelette as directed in the basic recipe (page 42). Spoon the apple and bacon onto the third of the omelette closest to the handle of the skillet and sprinkle with the cheese. Finish the omelette as directed and serve.

Makes 1 serving

Caramelized Onion, Ham and Gruyère Omelette

1 tablespoon unsalted butter

1 cup slivered onions

2 tablespoons finely chopped ham

Freshly ground black pepper

1 tablespoon grated Gruyère cheese

1. Melt the butter in a medium nonstick skillet with low, sloping sides. Add the onions and cook over very low heat, stirring often, until soft and golden, about 15 minutes. Stir in the ham and a grinding of pepper. Transfer to a small bowl and set aside.

2. Prepare the omelette as directed in the basic recipe (page 42). Spoon the filling and the cheese onto the third of the omelette closest to the handle of the skillet. Finish the omelette as directed. Serve immediately.

Makes 1 serving

Omelette Wisdom from Two Great Women

When I was in college, I decided to write an essay about omelettes and so sought out the celebrated Madame Romaine de Lyon, who reputedly made more than 500 varieties of omelettes in her tiny restaurant near Park Avenue in New York City. She prepared for me an authentic French omelette and gave me a signed copy of her small book, *The Art of Cooking Omelettes*, which I still use today. Of all the words of wisdom she shares about egg cookery, these are my favorite: "The superior omelette is far more than breaking the eggs into the pan and applying heat. One begins with principles and practice . . . the love and delicacy come naturally, if they are to come at all."

Years later, I got another glimpse into the mystery of omelette making when my daughter, Stephanie, and I visited the towering abbey of Mont-Saint-Michel on the coast of Normandy. As we walked along the narrow stone path that leads through the ancient ramparts, we heard a soft, rhythmic metallic sound, repeated over and over—"shu, shu, shu-shing; shu, shu, shu-shing." What could it be?

Turning into a medieval courtyard, we came upon the source of the sound: four women in old-fashioned long skirts, seated upon low wooden benches, each holding a large copper bowl between her knees. The bowls were filled with eggs, and the women were whipping them with huge balloon whisks, creating the "shu-shing" sound that emanated from the courtyard. Here was a world-famous dish in the making. The beaten eggs were to become *omelettes Poulard,* a fluffy delicacy first created over a century ago by a legendary cook, Annette Poulard. Of course, Stephanie and I enjoyed omelettes for lunch that day at the restaurant she founded, La Mère Poulard.

Madame Poulard was besieged by chefs and writers who wanted to learn the secret ingredient of her light, delicate egg dish. She finally relented in 1932 in a letter she sent to an admirer. She wrote, "Here is the recipe for the omelette: I break some good eggs in a bowl, I beat them well, I put a good piece of butter in the pan, I throw the eggs into it and I shake it constantly. I am happy, monsieur, if this recipe pleases you."

Though Madame Poulard obviously wanted to keep her omelette a mystery, the sight of the women in the courtyard that day provided me with an important clue. It's the long rhythmic whisking of the eggs, I believe, that makes them thick and airy and thus gives the *omelette Poulard* its extraordinary texture.

Salmon Caviar, Sour Cream and Dill Omelette

3 tablespoons sour cream

1 tablespoon salmon caviar

2 teaspoons minced fresh dill
  Freshly ground black pepper

1. Prepare the omelette as directed in the basic recipe (page 42). Spoon the sour cream onto the third of the omelette closest to the handle of the skillet and sprinkle with the caviar, 1 teaspoon of the dill and a grinding of pepper.

2. Finish the omelette as directed, sprinkle with the remaining 1 teaspoon dill and serve immediately.

Makes 1 serving

If you prefer sturgeon caviar, buy the best you can afford and enjoy every sinfully delicious morsel.

Bacon, Avocado and Brie Omelette

1–2 slices bacon

½ cup diced ripe avocado

¼ cup ½-inch chunks chilled Brie cheese (rind removed)

1. Cook the bacon in a medium nonstick skillet with low, sloping sides until crisp; drain on paper towels. Crumble and set aside. Discard the bacon fat and wipe out the skillet.

2. Prepare the omelette as directed in the basic recipe (page 42). Spoon the bacon, avocado and cheese onto the third of the omelette closest to the handle of the skillet. Finish the omelette as directed and serve.

Makes 1 serving

Feta, Spinach and Tomato Omelette

2 tablespoons extra-virgin olive oil

½ garlic clove, minced

⅓ cup diced tomato

Pinch of kosher salt

¾ cup lightly packed torn spinach leaves

1 tablespoon minced fresh dill

2 tablespoons crumbled feta cheese

1. Combine 1 tablespoon of the oil and the garlic in a medium nonstick skillet with low, sloping sides and heat over low heat until the garlic begins to sizzle, about 1 minute. Add the tomato and salt and sauté for 30 seconds. Add the spinach and sauté for 30 seconds more. Transfer to a small bowl and set aside.

2. Wipe out the skillet. Heat the remaining 1 tablespoon oil in the skillet and prepare the omelette as directed in the basic recipe (page 42), using the oil in place of the butter. Spoon the spinach mixture onto the third of the omelette closest to the handle of the skillet and sprinkle with the dill and feta. Finish the omelette as directed and serve immediately.

Makes 1 serving

Avocado, Tomato and Monterey Jack Omelette

2 tablespoons diced avocado

2 tablespoons diced plum
tomato

1 tablespoon minced fresh
cilantro

½ teaspoon minced jalapeño,
or to taste

Pinch of kosher salt

2 tablespoons grated Monterey
Jack cheese

1. Combine the avocado, tomato, cilantro, jalapeño and salt in a small bowl.

2. Prepare the omelette as directed in the basic recipe (page 42). Spoon the avocado mixture onto the third of the omelette closest to the handle of the skillet and sprinkle with the cheese. Finish the omelette as directed and serve.

Makes 1 serving

Sour Cream and Chutney Omelette

2 tablespoons prepared
  chutney
2 tablespoons sour cream

Prepare the omelette as directed in the basic recipe (page 42). Spoon the chutney and sour cream onto the third of the omelette closest to the handle of the skillet. Finish the omelette as directed and serve.

Makes 1 serving

Egg Fu Yung

These little pancakes, a Chinese-American classic, can be made with bits of meat or shrimp, bamboo shoots and water chestnuts. This version uses slivered bok choy for crunch. I like to serve Egg Fu Yung in several ways: as a side dish, floating in steaming broth or on top of freshly cooked rice.

4 **large eggs**

¼ **cup cold water**

2 **teaspoons soy sauce**

½ **teaspoon toasted sesame oil**
   Pinch of kosher salt

1 **cup thinly sliced bok choy (stems and leafy tops)**

¼ **cup grated carrot**

¼ **cup thinly sliced scallions (white and light green parts)**

1 **garlic clove, minced**

1 **teaspoon grated ginger**
   Vegetable oil

1. Whisk the eggs, water, soy sauce, sesame oil and salt in a large bowl until blended. Add the bok choy, carrot, scallions, garlic and ginger and stir vigorously to blend.

2. Heat a large skillet with low, sloping sides over medium heat. Add 1 inch of vegetable oil to the pan, then add a crust of bread to the oil; when it browns, the oil is hot enough. Remove and discard the bread crust.

3. Stir the egg mixture to distribute the ingredients evenly. Ladle ⅓ cup of the egg mixture into the hot skillet, pushing the edges in to form a 3-inch pancake. Add two more ladles of egg mixture to form two more pancakes. When the pancakes are set, about 2 minutes, turn and cook until set and lightly browned on the other side. Transfer to paper towels to drain. Repeat, cooking two or three pancakes at a time. Arrange on a serving platter and serve hot.

Makes 8 pancakes

Lemon Curd Omelette with Fresh Berries and Mint

2 tablespoons Lemon Curd
(page 369)

¼ cup mixed blueberries,
raspberries and
sliced strawberries
(or at least two kinds)

2 fresh mint leaves, finely
chopped

Confectioners' sugar

Prepare the omelette as directed in the basic recipe (page 42). Spread the lemon curd onto the third of the omelette closest to the handle of the skillet, then sprinkle with the berries and mint leaves. Finish the omelette as directed, sprinkle with confectioners' sugar and serve.

Makes 1 serving

SWEET OMELETTES
Omelettes filled with sweet fillings like jam, fresh fruit, toasted nuts and sweet cheese are a personal favorite. They can be easily made from ingredients on hand, such as jam or fresh fruit. The examples on the following pages are only the beginning. Feel free to improvise with sliced bananas, pears sautéed in butter or simply cream cheese and jelly.

Ricotta and Strawberry Omelette

⅓ cup thinly sliced strawberries

1 teaspoon sugar

2 tablespoons ricotta cheese

Cinnamon sugar

1. Combine the strawberries and sugar in a small bowl and set aside.

2. Prepare the omelette as directed in the basic recipe (page 42). Spoon the strawberries and ricotta onto the third of the omelette closest to the handle of the skillet. Finish the omelette as directed, sprinkle generously with cinnamon sugar and serve.

Makes 1 serving

Sweet Jam Omelette

1–2 **tablespoons whole fruit jam**

1 **tablespoon sliced natural almonds, lightly toasted (see box)**

Confectioners' sugar

Prepare the omelette as directed in the basic recipe (page 42). Spoon the jam onto the third of the omelette closest to the handle of the skillet. Finish the omelette as directed, sprinkle with the almonds and confectioners' sugar and serve.

Makes 1 serving

> *To toast nuts, place in a small dry skillet and heat over medium-low heat, stirring often, until they begin to color, 3 to 5 minutes.*

Peach, Honey and Toasted Almond Omelette

¼–½ cup thinly sliced peeled
   peaches

1 teaspoon honey

   Drop of pure vanilla extract

1 tablespoon sliced natural
   almonds, lightly toasted
   (page 56)

   Confectioners' sugar

1. Stir together the peaches, honey and vanilla in a small bowl.

2. Prepare the omelette as directed in the basic recipe (page 42). Spoon the peach mixture onto the third of the omelette closest to the handle of the skillet. Finish the omelette as directed, sprinkle with the almonds and confectioners' sugar and serve.

Makes 1 serving

You can also use nectarines or plums.

Puffed Omelette

A puffed omelette is sometimes called a souffléed omelette because the eggs are separated and the whites are beaten until soft peaks form, then folded into the gently beaten yolks. Cooked partly on top of the stove and partly in the oven, the omelette emerges puffed and tender, almost soufflélike. A puffed omelette can be filled with the same fillings used for other conventional omelettes, then folded in half and turned out of the pan.

4 **large eggs, separated**
   Freshly ground black pepper
¼ **cup cold water**
½ **teaspoon kosher salt**
1 **tablespoon unsalted butter**

Filling (optional)
1 **tablespoon unsalted butter**
1 **cup sliced mushrooms**
1 **tablespoon minced fresh parsley**
1 **garlic clove, minced**
1 **teaspoon minced fresh thyme**
   Kosher salt and freshly ground black pepper
1 **tablespoon grated Gruyère, cheddar or other cheese (optional)**

Be careful not to overcook the omelette, or the eggs will toughen.

1. Preheat the oven to 350°F. Whisk the egg yolks and a grinding of pepper in a large bowl until blended. In a separate large bowl, whisk the egg whites until foamy. Add the water and salt and whisk until soft peaks form. Gently fold the whites into the yolks until blended.

2. Melt the butter over low heat in an ovenproof 9-to-10-inch nonstick skillet with low, sloping sides. Swirl to coat the bottom and sides evenly with melted butter and pour the egg mixture into the skillet.

3. Cook, without stirring, over low heat until the bottom is set, about 3 minutes. Transfer to the oven and bake until golden and puffed, 12 to 15 minutes.

4. **Meanwhile, prepare the filling, if using:** Melt the butter in a medium skillet. Add the mushrooms and cook, stirring, until browned and tender, about 5 minutes. Add the parsley, garlic and thyme; cook for 1 minute more. Add salt to taste and a grinding of pepper and remove from the heat.

5. To serve, loosen the sides of the omelette. Place the filling, if using, in a strip down the center and sprinkle with cheese, if using. With a spatula, fold the omelette in half and turn out of the skillet. Serve at once.

Makes 2 servings

Omelette Pancake

Part pancake and part omelette, this thin, delicate omelette can be used in a variety of ways. I like to roll it up, cut it into half-inch-wide strips and add it to soups. The egg strips are also delicious in salads or as a topping for fried or steamed rice. Or roll the omelette up around shredded chicken moistened with a little mayonnaise and fresh herbs, or around a chopped salad of ripe tomatoes and fresh basil seasoned with olive oil.

2　**large eggs**

1　**tablespoon cold water**

2　**teaspoons vegetable oil, plus more for the skillet**

　　Pinch of kosher salt and freshly ground black pepper

1. In a small bowl, whisk the eggs, water, 2 teaspoons oil, salt to taste and a grinding of pepper until blended; let stand for a few minutes to allow any foam to subside.

2. Heat a 9-to-10-inch nonstick skillet with low, sloping sides over medium heat until hot enough to sizzle a drop of water. Brush with a thin film of oil. Add the egg mixture to the pan, lifting the pan off the heat and tilting and swirling it so the eggs cover the bottom of the skillet evenly.

3. Cook, without stirring, over low heat until the pancake is set, 3 to 5 minutes. Slide the pancake onto a plate and serve.

Makes 1 serving

VARIATIONS

ITALIAN:　Substitute olive oil for the vegetable oil. After the pancake has cooked for 1 minute, press 4 or 5 fresh flat-leaf parsley leaves onto the surface. Cook for 2 to 4 minutes more. Sprinkle with 1 tablespoon freshly grated Parmigiano-Reggiano cheese; cover and cook for 1 minute more; serve.

ASIAN:　Substitute toasted sesame oil for the vegetable oil. After the pancake has cooked for 1 minute, scatter 1 tablespoon thinly sliced scallion greens and ½ teaspoon sesame seeds over the top. Cook for 2 to 4 minutes more; serve.

Basic Frittata Technique

 1. Heat the oil in a large nonstick skillet with low, sloping sides. Sauté the filling ingredients until tender if raw or until heated through if precooked.

2. Meanwhile, whisk the eggs (at least 2 for each serving) in a large bowl. Add a pinch of salt and a grinding of black pepper, plus any other seasonings, such as grated cheese or minced parsley.

3. Pour the egg mixture into the skillet. Reduce the heat to low and cook the frittata until the edges are set and bubbling up a little, about 2 minutes. Tilt the pan slightly and lift the set edges so the raw egg in the center can flow to the edges. The surface should be moist but not liquid.

4. The frittata is now ready to finish in one of four ways.

Four Ways to Finish a Frittata

 I use a variety of methods to make sure that my frittatas are set on top and that the prettiest side of the disk is showing when served.

♦ When I'm in a hurry, I often use the simplest method, which is to cook the frittata completely on the stovetop, covered, until the eggs are set on top.

♦ If I want the top to be browned—or if I want to melt any cheese added at the end—I finish the frittata under the broiler. To do this, preheat the broiler while the frittata is cooking, then set the (ovenproof) skillet under the broiler for about 1 minute.

♦ Traditionally, frittatas are turned over in the pan to finish cooking. I like to finish lighter frittatas without cheese in this fashion. While this technique is slightly trickier than the first two, the eggs cook more evenly and both top and bottom will be lightly browned. The easiest way to flip a frittata without breaking it is to slide it out onto a large plate. Then place the skillet upside down over the frittata on the plate. Protecting your hands with a heavy kitchen towel or pot holders, hold the plate and pan tightly together and quickly invert so the frittata drops into the pan, browned side up. Cook for about 1 minute more, then slide the finished frittata back onto the plate and serve.

♦ You can also finish a frittata in a hot oven. Set the (ovenproof) skillet on the upper rack of a preheated 450°F oven and bake for 2 to 5 minutes, until the top is set and lightly colored.

Asparagus and Parmesan Frittata

I like to serve thin wedges of this attractive frittata at room temperature before dinner with a glass of wine.

12 ounces asparagus, trimmed

2 tablespoons extra-virgin olive oil

1 garlic clove, minced
   Kosher salt and freshly ground black pepper

8 large eggs

½ cup freshly grated Parmigiano-Reggiano cheese, plus a wedge of cheese for shaving

1 tablespoon fresh thyme leaves (no substitutions), plus sprigs of thyme for garnish

1. Cut the stems of the asparagus into ¼-inch slices; leave the tips whole.

2. In a large nonstick skillet with low, sloping sides, heat the oil over medium heat. Add the asparagus and cook, stirring, until crisp-tender, about 3 minutes. Add the garlic and cook just until it begins to sizzle, about 30 seconds. Sprinkle with salt and a grinding of pepper.

3. Meanwhile, in a large bowl, whisk the eggs, grated cheese and a grinding of pepper. Add the egg mixture to the skillet, reduce the heat to medium-low and cook until the eggs are set on the bottom and around the edges, about 4 minutes. Sprinkle with the thyme leaves. With a spatula, lift one side of the frittata and tilt the pan so the raw eggs flow under the set edges. Repeat at least twice at different places around the edge until the egg is no longer runny, about 2 minutes. Using a vegetable peeler, pare shavings from the cheese wedge, covering the top of the frittata.

4. Cover the frittata and cook over low heat until set, 10 to 15 minutes. If you prefer the top browned, preheat the broiler, then set the (ovenproof) skillet under the heat just until the top is lightly browned, 1 to 2 minutes.

5. To serve, loosen the edges with a spatula and slide the frittata onto a serving plate, garnish with the thyme sprigs and serve warm or at room temperature.

Makes 4 main-course or 8 appetizer or hors d'oeuvre servings

Green Bean and Goat Cheese Frittata with Garlic

Frittatas can be made from the simplest ingredients. I first created this frittata to use up some leftover cooked green beans. It was so good that now I boil beans especially for it.

2–2½ cups cooked 1-inch green-bean pieces, or 1 pound fresh green beans, trimmed and cut into 1-inch lengths

¼ cup extra-virgin olive oil

1 tablespoon minced garlic

½ teaspoon crushed red pepper flakes

8 large eggs

½ teaspoon kosher salt

Freshly ground black pepper

2 ounces mild goat cheese, crumbled

1. If using raw green beans, cook them in a large pot of boiling salted water until crisp-tender, about 6 minutes. Drain well and set aside.

2. Combine the oil, garlic and red pepper flakes in a large nonstick (ovenproof) skillet with low, sloping sides and cook over medium heat just until the garlic begins to sizzle (do not let it brown), about 30 seconds. Add the green beans and cook for 1 minute more.

3. Meanwhile, in a large bowl, whisk the eggs, salt and a generous grinding of pepper until blended. Pour the eggs evenly over the green beans. Cook over low heat until the edges begin to set, about 2 minutes. With a spatula, lift one side of the frittata and tilt the pan so the raw eggs flow under the set edges. Repeat at least twice at different places around the edge until the egg is no longer runny, about 2 minutes. Cover and cook until the frittata is almost set, 10 to 15 minutes.

4. Meanwhile, preheat the broiler. Sprinkle the cheese over the frittata and broil until the top is lightly browned, 2 to 3 minutes.

5. To serve, loosen the edges with a spatula and slide the frittata onto a serving plate. Serve warm or at room temperature, cut into wedges.

Makes 4 to 6 servings

Potato, Sun-Dried Tomato and Rosemary Frittata

I make this frittata when I have leftover baked or boiled russet potatoes on hand.

3 tablespoons extra-virgin olive oil

2 medium russet potatoes (about 1 pound total), cooked, peeled and cut into ¼-inch dice

¼ cup diced red bell pepper

¼ cup diced onion

¼ cup sliced oil-packed sun-dried tomatoes, drained and patted dry with paper towels

½ teaspoon minced fresh rosemary or 1 teaspoon dried, crumbled

½ teaspoon kosher salt
Freshly ground black pepper

8 large eggs

½ cup freshly grated Parmigiano-Reggiano cheese

Serve with a green salad for lunch or a light supper.

1. In a large nonstick skillet with low, sloping sides, heat the oil over medium heat. Add the potatoes and cook, turning as they brown, until golden, about 10 minutes. Add the bell pepper and onion and cook over medium-low heat until tender, about 5 minutes. Add the sun-dried tomatoes, rosemary, salt and a generous grinding of pepper.

2. Meanwhile, in a large bowl, whisk the eggs and cheese until blended. Add the egg mixture to the skillet and cook until the eggs are set on the bottom and around the edges, about 4 minutes. With a spatula, lift one side of the frittata and tilt the pan so the raw eggs flow under the set edges. Repeat at least twice at different places around the edge until the egg is no longer runny.

3. Cover the frittata, reduce the heat to low and cook until set, 10 to 15 minutes. If you prefer the top browned, preheat the broiler, then set the (ovenproof) skillet under the heat just until the top is lightly browned, 1 to 2 minutes.

4. To serve, loosen the edges with a spatula and slide the frittata onto a platter or turn out, browned side up, by inverting the serving plate on the skillet and turning the frittata out. Serve warm or at room temperature, cut into wedges.

Makes 4 to 6 servings

Pancetta, Broccoli and Sweet Onion Frittata

Pancetta is a rolled Italian bacon seasoned with black pepper. It can be found in Italian delis and specialty markets, but thick-cut bacon can be substituted if pancetta is not available.

3 ¼-inch-thick slices pancetta
or 3 slices thick-cut bacon,
cut into ¼-inch dice

1 tablespoon extra-virgin
olive oil

1 cup thin lengthwise slices
sweet onion

2 cups cooked 1-inch broccoli
pieces
Freshly ground black pepper

8 large eggs

¼ teaspoon kosher salt, or
to taste

¼ cup freshly grated
Parmigiano-Reggiano cheese
(optional)

1. Combine the pancetta or bacon and oil in a large nonstick skillet with low, sloping sides and cook over medium heat until the pancetta or bacon begins to turn golden, about 3 minutes. Stir in the onion and cook until crisp-tender, about 5 minutes. Add the broccoli and a grinding of pepper and cook, stirring, until heated through, about 1 minute.

2. Meanwhile, in a large bowl, whisk the eggs, salt and a grinding of pepper until blended. Add the eggs to the skillet, reduce the heat to medium-low and cook until the eggs are set on the bottom and around the edges, about 4 minutes. With a spatula, lift one side of the frittata and tilt the pan so the raw eggs flow under the set edges. Repeat at least twice at different places around the edge until the egg is no longer runny.

3. Sprinkle the frittata with the cheese, if using, cover and cook over low heat until set, 10 to 15 minutes. If you prefer the top browned, preheat the broiler, then set the (ovenproof) skillet under the heat just until the top is lightly browned, 1 to 2 minutes.

4. To serve, loosen the edges with a spatula and slide the frittata onto a platter. Serve warm or at room temperature, cut into wedges.

Makes 4 to 6 servings

Make this frittata with broccoli rabe instead of ordinary broccoli or with a combination of broccoli and cauliflower.

Fresh Tomato and Basil Frittata with Asiago

Asiago is a tangy, semihard cow's milk cheese. Make this frittata with a combination of red, green and yellow tomatoes during the height of tomato season.

8 **large eggs**

1 **cup grated Asiago cheese (about 4 ounces)**

Kosher salt and freshly ground black pepper

2 **cups cubed (½ inch) tomatoes**

¼ **cup torn fresh basil leaves**

2 **tablespoons extra-virgin olive oil**

1 **garlic clove, minced**

You can substitute grated Parmigiano-Reggiano or fontina or crumbled ricotta salata for the Asiago.

1. In a large bowl, whisk the eggs, ½ cup of the cheese, ¼ teaspoon salt and a grinding of pepper until blended.

2. In a medium bowl, toss the tomatoes with the basil, 1 tablespoon of the oil, salt to taste and a grinding of pepper; set aside.

3. In a large nonstick skillet with low, sloping sides, heat the remaining 1 tablespoon oil and the garlic over medium-low heat. When the garlic begins to sizzle, add the egg mixture and stir to blend with the oil. Spoon the tomato mixture evenly over the top. Cook until the eggs are set on the bottom and around the edges, about 4 minutes. With a spatula, lift one side of the frittata and tilt the pan so the raw eggs flow under the set edges. Repeat at least twice at different places around the edge until the egg is no longer runny.

4. Sprinkle the top with the remaining ½ cup cheese, reduce the heat to low, cover and cook until the frittata is set, 10 to 15 minutes. If you prefer the top browned, preheat the broiler, then set the (ovenproof) skillet under the heat just until the top is lightly browned, 1 to 2 minutes.

5. To serve, loosen the edges with a spatula and slide the frittata onto a platter. Serve hot, warm or at room temperature, cut into wedges.

Makes 4 to 6 servings

Broccoli Rabe Frittata with Pecorino Romano

Broccoli rabe, a slightly bitter Italian green, makes an especially delicious lunch or brunch frittata, served with roasted red peppers and a plate of salami or prosciutto.

Kosher salt

¾ **pound broccoli rabe, washed, large leaves and thick stems trimmed, and cut into 2-inch lengths (about 4 cups)**

2 **tablespoons extra-virgin olive oil**

2 **garlic cloves, minced**

⅛ **teaspoon crushed red pepper flakes, or to taste**

8 **large eggs**

3 **tablespoons freshly grated Pecorino Romano**

Freshly ground black pepper

I especially like this frittata as a sandwich filling.

1. Bring a large pot of water to a boil and add 1 tablespoon salt. Add the broccoli rabe and cook, stirring occasionally, until tender and bright green, 4 to 6 minutes. Drain well and pat dry with paper towels.

2. In a large nonstick skillet with low, sloping sides, heat the oil and garlic over medium-low heat until the garlic sizzles. Add the broccoli rabe and red pepper flakes and cook, stirring, until heated through, about 1 minute.

3. Meanwhile, in a large bowl, whisk the eggs until blended. Whisk in the cheese and a grinding of pepper. Pour the egg mixture over the broccoli rabe. Cook over low heat until the bottom and sides are set, about 4 minutes. With a spatula, lift one side of the frittata and tilt the pan so the raw eggs flow under the set edges. Repeat at least twice at different places around the edge until the egg is no longer runny.

4. Cover the frittata and cook over low heat until set, 10 to 15 minutes. Loosen the edges with a spatula and slide the frittata onto a large plate. Invert the skillet over the frittata and, holding it firmly against the plate, invert the plate so the frittata falls back into the skillet. Cover and cook over low heat for 1 minute more.

5. To serve, slide the frittata onto a platter and serve warm or at room temperature, cut into wedges or small squares.

Makes 3 to 4 main-course or 6 appetizer servings

Zucchini and Red Onion Frittata with Goat Cheese and Mint

If you can, make this frittata with a variety of different-colored zucchini. In my farmers' market, I often find dark green and golden yellow zucchini, even pale green ones with dark green stripes.

3–4   **medium zucchini (about 1 pound total), trimmed**

2   **tablespoons extra-virgin olive oil**

1   **cup diced red onions**

⅓   **cup chopped fresh mint**
    Kosher salt and freshly ground black pepper

8   **large eggs**

¼   **cup milk (optional)**

½   **cup crumbled fresh goat cheese, mild-flavored feta or ricotta salata**

1. Quarter each zucchini lengthwise and then cut into ½-inch slices. You should have about 3 cups.

2. In a large nonstick (ovenproof) skillet with low, sloping sides, heat the oil over medium heat. Add the zucchini and onions and cook, stirring, for 1 minute. Cover, reduce the heat to medium-low and cook until the zucchini is tender but not mushy, about 5 minutes, stirring once or twice. Add the mint and cook, stirring, over high heat to evaporate any moisture, about 1 minute. Sprinkle with salt to taste and a grinding of pepper.

3. Meanwhile, in a large bowl, whisk the eggs, milk, if using, ½ teaspoon salt and a generous grinding of pepper until blended. Reduce the heat to medium-low, add the egg mixture to the skillet and cook until the eggs are set on the bottom and around the edges, about 4 minutes. With a spatula, lift one side of the frittata and tilt the pan so the raw eggs flow under the set edges. Repeat at least twice at different places around the edge until the egg is no longer runny.

4. Cover the frittata and cook over low heat until set, about 2 minutes.

> *I like the richness that a little milk stirred into the beaten eggs adds, but you can omit it if you prefer.*

5. Meanwhile, preheat the broiler. Sprinkle the cheese evenly over the frittata. Broil just until the top is golden, 1 to 2 minutes.

6. To serve, loosen the edges with a spatula and slide the frittata onto a platter. Serve warm or at room temperature, cut into wedges.

Makes 4 to 6 servings

Cabbage, Green Olive and Onion Frittata

Cabbage and green olives are an unusual combination, but when you taste it, you will be surprised at how good it is.

3 tablespoons extra-virgin olive oil

1 tablespoon unsalted butter

1 large onion, halved lengthwise and cut lengthwise into thin slivers (about 2 cups)

1 garlic clove, minced

¼ teaspoon crushed red pepper flakes, or to taste

½ large cabbage (1¼ pounds), cored and thinly sliced (about 8 cups)

10 green olives, pitted and coarsely chopped

8 large eggs

1 teaspoon kosher salt
Freshly ground black pepper

4 ounces Teleme, mozzarella or other quick-melting cheese, cut into thin slivers

1. In a large nonstick skillet with low, sloping sides, heat 1 tablespoon of the oil and the butter over medium-low heat. Add the onion and cook, stirring, until golden, about 10 minutes. Stir in the garlic and red pepper flakes and cook for 1 minute. Stir in the cabbage, a handful at a time, then drizzle the remaining 2 tablespoons oil on top. Cover, reduce the heat to low and cook for 2 minutes. Uncover and stir well to mix the cooked cabbage from the bottom with the crisper cabbage on top, then cook, stirring, until all the cabbage is wilted, about 2 minutes. Stir in the green olives.

2. Meanwhile, in a large bowl, whisk the eggs, salt and a grinding of pepper until blended. Pour over the cabbage and cook until the eggs are set on the bottom and around the edges, about 4 minutes. With a spatula, lift one side of the frittata and tilt the pan so the raw eggs flow under the set edges. Repeat at least twice at different places around the edge until the egg is no longer runny. Cover the frittata and cook over low heat until set, 10 to 15 minutes.

3. Loosen the edges with a spatula and slide the frittata onto a large plate. Invert the skillet over the frittata and, holding it firmly against the plate, hands protected with oven mitts or a towel, invert the frittata into the skillet, moist side down. Scatter the cheese over the top of the frittata and cook, covered, until the cheese melts and the bottom is set, about 2 minutes.

Serve cold or at room temperature with drinks before dinner, or serve warm as a light main course.

4. Loosen the edges with a spatula and slide the frittata onto a platter. Serve warm, at room temperature or cold, cut into wedges or squares.

Makes 4 main-course or 8 appetizer servings

John's Hangtown Fry
(Frittata with Fried Oysters and Bacon)

According to legend, Hangtown Fry was born when a miner who struck it rich during the California Gold Rush sauntered into a saloon and ordered a feast worth its weight in gold. The cook took the most expensive ingredients in his larder—eggs, bacon and oysters— and whipped up this delightful dish. We can only guess how Hangtown Fry found its way from the Wild West to the relative gentility of a restaurant called Gage & Tollner in Brooklyn, New York. This version from my husband, John, who was once a partner there, is rich, sumptuous and perfect for oyster lovers.

4	slices bacon
½	cup all-purpose flour
	Kosher salt and freshly ground black pepper
8	ounces (½ pint, about 8) shucked oysters, drained and patted dry
6–8	large eggs
¼	cup minced onion
2	tablespoons unsalted butter
	Toasted French or sourdough bread

1. Cook the bacon in a large nonstick skillet with low, sloping sides until crisp; drain on paper towels. Drain off all but 1 tablespoon bacon fat from the skillet; set the skillet aside. Crumble the bacon and set aside.

2. Mix together the flour, ½ teaspoon salt and a grinding of pepper on a sheet of waxed paper. Lightly coat the oysters with the flour, shaking off the excess.

3. In a medium bowl, whisk the eggs with a pinch of salt and a grinding of pepper until blended. Set aside.

4. Return the skillet to medium heat, add the onion and cook, stirring, until just golden, about 5 minutes. Add the bacon and butter. When the butter foams, add the oysters and sauté for about 1 minute per side. Do not overcook.

5. Preheat the broiler if you want to use it to finish the frittata. Increase the heat under the skillet to medium-high and pour the eggs over the oysters. Reduce the heat to medium-low. With a spatula, lift one side of the frittata and tilt the pan so the raw eggs flow under the set edges. Repeat at least twice at different places around the edge until the eggs are partially set, about 3 minutes.

6. To finish cooking the frittata, place the (ovenproof) skillet under the broiler for about 3 minutes. Or place a plate over the skillet and invert the frittata onto the plate, then slide it back into the skillet and cook until set, about 3 minutes more.

7. Slide onto a platter and cut into 4 wedges. Serve with the toast and plenty of softened butter.

Makes 4 servings

Roasted Red Pepper and Italian Sausage Frittata

Roasted red bell peppers and sweet Italian sausage make this frittata perfect for a hearty supper. Serve with steamed broccoli or cooked greens.

1 tablespoon extra-virgin olive oil

3 links (about 8 ounces) sweet Italian sausage, casings removed and meat separated into small lumps

2 large red bell peppers, roasted and cut into ½-inch-wide strips (see box)

1 garlic clove, minced

8 large eggs

2 tablespoons minced fresh flat-leaf parsley

½ teaspoon kosher salt

Freshly ground black pepper

½ cup grated mozzarella cheese

1. In a large nonstick skillet with low, sloping sides, heat the oil over medium heat. Add the sausage and cook, breaking it up with a wooden spoon, until browned, about 5 minutes; pour off the fat. Add the roasted peppers and garlic and cook, stirring, until heated through, about 1 minute. Reduce the heat to low.

2. Meanwhile, in a large bowl, whisk the eggs, parsley, salt and a grinding of pepper until blended. Add the egg mixture to the skillet, increase the heat to medium-low and cook until the eggs are set on the bottom and around the edges, about 4 minutes. With a spatula, lift one side of the frittata and tilt the pan so the raw eggs flow under the set edges. Repeat at least twice at different places around the edge until the egg is no longer runny.

3. Sprinkle the top of the frittata with the cheese, cover, reduce the heat to low and cook until set, 10 to 15 minutes. If you prefer the top browned, preheat the broiler, then set the (ovenproof) skillet under the heat just until the top is lightly browned, 1 to 2 minutes.

4. Slide the frittata onto a platter. Serve warm or at room temperature, cut into wedges.

Makes 4 to 6 servings

How to Roast Peppers

Position the broiler rack about 2 inches from the heat source and preheat the broiler. Place a sheet of foil on a baking sheet and arrange the peppers on it shoulder to shoulder. Broil, turning the peppers with tongs as they blacken, until evenly charred, about 20 minutes. Remove the pan from the broiler. Fold the foil up over the peppers and seal. As the peppers cool, the skins will loosen.

When they have cooled, peel the peppers with a small paring knife or your fingertips, working over the foil to catch the juices. Separate the peppers into halves or quarters, following their natural contours. Lift out the seeds and stems, then pull out any thick white ribs. Do not rinse the peppers: rinsing would wash away all the good flavors. Strain the juices left on the foil and pour over the peppers.

Oven-Baked Spaghetti Frittata

Italians often use their leftover pasta in frittatas. The result is a sturdy frittata that can be cut into nice thick wedges and makes a hearty meal. This frittata is easier to handle if it is baked in the oven rather than on top of the stove. I use a cast-iron skillet that is about 9 inches across and 2 inches deep, but any baking pan or heavy skillet with an ovenproof handle will do.

2 tablespoons fine dry bread crumbs

¼ cup extra-virgin olive oil, plus more to drizzle on top

2 garlic cloves, minced

8 ounces spaghetti, cooked until al dente and drained (about 2 cups)

1 3½-ounce can imported tuna in olive oil, drained and flaked

¼ cup chopped pitted green olives

2 tablespoons finely chopped fresh flat-leaf parsley

6 large eggs

1. Preheat the oven to 375°F. Generously butter a medium cast-iron skillet and sprinkle with the bread crumbs to coat.

2. Combine the oil and garlic in a large skillet and heat just until the garlic begins to sizzle. Remove from the heat, add the spaghetti and toss to coat with the oil. Add the tuna, olives and parsley.

3. Whisk the eggs in a large bowl until blended. Add to the spaghetti mixture and, using a fork, move the ingredients to distribute the eggs evenly. Transfer to the bread-crumb coated skillet. Top with a drizzle of oil.

4. Place in the oven and bake until the edges are browned and the frittata is set in the center, 25 to 30 minutes. Cool in the skillet for 10 minutes, then loosen the edges with a spatula and turn out the frittata onto a platter. Cut into wedges and serve.

Makes 4 to 6 servings

The flavorings in oven frittatas, like conventionally cooked frittatas, can be as varied as the leftovers in your refrigerator or the staples in your pantry. Cheese, roasted chicken, shrimp, roasted peppers, mushrooms and other herbs are all possibilities.

Fresh Fig and Prosciutto Frittata with Mild Asiago

Sweet fresh figs, tangy young Asiago cheese and salty prosciutto provide the perfect balance in this unusual frittata. Because the filling is chunky, it's easier to finish the frittata under the broiler than to flip it. This frittata is excellent accompanied by a salad of bitter greens tossed with a drizzle of balsamic vinegar.

10 large eggs

1 teaspoon kosher salt

Freshly ground black pepper

2 tablespoons extra-virgin olive oil

4–5 slices (about 2 ounces) prosciutto, trimmed of excess fat and chopped

10–12 ripe figs, stems trimmed, cut into 1-inch chunks (about 1½ cups)

½ cup diced (¼ inch) young Asiago (about 2 ounces)

1. In a large bowl, whisk the eggs, salt and a generous grinding of pepper until blended.

2. In a large nonstick (ovenproof) skillet with low, sloping sides, heat the oil over low heat. Add the eggs and cook until set on the bottom and around the edges, about 4 minutes. With a spatula, lift one side of the frittata and tilt the pan so the raw eggs flow under the set edges. Repeat at least twice at different places around the edge until the egg is no longer runny.

3. Sprinkle the frittata with the prosciutto and then arrange the figs evenly over the frittata. Cover and cook until barely set, 10 to 15 minutes.

4. Meanwhile, preheat the broiler. Sprinkle the cheese over the frittata and broil just until the top is golden, 1 to 2 minutes. Let stand a few minutes before serving.

5. Slide the frittata onto a platter. Serve warm or at room temperature, cut into wedges.

Makes 5 to 6 servings

If a young, soft-textured, mild Asiago is not available, use fontina, Havarti, Monterey Jack, cold or chilled Teleme or another mild semisoft cheese with a slight tang.

Tortilla Española with Roasted Red Pepper and Almond Sauce (Spanish Frittata with Potato)

In Spain, this classic layered potato and egg dish, half omelette, half frittata, is known as a *tortilla*. I often make Tortilla Española for informal dinners or lunches, serving it in big wedges with roasted red pepper sauce on top and a green salad on the side.

¾ cup extra-virgin olive oil

4 large baking potatoes (about 2 pounds total), peeled and thinly sliced

1 large onion, halved and thinly sliced

1 teaspoon kosher salt

6 large eggs

Roasted Red Pepper and Almond Sauce (page 80)

1. In a large nonstick skillet with low, sloping sides, heat the oil over medium-low heat. Arrange the potato and onion slices in alternating layers in the pan. Bring to a simmer and cook, turning occasionally, until the potatoes are tender, about 15 minutes. Do not let them brown.

2. Drain the potatoes and onions in a colander; reserve 2 tablespoons of the oil. Pat the potatoes dry with paper towels to absorb the excess oil. Sprinkle with the salt.

3. In a large bowl, whisk the eggs until blended. Add the potatoes and onions and press down into the eggs with a spoon. Let stand for 15 minutes.

4. Heat 1 tablespoon of the reserved oil in the skillet over medium heat until very hot. Tilt to coat the skillet evenly with oil, then add the potato mixture all at once and spread in an even layer. Reduce the heat to low and cook, shaking the pan frequently, until the bottom is lightly browned, 8 to 10 minutes. Place a plate on top of the skillet and invert. Add the remaining 1 tablespoon oil to the skillet, then slide the tortilla, browned side up, back into the skillet and cook, shaking the pan, until the bottom is browned, 8 to 10 minutes.

The sauce is excellent served over warm hard-cooked eggs (page 162), so I usually make a double batch.

5. Loosen the sides with a spatula and slide the tortilla onto a platter. Serve warm, at room temperature or cold, cut into wedges or squares and topped with the Roasted Red Pepper and Almond Sauce.

Makes 6 to 8 servings

Roasted Red Pepper and Almond Sauce

½ cup whole natural almonds

2 garlic cloves, coarsely chopped

3 red bell peppers, roasted, with their juices (page 75)

2 tablespoons chopped fresh flat-leaf parsley

½ teaspoon kosher salt

¼ teaspoon crushed red pepper flakes

Freshly ground black pepper

2 tablespoons sherry vinegar

6–8 tablespoons extra-virgin olive oil

1. Preheat the oven to 350°F. Spread the almonds on a baking sheet and toast until golden brown, about 10 minutes. Cool slightly.

2. Place the almonds and garlic in a food processor and finely chop. Add the roasted peppers (reserve the juices), parsley, salt, red pepper flakes and a grinding of pepper and process until pureed. With the motor running, gradually add the reserved pepper juices and the vinegar and process until incorporated, then add the oil in a slow, steady stream, processing until the sauce is smooth.

3. Serve with Tortilla Española (page 78) or over halved hard-cooked eggs as a luncheon dish, a side dish or an appetizer. The sauce will keep refrigerated for about 5 days.

Makes about 1 ½ cups

CHAPTER 3   *Baked and Poached Eggs*

CROWNING GLORIES

"Egg dishes have a kind of elegance, a freshness, an allure, which sets them apart from any other kind of food."
—ELIZABETH DAVID

aking and poaching are gentle, almost foolproof modes of cooking that "set" eggs into shapely ovals, with a compact, tender white surrounding a lightly veiled mound of soft golden yolk. I have given these beautifully formed eggs a score of savory "settings," arranging them on platforms of fried and whipped potatoes, polenta or rice, black beans or lentils; nestling them into vegetable stews or sauces; or perching them on pan-crisped seafood and meat hashes.

In these settings, the eggs are indeed "crowning glories," shimmering on top of a large casserole or in individual gratin dishes. A simple baked or poached egg can transform a wide variety of everyday side dishes (and leftovers) into satisfying meals, good for breakfast, lunch or supper. The sweet, mild flavor of the egg complements all kinds of savory and spicy combinations, from cheesy creamed spinach to curried lentils, and the soft, runny yolks provide a natural sauce, pulling all the elements together.

Of these two cooking methods, you may find baking eggs simpler in several respects. Once you've made the savory base and placed it in the baking dish, you create small hollows in the top and crack the eggs into them. In the heat of the oven, they set in a perfect shape.

Poached eggs present a slightly greater challenge, as the eggs are cooked on their own in a pan of simmering water, then placed on top of their base just before serving. Poaching eggs is fundamentally quite easy, but producing a compact shape requires fresh eggs, gentle handling, close attention to the heat of the poaching liquid and careful timing.

Remember that eggs can be poached in almost any liquid, not just water. I use tomato sauce and wine sauce in a couple of the recipes in this chapter, and I have often poached eggs in the gravy left from short ribs, veal or beef bourguignon. Stock or broth, milk and tomato juice work very well too.

Plain Baked Eggs
The Basics

Baked eggs don't need a savory base like polenta or rice pilaf to be delicious. You can easily bake a plain egg—adorned with nothing more than a bit of butter and some seasonings —for an easy breakfast or lunch. There are two basic types of baked eggs: shirred eggs and eggs *en cocotte*. "Shirred" is a fancy name for eggs that are cracked into a flat gratin dish and baked until softly set. *En cocotte* is a French term referring to eggs that are cracked into small ramekins or custard cups, which are then placed in a water bath and baked until set.

Shirred Eggs

Position a rack in the center of the oven and preheat the oven to 325°F. Lightly butter a round or an oval gratin or other baking dish about 5 inches in diameter. Break 2 eggs into the dish. Dot with 1 teaspoon butter cut into small pieces. Bake until the whites are set and the yolks are thickened, 15 to 18 minutes. Season with salt and pepper and sprinkle with minced fresh tarragon just before serving. You can vary the seasonings and/or herb, or top the eggs with a sauce, bread crumbs or grated cheese.

Eggs *en Cocotte*

Position a rack in the center of the oven and preheat the oven to 325°F. For each serving, lightly butter a 5-ounce ramekin. Crack an egg into each ramekin and add 1 tablespoon heavy cream, a small pinch of grated lemon zest and 1 teaspoon butter. (For other seasoning ideas, see page 107.) Place the ramekins in a baking pan, add enough boiling water to the pan to come halfway up the sides of the ramekins and bake until the whites are set and the yolks are thickened, 15 to 20 minutes. Season with salt and pepper just before serving.

Eggs Baked in Fresh Tomato Salsa with Melted Cheese

Make your own fresh tomato salsa, or buy a good-quality refrigerated fresh salsa from the supermarket. The flavors are best if you prepare the salsa just before baking and serving. The entire dish, including preparation and cooking times, takes less than 30 minutes.

Extra-virgin olive oil

Tomato Salsa

2½ **cups diced (¼ inch) tomatoes (2–3 large ripe tomatoes)**

¼ **cup finely chopped sweet onion**

2 **tablespoons extra-virgin olive oil**

2 **tablespoons chopped fresh cilantro or basil**

2 **teaspoons fresh lime or lemon juice**

1–2 **teaspoons minced jalapeño**

½ **teaspoon kosher salt**

4 **large eggs**

1 **cup grated Monterey Jack or mozzarella cheese (about 4 ounces)**

Toasted bread

1. Preheat the oven to 400°F. Brush four (8-ounce) ramekins or small gratin dishes (about 5 inches in diameter and 1 inch deep) with oil. Set the dishes on a baking sheet.

2. **Make the salsa:** Combine the tomatoes, onion, oil, cilantro or basil, lime or lemon juice, jalapeño and salt in a medium bowl and stir to blend.

3. Distribute the salsa evenly among the prepared dishes. Make an indention in the middle of the salsa in each dish. Break the eggs one at a time into a cup and slip an egg into each dish. Sprinkle with the cheese, dividing evenly.

4. Bake until the whites are set, about 8 minutes. Serve at once, with the toast.

Makes 4 servings

Vary the seasoning in the salsa depending on your preference. A little wine vinegar can be used instead of the lime or lemon juice. Red onion and a mix of red and yellow tomatoes are also good.

Eggs Baked in Roasted Summer Vegetables

In the summertime, I like to start with tomatoes, eggplant and red bell peppers and then add whatever else looks good at my local farmers' market.

2 pounds ripe plum tomatoes, cored and halved lengthwise

½ large or 1 small eggplant, stem trimmed, cut into 1-inch chunks

1 red bell pepper, cored, seeded and cut into ½-inch chunks

1 small yellow summer squash, trimmed and cut into 1-inch chunks

1 small zucchini, trimmed and cut into 1-inch chunks

1 onion, cut into thin wedges

2 garlic cloves, chopped

½ cup extra-virgin olive oil

Kosher salt and freshly ground black pepper

1 tablespoon chopped fresh basil

1 teaspoon fresh thyme leaves

1 teaspoon fresh oregano leaves

1. Preheat the oven to 400°F. Spread the tomatoes, eggplant, bell pepper, summer squash, zucchini, onion and garlic evenly on one large or two small baking sheets. Drizzle with the oil and sprinkle with salt to taste and a grinding of pepper.

2. Roast the vegetables, stirring occasionally, until browned and tender, about 1 hour 5 minutes. (You can roast the vegetables several days ahead and store in an airtight container in the refrigerator. Bring to room temperature before baking.)

3. Transfer the vegetable mixture to a 13-x-9-inch baking dish. Stir in the basil, thyme, oregano and more salt and pepper to taste. Cover with foil and bake until the vegetables are very hot, about 20 minutes.

Experiment with different fresh herbs. Basil, thyme and oregano are excellent, but chervil, mint and flat-leaf parsley are very good too.

4 large eggs

1½ cups grated aged Gouda, fontina, Emmentaler or other cheese (about 6 ounces)

4. With a large spoon, make 4 evenly spaced indentations in the vegetables. Break the eggs one at a time into a cup and slip each egg into an indentation. Sprinkle the cheese over the vegetables and eggs.

5. Bake, uncovered, until the eggs are set and the cheese is melted, 12 to 15 minutes. Serve at once.

Makes 4 servings

Eggs Baked in Roasted Tomato Sauce

To coax flavor from out-of-season tomatoes, I roast them. In this recipe, pureed roasted plum tomatoes make a sauce with wonderful depth of flavor.

Roasted Tomato Sauce

- 3 **pounds plum tomatoes, cored and halved**
- ½ **onion, thinly sliced**
- 3 **garlic cloves, bruised with the side of a knife**
- ¼ **cup extra-virgin olive oil**
  Kosher salt and freshly ground black pepper
- 1 **teaspoon fresh thyme leaves**

- 4–8 **large eggs**
- 1 **cup grated Gruyère or mozzarella cheese (about 4 ounces)**
  Toasted Italian bread

You can substitute smoked mozzarella or Gouda for the cheese.

1. **Make the sauce:** Preheat the oven to 400°F. Arrange the tomatoes, cut side up, on a heavy baking sheet with sides or in a large roasting pan. Scatter the onion and garlic over the top. Drizzle with the oil and sprinkle lightly with salt and a grinding of pepper.

2. Roast for 20 minutes. Turn the tomatoes cut side down, sprinkle with salt and the thyme and spoon the juices and oil over the tomatoes. Roast for 20 to 30 minutes more, or until the skins are slightly blackened. Remove and let cool slightly. Leave the oven on.

3. Set a food mill over a large saucepan and transfer the tomatoes, onion, garlic and all the juices to the food mill. Press through the mill. (If you don't have a food mill, transfer to a food processor and finely chop, then press through a strainer with a rubber spatula; discard the solids.) You should have 2 to 2½ cups sauce. (The sauce can be made 1 or 2 days ahead.)

4. Heat the sauce to a simmer. Pour it into a shallow 2-quart baking dish, or divide it among four (8-ounce) gratin dishes (about 1 inch deep and 5 inches in diameter) and place them on a baking sheet. Break the eggs one at a time into a cup and slip into the hot sauce. Top with the cheese.

5. Bake just until the eggs are set, the cheese is melted and the sauce is bubbly, 15 to 20 minutes. Serve at once with the toast.

Makes 4 servings

Eggs Baked in Mushrooms

If you have them on hand, soak a few dried shiitake or porcini mushrooms in warm water until softened, squeeze them dry, chop and add to the mix of fresh mushrooms. Mix and match white button, cremini, shiitake and oyster mushrooms, selecting a few of each until you have a total of one pound.

1   **pound mixed fresh mushrooms**

3   **tablespoons extra-virgin olive oil**

½   **cup chopped onion**

2   **garlic cloves, minced**

1   **cup diced seeded ripe tomatoes, with their juices**

2   **tablespoons finely chopped fresh flat-leaf parsley**

2   **tablespoons chopped fresh basil**

    Kosher salt and freshly ground black pepper

4   **large eggs**

¼   **cup grated Asiago or other semisoft cheese (see box)**

    Toasted bread

Gruyère, mild cheddar, Monterey Jack and even fontina are all excellent substitutes for the Asiago cheese.

1. Preheat the oven to 400°F. Generously butter four (8-ounce) ramekins or small gratin dishes (about 1 inch deep and 5 inches in diameter). Set the dishes on a baking sheet.

2. Wipe the mushrooms clean with a damp paper towel. Remove and discard the stems of shiitake mushrooms, if using. Chop the mushrooms into ¼-inch pieces. You should have about 7 cups.

3. Heat the oil in a large skillet over medium heat. Add the mushrooms and onion and sauté until the mushrooms are tender and lightly browned, 5 to 8 minutes. Stir in the garlic and cook, stirring, for 2 minutes. Add the tomatoes and their juices, parsley and basil. Cook, stirring, until the tomatoes are soft and the mixture is evenly moistened, about 2 minutes. Add salt to taste and a grinding of pepper.

4. Transfer the mushroom mixture to the prepared dishes. With the back of a spoon, make an indentation in the center of the mushroom mixture in each dish. Break the eggs one at a time into a cup and slip an egg into each dish. Sprinkle with the cheese.

5. Bake until the whites are set, about 8 minutes. Serve at once with the toast.

Makes 4 servings

Eggs Baked in Creamed Spinach

This is my version of eggs Florentine. You can make the spinach mixture up to one day ahead. Reheat before putting in the gratin dishes. Add the eggs and bake just before serving. Serve for breakfast, brunch, lunch or supper with a tomato or roasted-pepper salad on the side.

2 tablespoons unsalted butter

¼ cup minced onion

2 10-ounce packages frozen chopped spinach, thawed, drained and squeezed dry

½ cup heavy cream

Freshly grated nutmeg

Kosher salt and freshly ground black pepper

4 large eggs

¼ cup freshly grated Parmigiano-Reggiano cheese

Toasted bread

1. Preheat the oven to 400°F. Generously butter four (8-ounce) ramekins or small gratin dishes (about 1 inch deep and 5 inches in diameter). Set the dishes on a baking sheet.

2. Melt the butter in a large nonstick skillet over low heat. Add the onion and sauté until soft, about 5 minutes. Stir in the spinach and cream; cook over medium heat until boiling. Continue to cook until blended and creamy, about 2 minutes. Add the nutmeg, salt to taste and a grinding of pepper.

3. Transfer the spinach mixture to the prepared dishes. With the back of a spoon, make an indentation in the center of the spinach mixture in each dish. Break the eggs one at a time into a cup and slip an egg into each dish. Sprinkle with the cheese.

4. Bake until the whites are set, about 8 minutes. Serve at once with the toast.

Makes 4 servings

For the frozen spinach, substitute two 10-ounce bags fresh spinach, trimmed and steamed over boiling water until wilted, about 3 minutes. Cool, drain, squeeze dry and chop. Equal weights of frozen and fresh spinach will yield ¾ to 1 cup when cooked and chopped.

Eggs Baked in Potatoes

An egg baked inside a russet potato whose flesh has been mashed with grated Parmesan cheese and olive oil or butter makes an especially comforting and nourishing meal. Serve with a side dish of broccoli tossed with garlic and lemon juice.

2 large russet potatoes, scrubbed and pierced with the tines of a fork

2 tablespoons extra-virgin olive oil or unsalted butter

¼ cup freshly grated Parmigiano-Reggiano cheese

Kosher salt and freshly ground black pepper

2 large eggs

1. Preheat the oven to 400°F. Bake the potatoes until the skin is crisp and the interior feels soft when pierced with a skewer, about 1 hour.

2. Slash the potatoes lengthwise about halfway down into the flesh. Protecting your hands with a kitchen towel, hold onto both ends and push so that the slash opens up to expose the interior of each potato.

3. Using a tablespoon, scoop about ½ cup of the flesh from each potato into a small bowl. Add the oil or butter, half of the cheese, a pinch of salt and a grinding of pepper and mash with a fork until blended. Spoon back into the potato, pressing down and making an indentation in the center. Place the potatoes in a small baking dish. Break the eggs one at a time into a cup and slip an egg into the center of each potato. Sprinkle with the remaining cheese.

4. Bake until the egg white is set to the desired doneness, 10 to 15 minutes. Serve at once.

Makes 2 servings

Mom's Ciambotta with Baked Eggs

Make this hearty stew with or without the sausage, or if you prefer, grill the sausage and serve on the side. Mom served it as either a vegetable side dish or a vegetable-and-sausage main dish. The eggs and cheese are my idea.

2 pounds plum tomatoes or one 28-ounce can plum tomatoes, with their juices

¼ cup extra-virgin olive oil

8–12 ounces Italian sausage, preferably sweet, casings removed and meat broken into small lumps

1 large sweet onion, cut lengthwise into thin slices

1 serrano or other hot chile, seeded and chopped, or ¼–½ teaspoon crushed red pepper flakes

2 garlic cloves, minced
   Kosher salt and freshly ground black pepper

2 pounds zucchini (all green or a mixture of green and yellow), trimmed, quartered lengthwise and cut crosswise into ½-inch pieces

¼ cup torn fresh basil or flat-leaf parsley leaves

1. If using fresh tomatoes, fill a saucepan half-full with water and bring to a boil. Add the tomatoes, remove from the heat and let stand for 20 seconds. Drain and transfer to a large bowl. When the tomatoes are cool enough to handle, remove and discard the skins and cores. Cut the tomatoes into ½-inch cubes, reserving the juices. You should have about 3 cups.

2. Heat the oil in a large, wide saucepan over medium-low heat. Add the sausage, breaking it up as needed, and cook, stirring, until no longer pink, about 5 minutes. Stir in the onion and cook until it softens and starts to turn golden, about 5 minutes. Add the hot chile or red pepper flakes and garlic and cook for 1 minute. Add the fresh or canned tomatoes with their juices, a pinch of salt and a grinding of pepper and bring to a boil. Cover and simmer for 20 minutes.

3. Add the zucchini to the tomatoes, cover and cook, stirring occasionally, until very tender, about 15 minutes. Add the basil or parsley. Taste and add more salt and pepper, if needed. If the mixture is watery, boil, uncovered, until slightly thickened, about 5 minutes. (The dish can be made a day or two ahead to this point; reheat before proceeding.)

4 large eggs

1–2 cups shredded fontina,
     mozzarella, Gruyère, young
     Pecorino Romano or Dry Jack
     cheese (4–8 ounces)

4. Meanwhile, preheat the oven to 400°F. Spoon the hot zucchini mixture into a 13-x-9-inch baking dish. With a large spoon, make 4 evenly spaced indentations in the zucchini mixture. Break the eggs one at a time into a cup and slip an egg into each indentation. Sprinkle with the cheese.

5. Bake until the cheese is melted and the eggs are set to the desired doneness, 15 to 20 minutes. Scoop each egg into a shallow bowl and surround with the vegetable stew. Serve immediately.

Makes 4 servings

Eggs Baked in Green Bean and Tomato Sauce

In this recipe, the eggs are baked in a rich green bean and tomato sauce flavored with bay leaf and a pinch of crushed red pepper flakes.

2 tablespoons extra-virgin olive oil

½ cup finely chopped onion

1 slice bacon, cut into ¼-inch dice

1 28-ounce can plum tomatoes, with their juices

1 bay leaf

Pinch of crushed red pepper flakes, or more to taste

1¼ pounds green beans (either snap beans or wide Italian), trimmed and cut into ½-inch lengths

Kosher salt and freshly ground black pepper

4 large eggs

1 cup coarsely shredded mozzarella cheese (8 ounces)

1. Heat the oil in a large, deep ovenproof skillet over medium-low heat. Add the onion and bacon and cook, stirring, until the onion is soft and the bacon is golden, about 5 minutes.

2. Meanwhile, using kitchen shears, cut each tomato into 6 or more pieces. Add the tomatoes and their juices, the bay leaf and red pepper flakes to the skillet and bring to a boil.

3. Add the green beans, salt to taste and a grinding of pepper. Cover, increase the heat to medium and cook until the beans are very tender, about 25 minutes. Uncover and simmer until the tomato sauce thickens slightly, about 10 minutes. Taste and add more red pepper flakes, salt or pepper, if needed. Remove from the heat.

4. Meanwhile, preheat the oven to 400°F. With a large spoon, make 4 evenly spaced indentations in the sauce. Break the eggs one at a time into a cup and slip an egg into each indentation. Sprinkle with the cheese.

5. Bake until the eggs are set and the cheese is bubbly, about 15 minutes. Serve at once.

Makes 4 servings

Eggs Baked in Polenta Casserole

I especially like this baked egg and polenta dish with Italian fontina or Taleggio cheese melted over the top. Or try it with mild Gorgonzola. Almost any cheese will work.

6 cups water

1½ cups cornmeal

1 tablespoon kosher salt

1 cup milk

4 tablespoons (½ stick) unsalted butter

½ cup freshly grated Parmigiano-Reggiano cheese

Freshly grated nutmeg (optional)

8 large eggs

6 ounces Taleggio or Italian fontina, slivered (about 1½ cups)

Warm buttered toast

1. Bring 4 cups of the water to a boil in a large, wide saucepan. In a small bowl, stir the cornmeal into the remaining 2 cups water until blended. Stir the cornmeal mixture into the boiling water, add the salt and cook, stirring frequently, until thickened and smooth, about 25 minutes.

2. Stir in the milk and butter and cook, stirring, for 5 minutes more. Add the Parmigiano-Reggiano and a grating of nutmeg, if using. (The polenta can be made ahead.) Transfer it to the top of a double boiler and keep warm over hot — not boiling   water until ready to serve. If it gets too thick, stir in a small amount of milk to thin it.

3. Meanwhile, preheat the oven to 350°F. Lightly butter a shallow 1½-to-2-quart baking dish or four 2-cup casseroles. Pour the hot polenta into the dish(es). Make 8 indentations in the polenta with a large spoon. Break the eggs one at a time into a cup and slip an egg into each indentation. Sprinkle with the cheese.

4. Bake until the polenta is golden around the edges and the eggs are soft-cooked, 10 to 12 minutes. (The eggs will continue cooking after they are removed from the oven.) Let stand for 3 minutes before serving. Serve with the toast.

Makes 4 servings

Potato, Sausage and Fontina Casserole with Baked Eggs

In this dish, soft-cooked egg yolks make a luscious sauce as they seep over and around the potatoes when the casserole is served.

2½ **pounds Yukon Gold or other all-purpose potatoes**

8 **ounces sweet Italian sausage, casings removed and meat broken into small lumps**

1 **10-ounce bag spinach, trimmed and washed**

Unsalted butter

2 **cups grated fontina cheese (about 8 ounces)**

4 **large eggs**

1. Cook the potatoes in a large pot of boiling salted water to cover until tender, about 30 minutes. Drain. When the potatoes are cool enough to handle, peel them and cut into ¼-inch-thick slices.

2. Meanwhile, in a large skillet, cook the sausage over medium-high heat, breaking up with the side of a spoon, if necessary, until golden brown, about 10 minutes. Drain off any fat and let cool.

3. Bring about 1 inch of water to a boil in a large saucepan fitted with a steamer basket. Add the spinach, cover and steam until just wilted, about 2 minutes. Transfer to a strainer and drain well, pressing down on the spinach to remove as much water as possible.

4. Preheat the oven to 350°F. Generously butter a 2-quart casserole or soufflé dish. Layer one-third of the potatoes in the casserole. Top with one-third of the sausage and half of the spinach. Make another layer with one-third of the potatoes and top with half of the remaining sausage and the remaining spinach. Make another layer with the remaining potatoes and top with the remaining sausage and 1½ cups of the cheese.

5. Bake until the cheese is browned and bubbly, about 25 minutes. Remove from the oven and immediately break the eggs over the top (they will all cook together). Sprinkle with the remaining ½ cup cheese and bake until the eggs are soft-cooked, about 15 minutes. Serve at once.

Makes 4 servings

Baked Eggs on Salmon Hash with Dill and Orange

Since I cook salmon more often than lamb or beef, I frequently make salmon hash. It is light, delicious and quite healthful (especially with the good omega-3 fatty acids of the salmon). This makes a great "leftovers" meal that may be even better than the original.

2 tablespoons unsalted butter

2 tablespoons extra-virgin olive oil or vegetable oil

1¼ pounds all-purpose or new potatoes, cooked, peeled and cut into ¼-inch dice (about 3 cups)

1 cup chopped onions

¼ cup finely chopped green bell pepper

¼ cup finely chopped red bell pepper

2 cups skinned, flaked cooked salmon

1 tablespoon minced fresh dill, plus small sprigs for garnish

1 tablespoon chopped fresh flat-leaf parsley

1 garlic clove, minced

½ teaspoon grated orange zest
Kosher salt and freshly ground black pepper

½ cup sour cream, at room temperature

4 large eggs

1. Heat the butter and oil in a large skillet over medium heat. When hot enough to sizzle a piece of potato, spread the potatoes evenly in the skillet. Cook, without stirring, just until the bottom begins to turn golden, about 3 minutes. Turn the potatoes, sprinkle the onion on top and cook, adjusting the heat to maintain a steady sizzle and stirring occasionally, until the potatoes are browned and the onions are golden, about 5 minutes more.

2. Add the bell peppers and cook, stirring, for 2 minutes. Add the salmon, minced dill, parsley, garlic and orange zest. Sprinkle generously with salt and pepper and cook, turning gently with a spatula so as not to break up the salmon too much, just until the salmon is heated through, about 2 minutes.

3. Stir the sour cream in a small bowl until smooth. Drizzle over the top of the hash and stir once or twice just to combine. Reduce the heat to medium-low and spread the hash in a fairly even layer. Make 4 evenly spaced slight indentations in the hash with the back of a large spoon. Break the eggs one at a time into a cup and slip an egg into each indentation. Cover and cook until the eggs are cooked to the desired doneness, 3 to 5 minutes.

Serve with warm buttered toast, preferably sourdough.

4. Transfer to four plates, using a large spatula to avoid breaking the eggs. Garnish with dill sprigs and serve.

Makes 4 servings

Perfect Poached Eggs
The Basics

The first key to success when poaching eggs is to use the freshest eggs possible. A freshly laid egg has a thick viscous albumen and a rounded yolk, which will poach into a perfectly plump oval with the yolk sitting pertly on top. But as an egg ages, the white becomes thinner and the yolk flattens. When the egg is lowered into hot water—especially if it is boiling rapidly—the thinner portions of the white will disperse and cook into lacy, featherlike strands. Therefore, I usually don't poach eggs unless I have bought them guaranteed "farm fresh" at my local farmers' market or from a supermarket that I know has only the freshest eggs. I add a bit of vinegar and salt to the poaching water, which helps the whites to coagulate, and keep the water at a bare simmer, which also helps prevent feathering. If you are uncertain about the age of your eggs, be sure to read the tip below about "preboiling," but you may want to try cooking them in a metal poacher, a mold or a coddler, as detailed in the sidebar on page 106.

♦ Fill a deep 10-inch skillet or sauté pan with water, adding 1 tablespoon white vinegar and 1 teaspoon salt for each 2 quarts of water.

♦ Heat the water to a bare simmer.

♦ Use cold eggs straight from the refrigerator, because a chilled white is thicker and will be less likely to feather than a warm one. Break the eggs one at a time into a cup or saucer and slip gently into the water (I usually poach no more than 4 at a time). Add the eggs in a clockwise pattern, so that you can remove them in the same order, ensuring equal cooking times.

♦ If using older eggs, you can give them a "preboil" in the shell before poaching to set the whites slightly and help control feathering. Bring the water to a boil and lower each egg (still in the shell) into the pan—immerse the eggs for only 8 seconds, then remove. Reduce the heat, and proceed to crack each egg into a cup and slip it into the simmering water.

♦ Adjust the temperature as necessary to maintain the simmer, but do not allow the water to boil, as the turbulence would cause feathering and toughen the egg whites.

♦ Cook the eggs for 1 minute, until partially set, then gently loosen them from the bottom of the pan with a spatula. If necessary, gently shape the whites into ovals.

♦ Poach until the yolks and whites are cooked to the desired doneness, 3 to 5 minutes.

♦ Remove the eggs one at a time with a slotted spoon in the order that they went into the pan. Drain each egg by holding the spoon on a cloth towel or paper towels for 2 seconds, then slip it onto a plate.

♦ If necessary, trim any ragged edges of white with a small knife or scissors.

♦ To hold poached eggs for later use, slip them directly into a bowl half-filled with cold water when you remove them from the poaching liquid. To reheat the eggs, carefully remove them from the water with a slotted spoon and lower them into a pan of very hot water for 1 minute before serving.

Eggs Poached in Spicy Tomato Sauce

This classic dish is also called eggs in purgatory. Sometimes I brown crumbled Italian fennel sausage meat and add it to the sauce. It makes for a richer dish, and the fennel imparts a nice sweet flavor that balances the spiciness of the crushed red pepper flakes.

2   **28-ounce cans plum tomatoes, with their juices**

2   **tablespoons extra-virgin olive oil**

½   **cup finely chopped onion**

1   **small garlic clove, minced**

¼   **teaspoon crushed red pepper flakes, or to taste**

2   **tablespoons chopped fresh flat-leaf parsley**

2   **tablespoons chopped fresh basil**

½   **teaspoon dried oregano**
    Kosher salt and freshly ground black pepper

4   **large eggs**

4–8   **slices Italian bread, toasted**
    Freshly grated Pecorino Romano cheese

1. Pass the tomatoes, with their juices, through a food mill into a bowl. (Or puree them in a food processor, then press through a strainer; discard the solids.) Heat the oil in a large saucepan over medium heat. Add the onion and sauté, stirring, until golden, about 5 minutes; do not brown. Add the garlic and red pepper flakes and cook for 1 minute more. Add the tomatoes and bring to a boil. Add the parsley, basil and oregano and simmer, uncovered, until thickened, about 50 minutes. Season with salt to taste and a grinding of pepper.

2. Break the eggs one at a time into a cup and slip them into the simmering sauce, spacing them evenly. Cover and cook until the egg whites and yolks are set to your liking, 6 to 8 minutes.

3. Place 1 or 2 slices of toast in the bottom of four shallow bowls. Top with the eggs, ladle the sauce around the eggs and sprinkle with the cheese. Pass red pepper flakes at the table for those who like more heat.

Makes 4 servings

VARIATION

Remove the casings from 4 links of Italian fennel sausage. Cook the sausage in a medium skillet, stirring and breaking it up with a spatula, until lightly browned. Add to the tomato sauce halfway through cooking and simmer for 10 to 20 minutes.

Skillet Eggs with Chipotle Peppers and Black Beans

Chipotle chiles add an especially delicious flavor to black beans and eggs smothered with melted Monterey Jack cheese. Serve this easy-to-prepare dish for brunch or dinner, with a tomato and avocado salsa seasoned with fresh cilantro and lemon or lime juice.

2 tablespoons extra-virgin olive oil

1 cup chopped onions

⅓ cup finely chopped green bell pepper

⅓ cup finely chopped red bell pepper

1 garlic clove, minced

4 cups cooked black beans or two 15-ounce cans, drained (not rinsed)

2–3 teaspoons minced canned chipotle chiles in adobo sauce (see box)

2 teaspoons ground cumin

Kosher salt and freshly ground black pepper

4 large eggs

½ cup grated Monterey Jack cheese

Tomato-Avocado Salsa (page 14)

4 large flour tortillas, wrapped in foil and warmed in the oven

1. Heat the oil in a large nonstick skillet over medium heat. Add the onions and bell peppers and cook, stirring, until the onions are golden and the bell peppers are lightly browned, about 10 minutes. Add the garlic and cook for 1 minute. Stir in the beans, chipotles and cumin, cover, reduce the heat to low and cook for 5 minutes. Season with salt to taste and a grinding of pepper.

2. Break the eggs one at a time into a small cup and place on top of the bean mixture, spacing them evenly. Sprinkle with the cheese. Cover, increase the heat to medium and cook until the whites are set and the yolks are cooked to the desired doneness, 5 to 8 minutes.

3. Transfer to plates and garnish with the Tomato-Avocado Salsa and serve with the tortillas.

Makes 4 servings

Chipotles are dried smoked jalapeños that are fiery hot and have a distinctively smoky flavor. They are available canned in adobo sauce in supermarkets that have a good selection of Latin American food items. Once I've opened a can, I freeze what I haven't used in a small plastic container and chip away at it as needed.

Eggs Meurette

Oeufs en Meurette is a French specialty featuring eggs poached in a red wine sauce, served with crisp bacon and sautéed mushrooms over slices of French bread that have been fried in garlic butter. I first tasted this dish at Balthazar, a French brasserie in New York City.

4½ slices (¼ inch thick) bacon, minced

½ cup diced onion

½ cup finely chopped carrot

2 garlic cloves, minced, plus ½ garlic clove

1 bay leaf

2 tablespoons chopped fresh flat-leaf parsley

2 teaspoons fresh thyme leaves

2 cups red wine (Pinot Noir or Burgundy)

2 cups canned reduced-sodium beef or chicken broth

4 tablespoons (½ stick) unsalted butter

2 cups sliced mushrooms (about 4 ounces)

Kosher salt and freshly ground black pepper

8 slices French bread

8 large eggs

1 tablespoon all-purpose flour

1. Mince 1½ slices of the bacon and cook in a large, heavy skillet over medium heat until the fat begins to render. Add the onion and carrot and cook, stirring, until very soft and lightly browned, about 5 minutes. Add the minced garlic and cook for 1 minute. Add the bay leaf, 1 tablespoon of the parsley and 1 teaspoon of the thyme. Stir in the wine and bring to a boil; boil for 1 minute. Add the broth; reduce the heat to a slow boil and cook, uncovered, until reduced to 1½ cups, 15 to 20 minutes.

2. Set a strainer over a heatproof bowl and strain the sauce, pressing down on the solids to extract as much flavor as possible. Discard the solids.

3. Meanwhile, cut the remaining 3 slices bacon into ¼-inch pieces. Cook in a large skillet over medium heat until crisp and browned. With a slotted spoon, transfer to a paper towel to drain; set aside. Add 1 tablespoon of the butter to the drippings in the skillet and heat until melted. Add the mushrooms and cook, stirring, until lightly browned and tender, about 5 minutes. Sprinkle with the remaining 1 tablespoon parsley and 1 teaspoon thyme, a pinch of salt and a grinding of pepper. Transfer to a bowl; cover with foil and keep warm until ready to serve.

4. In the same skillet, melt 2 tablespoons of the butter. Lightly rub the bread slices on one side with the cut side of the ½ garlic clove. Sauté the bread, in batches if

necessary, in the butter over medium-low heat, turning until lightly browned on both sides, about 5 minutes.

5. Transfer the wine sauce to a deep medium skillet or sauté pan and bring to a boil. Reduce the heat to maintain a gentle simmer. Break 4 of the eggs one at a time into a cup and gently slip into the sauce. Cook, spooning the sauce over the tops of the eggs, until the whites are set and the yolks are cooked to the desired doneness, 4 to 5 minutes. Using a slotted spoon, transfer the eggs to a platter; cover with foil and repeat the process with the remaining 4 eggs. Trim any ragged edges from the eggs.

6. Strain the wine sauce into a small saucepan (to remove any pieces of egg white) and heat to a simmer. Place the remaining 1 tablespoon butter on a saucer, add the flour and work into a paste with a fork. Form the mixture into a ball, stir into the simmering sauce and cook over low heat until thickened, about 1 minute. Remove from the heat; taste and correct the seasonings.

7. To serve, place 2 slices of toast on each of four dinner plates. Place a poached egg on top of each slice. Top with the mushrooms, spoon the wine sauce on top and garnish with the reserved crisp bacon. Serve immediately.

Makes 4 servings

Garnish with sprigs of fresh watercress or a salad of bitter greens tossed with a light dressing of lemon juice and olive oil.

Coddling Your Egg

Placing each egg in a small vessel before cooking keeps the white in a compact shape, even if the egg is old. Another advantage to this method is that you can add seasonings to the containers to flavor the eggs as they cook.

A coddled egg is cooked in a "coddler," a small porcelain cup with a screw top. (Egg terminology can be confusing, though: eggs cooked in the shell for 5 to 6 minutes are also called "coddled.") Coddlers—a British specialty—are often made of fine china and can be quite expensive. To make a coddled egg, break the egg into the buttered cup, cover tightly, set in a pan of simmering water and cook to the desired doneness. Coddled eggs are eaten straight from the coddler.

"Molded eggs" are cooked in oiled metal molds or small custard cups. The metal molds, which can be purchased at most cookware stores, resemble a round tray with indentations and are set in a pan over simmering water, like a double boiler. Custard cups or ramekins, on the other hand, are set directly into the water so it comes partway up the sides. The pan is covered, and the eggs cook until set. Then they are carefully lifted from the mold or loosened and tipped out of the ramekins and served on toast, as you would a poached egg, or with vegetables or sauces. (You can eat the eggs right from the ramekins, if you like, without unmolding them.)

Using a coddler or a ramekin allows you to add an assortment of tasty seasonings. I like to pour in a tablespoon of cream, put in the egg and add ½ teaspoon (or just a dab) of butter, a pinch of grated lemon zest and a few leaves of fresh thyme. I sprinkle on salt and pepper after the egg is cooked; if you do this before cooking, the salt and pepper will make ugly spots on the pretty yolk. Serve with pieces of toast to dip into the egg.

Here are some other delicious flavorings to place in the bottom of your coddler or ramekin:

♦ 1 tablespoon unsalted butter

♦ 1 tablespoon sour cream

♦ A pinch of grated orange zest

♦ 1 tablespoon finely chopped roasted red pepper

♦ 1 tablespoon each fresh corn kernels and diced fresh tomato mixed with a little chopped fresh cilantro and ½ teaspoon minced chile pepper

♦ 1 teaspoon chopped anchovy fillets, "melted" in 1 tablespoon unsalted butter with ½ teaspoon minced garlic

♦ 2 tablespoons chopped mushrooms and 1 teaspoon chopped shallot, sautéed in 1 tablespoon unsalted butter

♦ 1 tablespoon soft unsalted butter mixed with 1 teaspoon minced fresh parsley, ½ teaspoon thyme leaves and ¼ teaspoon minced fresh rosemary

Poached Eggs on Artichoke Bottoms

I like to serve this dish for a special breakfast when we've got overnight guests or friends coming to visit on a Saturday or Sunday morning. It's one of those recipes that encourages people to lend a hand in the kitchen. Then you can all sit down and feast together. Although this recipe requires a little organization and planning ahead, it is not difficult to do.

4 **large artichokes**

1 **garlic clove, bruised with the side of a knife**

2 **teaspoons kosher salt**

2 **tablespoons extra-virgin olive oil**

1 **tablespoon finely chopped fresh flat-leaf parsley or tarragon, plus small sprigs for garnish**

Freshly ground black pepper

2 **teaspoons red wine vinegar**

2 **tablespoons white vinegar**

4 **large eggs**

1½ **cups Roasted Red Pepper and Almond Sauce (page 80) or Orange Hollandaise (page 349), kept warm**

1. Slice off the stem and remove a few of the outside leaves from each artichoke. Turn each artichoke on its side and cut off about 1 inch of the top. Place in a large saucepan with the garlic and salt, add water to cover and bring to a boil. Cover and simmer until the artichokes are very tender when pierced with a skewer, 25 to 35 minutes, depending on the size. Remove the artichokes from the water, turn them cut side down to drain and let cool.

2. Pull off all the leaves from each artichoke and remove and discard the sharp purple-edged center core of leaves. Using a teaspoon, scrape away the fuzzy center (choke). With a paring knife, trim the bottoms (hearts) neatly. (The artichokes can be prepared ahead to this point; cover and refrigerate until ready to use.)

3. Just before serving, heat the oil in a large nonstick skillet over medium-low heat. Add the artichoke bottoms and cook, turning once or twice, until heated through. Season with the chopped parsley or tarragon, a grinding of pepper and the red wine vinegar.

Cook the artichokes a day or two ahead and reheat the bottoms just before serving. The red pepper sauce can also be made a day or two ahead and reheated. If using hollandaise, make it just before serving and keep warm.

4. Fill a deep skillet with water, bring to a boil and add the white vinegar. Reduce the heat to a simmer. Break the eggs one at a time into a cup and slip them into the water. Cook for 3 to 5 minutes, depending on the desired doneness. With a slotted spoon, remove the eggs in the order you added them to the pan and place on a folded kitchen towel or paper towel. Trim off any ragged whites.

5. To serve, place 1 artichoke bottom on each of four warm plates and place a poached egg on each artichoke. Spoon about ¼ cup sauce over each serving, top with the herb sprigs and serve at once.

Makes 4 servings

Anatomy of an Egg

 Here's a look at the main components of an egg, working from the outside in:

Shell: Although the color of an eggshell varies with the breed of the hen laying it, all shells have the same basic chemical composition: calcium carbonate with small amounts of magnesium carbonate, calcium phosphate and other organic matter, including protein. The strength of the shell is related to the hen's diet and her age. As the hen gets older, the size of her eggs increases, but the amount of shell material for each egg remains the same. Because the shell must be stretched to cover ever larger eggs, older hens produce eggs with thinner shells.

Bloom: A newly laid egg has a protective covering called the bloom, or "cuticle." This natural coating seals the thousands of tiny pores in the shell, preventing bacteria from entering and reducing moisture loss.

Membrane: Two membranes within the shell surround the white of the egg. Like the bloom, these layers protect the egg's contents from bacterial penetration.

Air cell: Soon after the egg is laid and begins to cool, an air cell forms between the two membranes at the widest end of the shell. As the egg ages, moisture and carbon dioxide escape through the pores of the shell and the air cell becomes larger. Thus the size of the air cell indicates freshness — the smaller the air cell, the fresher the egg.

Albumen: Albumen is the technical name for the egg white. A thick viscous substance, pearly or opalescent in appearance, albumen is actually made up of two components: a thin albumen and a thick albumen. In a fresh egg, the thin albumen is just inside the shell membranes, and the thick albumen surrounds the yolk. As the egg ages, the thick albumen becomes thinner and less distinguishable from the thin part.

An egg white contains more than half of the egg's total protein. Scientists use albumen as the standard for a nutritional scale they call the "biological value of protein," giving it the highest possible rating, 100 out of 100. The egg delivers the most complete protein of any food in our diet, containing all the essential amino acids in the most efficient amounts for use in the human body. Egg whites also provide niacin, riboflavin, chlorine, magnesium, potassium, sodium and sulfur.

Chalaza: Derived from the Greek word meaning hailstone, or small lump, the chalaza is composed of ropy strands of egg white that hold the yolk suspended in the white. The more prominent the chalaza, the fresher the egg. The chalaza is edible and does not interfere with cooking or whipping egg whites. But when making a sauce or pudding, it's advisable to strain the mixture to remove any lumpy bits of cooked chalaza.

Yolk: The yolk accounts for only about one-third of the weight of an egg but contains all its cholesterol and fat: on average, 5 grams of fat (about 1.6 grams saturated), 213 milligrams of cholesterol and 59 calories. The yolk contains almost half of an egg's protein, all of its vitamins A, D and E and the B vitamin known as biotin, which plays an important part in metabolism. The yolk also has the bulk of an egg's calcium, copper, iodine, iron, manganese, phosphorus, selenium, zinc and lecithin, which is important to brain function.

Contrary to popular belief, a blood spot on the yolk does not mean the egg has been fertilized. The spot results from a ruptured blood vessel on the yolk surface, created as the egg formed. A blood spot is harmless; it can either be ignored or be removed with the tip of a knife.

Eggs Benedict

Eggs Benedict is a classic: half a toasted English muffin topped with a slice of warm Canadian bacon or ham and a poached egg and covered with hollandaise sauce. Because the elements are so simple, this dish is ripe for all sorts of wonderful interpretations. Instead of an English muffin, the base can be toasted walnut bread, sourdough bread, brioche or any number of the other interesting breads now on the market. The meat can be smoked turkey or crumbled sausage, one of the more exotic flavored sausages, such as veal and artichoke or whiskey and fennel, or just perfectly seasoned breakfast sausage. For this special dish, I like to seek out great-tasting farm-fresh eggs at my local farmers' market. The sauce can be basic hollandaise or any of the variations, or try Roasted Red Pepper and Almond Sauce (page 80).

4 slices Canadian bacon or ham

2 tablespoons white vinegar

4 large eggs

2 English muffins, halved

Unsalted butter, at room temperature

Classic Hollandaise (page 346), kept warm

1. Grill or fry the bacon or ham just to heat through. Cover and keep warm.

2. Fill a deep skillet with water, bring to a boil and add the vinegar. Reduce the heat to a simmer. Break the eggs one at a time into a cup and slip them into the water. Cook for 3 to 5 minutes, depending on the desired doneness. With a slotted spoon, remove the eggs in the order you added them to the pan and place on a folded kitchen towel or paper towel. Trim off any ragged whites.

3. Meanwhile, toast the muffins and slather with butter.

4. Place half of an English muffin on each of four warm plates. Top each with a slice of bacon or ham and a poached egg. Spoon the Hollandaise over the top and serve at once.

Makes 4 servings

VARIATION

For vegetarian Eggs Benedict, substitute a sautéed portobello mushroom, a roasted red pepper half or a thick slice of grilled or baked eggplant and/or a slice of fresh tomato for the meat.

Poached Eggs on Saffron Rice

In this homey but elegant dish, poached eggs rest gracefully in individual ramekins of saffron-tinted rice laced with Parmesan cheese.

3   cups water

1   teaspoon kosher salt

1   cup medium-grain or
    Arborio rice

¼   teaspoon saffron threads

2   tablespoons unsalted butter

6   tablespoons freshly grated
    Parmigiano-Reggiano cheese

¼   cup heavy cream

2   tablespoons white vinegar

4   large eggs

Instead of preparing individual servings, you can make the rice and poached eggs in a shallow broilerproof pie plate. Serve with a green salad and ham or bacon on the side or with warm crusty bread and fresh fruit.

1. Combine the water and salt in a medium saucepan and bring to a boil. Stir in the rice and saffron, reduce the heat to low, cover and cook, stirring vigorously at least two times, for 20 minutes. Add the butter and 2 tablespoons of the cheese and stir until well blended and the rice is creamy.

2. Generously butter four (8-ounce) ramekins or small gratin dishes (about 5 inches in diameter and 1 inch deep). Spoon the rice into the prepared dishes and smooth the tops with a spatula. Drizzle with the cream. Place the dishes on a baking sheet and cover with foil to keep warm.

3. Preheat the broiler. Fill a deep skillet with water, bring to a boil and add the vinegar. Reduce the heat to a simmer. Break the eggs one at a time into a cup and slip them into the water. Cook for 1 minute. With a slotted spoon, remove the eggs in the order you added them to the pan and place on a folded kitchen towel or paper towel. Trim off any ragged whites.

4. Gently place the partially poached eggs on top of the rice. Sprinkle with the remaining ¼ cup cheese. Broil just until the eggs are cooked to the desired doneness and the cheese is lightly browned. Serve at once.

Makes 4 servings

Poached Eggs on Hash

Hash can be made with any finely chopped leftover meat or fish, but my favorites are roast beef and leg of lamb. Fresh herbs make all the difference in this dish.

3 tablespoons extra-virgin olive oil

4 large potatoes, preferably red-skinned, unpeeled, cut into ½-inch dice (about 4 cups)

1 small onion, chopped

½ red bell pepper, cut into ½-inch dice

1 garlic clove, minced
Kosher salt and freshly ground black pepper

2 cups diced cooked roast beef or lamb

2 tablespoons chopped fresh flat-leaf parsley

2 teaspoons minced fresh rosemary or thyme

2 tablespoons white vinegar

4 large eggs

1. Heat the oil in a large nonstick skillet over medium heat until very hot. Add the potatoes all at once and fry, stirring and turning frequently, until evenly crisp and golden, about 10 minutes.

2. Add the onion and bell pepper and cook, stirring, until golden, about 5 minutes. Add the garlic, salt to taste and a grinding of pepper and sauté for 1 minute. Add the beef or lamb, 1 tablespoon of the parsley and 1 teaspoon of the rosemary or thyme and cook, stirring, until heated through. Press down on the hash with a spatula, increase the heat and cook until the hash is a little crusty on the bottom, about 5 minutes. Turn the hash a spatulaful at a time and cook until crusty on the other side, about 5 minutes.

3. Meanwhile, fill a deep skillet with water, bring to a boil and add the vinegar. Reduce the heat to a simmer. Break the eggs one at a time into a cup and slip them into the water. Cook for 3 to 5 minutes, depending on the desired doneness. With a slotted spoon, remove the eggs in the order you added them to the pan and place on a folded kitchen towel or paper towel. Trim off any ragged whites.

4. Divide the hash among four plates, top each with an egg and sprinkle with the remaining 1 tablespoon parsley and 1 teaspoon rosemary or thyme. Serve at once.

Makes 4 servings

Poached Eggs Gratin with Whipped Potatoes

Ideally, this recipe is easily made with leftover whipped potatoes, but if your family is like mine, there will never be any whipped potatoes left in the pot, so start from scratch with a fresh batch. This is the ultimate comfort dish: whipped potatoes rich with butter, milk and Parmesan cheese, poached eggs nestled on top, sprinkled with cheese and broiled until the heat turns the cheese golden. Served with a green vegetable or salad, the dish makes a wonderful meal at almost any time of day.

Whipped Potatoes

- 4 **large russet potatoes (about 2 pounds total), peeled, quartered**
- 2 **teaspoons kosher salt**
- ½–1 **cup milk**
- 2 **tablespoons unsalted butter**
- ½ **cup freshly grated Parmigiano-Reggiano cheese**
  Freshly ground black pepper

- 2 **tablespoons white vinegar**
- 4 **large eggs**
- ½ **cup freshly grated Parmigiano-Reggiano cheese**
- 2 **tablespoons finely chopped fresh flat-leaf parsley (optional)**

1. **Make the whipped potatoes:** Place the potatoes and salt in a large saucepan, add water to cover and bring to a boil. Cover, reduce the heat to low and cook until the potatoes are tender when pierced with a skewer, about 35 minutes.

2. Drain the water from the saucepan, leaving the potatoes in the pan. Set the pan over low heat, add ½ cup of the milk and the butter and, using an electric mixer, whip the potatoes, adding small amounts of the remaining milk as necessary, until they are thick, smooth and creamy. Off the heat, beat in the cheese. Season with pepper to taste.

3. Generously butter four (8-ounce) ramekins or gratin dishes (about 5 inches in diameter and 1 inch deep). Spoon the potatoes into the prepared dishes and smooth the tops with a spatula. Place on a baking sheet and cover with foil to keep warm.

4. Preheat the broiler. Fill a deep skillet with water, bring to a boil and add the vinegar. Reduce the heat to a simmer. Break the eggs one at a time into a cup and slip them into the water. Cook for 1 minute. With a slotted spoon, remove the eggs in the order you added them to the pan and place on a folded kitchen towel or paper towel. Trim off any ragged whites.

I make this dish in individual ramekins, but if you don't have any, use a shallow 2-quart broilerproof baking dish.

5. Gently place the partially poached eggs on top of the potatoes and sprinkle with the cheese. Broil just until the cheese is lightly browned and the eggs are cooked to the desired doneness. Sprinkle with the parsley, if using, and serve at once.

Makes 4 servings

Carter House Potato "Risotto" with Poached Eggs

This dish, a breakfast specialty of the Carter House Restaurant 301 in Eureka, California, is made like a risotto, using finely diced potatoes instead of rice. As they're stirred, the cubed potatoes release their starch into the broth, making it thick and creamy.

3 pounds Yukon Gold potatoes (about 8), peeled

1½ cups canned reduced-sodium chicken broth

2 tablespoons unsalted butter

2 tablespoons minced shallot or onion

1 garlic clove, minced

½ teaspoon kosher salt, or to taste

1–2 teaspoons minced fresh thyme or a combination of fresh thyme, marjoram, oregano and rosemary

¼–½ cup heavy cream

Freshly ground black pepper

2 tablespoons white vinegar

4 large eggs

1. To dice the potatoes evenly, first cut them lengthwise into ¼-inch-thick slices. Stack the slices and cut them into ¼-inch-wide strips, then cut the strips crosswise into ¼-inch dice. Place the potatoes in a large bowl and rinse them with cold water. Drain in a colander and set aside.

2. Heat the broth in a small saucepan or in the microwave; keep hot.

3. Melt the butter in a deep skillet over low heat. Add the shallot or onion and garlic and cook, stirring, until tender, about 3 minutes; do not brown. Add the potatoes, salt and thyme or mixed herbs and cook, stirring, until the potatoes are heated through and coated with butter, about 2 minutes.

4. Increase the heat to medium-low and, stirring constantly, gradually add the hot broth. Cook, gently stirring a few times, until the potatoes are tender and the broth is partially absorbed and creamy, about 10 minutes. Gradually add the cream until the consistency of the "risotto" is loose and creamy. Add a grinding of pepper, remove from the heat and keep warm while you poach the eggs.

5. Fill a deep skillet with water, bring to a boil and add the vinegar. Reduce the heat to a simmer. Break the eggs one at a time into a cup and slip them into the water. Cook for 3 to 5 minutes, depending on the desired doneness. With a slotted spoon, remove the eggs in the order you added them to the pan and place on a folded kitchen towel or paper towel. Trim off any ragged whites.

6. Spoon the potato "risotto" into four shallow bowls and top each with a poached egg. Serve at once.

Makes 4 servings

Poached Eggs with Soft Polenta, Pancetta and White Corn

There are many different techniques for making polenta, but I prefer this slow-cooked double-boiler method because it ensures that the cornmeal cooks fully and the polenta is soft and creamy. And it sure beats standing over the pot stirring for what seems like an eternity. Also, with the double-boiler method, the polenta can be made ahead and reheated without drying up.

6 cups water

Kosher salt

1½ cups cornmeal

4 tablespoons (½ stick) unsalted butter

¼ cup freshly grated Parmigiano-Reggiano cheese, plus more for serving

2 tablespoons extra-virgin olive oil

2 ¼-inch-thick slices pancetta or 2 slices lightly smoked bacon or Danish bacon (about 2 ounces)

1 cup diced onions

½ cup diced red bell pepper (optional)

2 cups fresh white corn kernels (cut from 3–4 ears) or frozen white corn

Freshly ground black pepper

1. Bring 4 cups of the water to a boil in a large, wide saucepan and add 2 teaspoons salt. Meanwhile, stir the remaining 2 cups water into the cornmeal in a medium bowl.

2. Stir the cornmeal mixture into the boiling water and cook, stirring constantly with a wide heatproof rubber spatula or a flat-edged wooden spoon, until the mixture boils. Reduce the heat to low and cook, stirring frequently (adjust the heat so the polenta doesn't boil and splatter), for 15 to 20 minutes, or until very thick.

3. Transfer the polenta to the top of a double boiler set over hot, not boiling, water. Stir in the butter and ¼ cup cheese. Cover the polenta and let sit over low heat for at least 20 and up to 45 minutes, or until the polenta is thick and smooth.

4. Meanwhile, heat the oil in a medium skillet over medium-low heat. Add the pancetta or bacon, onions and bell pepper, if using. Cook, stirring, until the onions are golden and the pancetta or bacon is browned and crisp, about 5 minutes. Stir in the corn and cook, stirring, until crisp-tender, about 2 minutes. Season with salt to taste and a grinding of pepper.

2 tablespoons white vinegar

4–8 large eggs

¼ cup chopped fresh flat-leaf parsley

5. Fill a deep skillet with water, bring to a boil and add the vinegar. Reduce the heat to a simmer. Break 4 eggs one at a time into a cup and slip them into the water. Cook for 3 minutes. With a slotted spoon, remove the eggs in the order you added them to the pan and place on a folded kitchen towel or paper towel. Repeat with the remaining eggs, if using. Trim off any ragged whites.

6. Spoon the polenta into four shallow bowls; quickly reheat the corn mixture and spoon on top, dividing evenly. Top each bowl with 1 or 2 eggs. Sprinkle with the parsley and cheese and serve at once.

Makes 4 servings

VARIATION

Polenta with Poached Eggs and Melted Cheese

Substitute ½ cup grated or diced Teleme, fontina, mozzarella or any semisoft cheese for the Parmigiano-Reggiano, adding a pinch of nutmeg to the polenta along with the cheese. Spoon the hot polenta into bowls, top with the eggs, garnish with parsley, if desired, and serve.

Poached Eggs on Creamy Curried Lentils

Here's a hearty all-in-one supper. Because this dish is quite rich, the topping of fried onion is optional. For a flavor touch without the fat (and the labor of frying), add a sprinkling of chopped fresh cilantro. The recipe was inspired by one from cookbook author Dana Jacobi.

2 tablespoons extra-virgin olive oil or vegetable oil

½ cup chopped onion

⅓ cup chopped carrot

1 garlic clove, minced

2 teaspoons curry powder, preferably Madras-style

3 cups water

1½ cups brown lentils, rinsed and picked through

¾ cup diced (¼ inch), peeled red-skinned potatoes

½ cup heavy cream or milk, plus more as needed

Kosher salt and freshly ground black pepper

Fried Onion (optional)

3 tablespoons vegetable oil

1 onion, very thinly sliced into rings (about 1 cup)

2 tablespoons white vinegar

4 large eggs

¼ cup chopped fresh cilantro

1. Combine the oil, onion and carrot in a large saucepan and cook over medium heat, stirring, until the onion is golden, about 10 minutes. Stir in the garlic and cook for 2 minutes. Add the curry powder and stir to blend, then add the water, lentils and potatoes and bring to a boil. Reduce the heat to low, cover and cook, stirring often, until tender, about 25 minutes; add a little additional water, if necessary. Add the cream or milk, salt to taste and a grinding of pepper; remove from the heat and set aside.

2. **Make the fried onion, if using:** Heat the oil in a medium skillet until hot enough to sizzle a ring of onion. Add the onion and fry over medium-high heat, stirring, until browned and crisp, about 8 minutes. Drain on paper towels.

3. Fill a deep skillet with water, bring to a boil and add the vinegar. Reduce the heat to a simmer. Break the eggs one at a time into a cup and slip them into the water. Cook for 3 to 5 minutes, depending on the desired doneness. With a slotted spoon, remove the eggs in the order you added them to the pan and place on a folded kitchen towel or paper towel. Trim off any ragged whites.

4. Reheat the lentils and spoon into four deep bowls. Top each with an egg. Sprinkle with the cilantro and the fried onion, if using. Serve at once.

Makes 4 servings

CHAPTER 4 *Eggs and Bread*

"As always, my grandmother sliced little bread fingers for me, cut the larger tip off the soft-boiled egg and then sprinkled salt into it. I looked up from my seat next to hers and saw the sun beaming into the dining room. My grandmother's lavender dress caught the light of this beautiful, quiet morning. I had stepped into a realm of magic and legend."

—ANDRÉ ACIMAN

A warm soft-cooked egg, accompanied by carefully cut strips of toast slathered with butter, has been my favorite breakfast since childhood. With ritualistic care, I use the strips instead of a spoon to eat the egg, to soak up the runny yolk and scoop out the soft white—just as I did when I was a small child. For me, there's still nothing more divine than that little finger of crisp toast, salty with butter and dripping with golden yolk.

Among life's great pleasures, I am happy to say, the combination of bread and eggs is one of the most readily available. These two elemental foods are present in almost all kitchens—certainly ever present in mine—and they can be brought together in the minute or two it takes to soft-cook an egg and toast a piece of bread. But with a few minutes more preparation, you can make bread and egg dishes in almost infinite variety.

Sandwiches are an equally delicious way to bring bread and eggs together, and it's no surprise to me that fast-food chains are selling morning egg sandwiches by the billions. When I was a teenager working as a waitress in my uncle's diner in upstate New York, I served Western omelette sandwiches by the zillions! Today, with all the different breads in the market, sandwiches can be more creative than ever.

A more intimate way to bring bread and eggs together is to soak the bread in the eggs *before* cooking. This, of course, is the basis of the universally loved skillet-fried bread we call French toast, and the French call *pain perdu*. That means "lost bread," and it signifies that old bread has found a delicious new life (the French think that each morning's bread is old by the afternoon!). You'll find a basic Pain Perdu here and a treat that I call Eggs Cooked in Savory Toast.

Stratas take the concept further. To make them, you simply combine beaten eggs, bread slices and savory additions such as cheese and vegetables and leave them to soak together for hours, then bake them into a golden puffy casserole. This deservedly popular dish is perfect for a special brunch or dinner party, since all the work can be done the night before (or the morning of) your gathering.

Also in this chapter are some simple breadlike recipes that owe their extraordinary lightness and flavor to eggs, including popovers, the savory egg pastry bread called gougère and a sensational side dish known as spoon bread.

Pain Perdu

What we call French toast, the French call *pain perdu*. Fried in butter and served covered with confectioners' sugar, Pain Perdu is considered dessert in France. But I like to serve it for breakfast or brunch with maple syrup, like pancakes. The following version is oven-fried, making it easier to prepare for a crowd.

6	large eggs
1½	cups milk
1½	teaspoons pure vanilla extract
2	tablespoons sugar
½	teaspoon ground cinnamon
10–12	thick (½-to-⅓-inch) slices day-old French or Italian bread
4	tablespoons (½ stick) unsalted butter
	Confectioners' sugar
	Maple syrup (optional)

1. In a large bowl, whisk the eggs, milk, vanilla, sugar and cinnamon until blended. Arrange the bread in a large shallow baking dish, layering or slightly overlapping the slices, if necessary. Pour the milk mixture over the bread and let stand for at least 30 minutes, carefully turning the bread with a wide spatula and rearranging it so it is evenly moistened halfway through the standing time.

2. Position one oven rack in the upper third of the oven and one in the lower third and preheat the oven to 400°F. Put 2 tablespoons of the butter on each of two baking sheets with sides and place in the oven until the butter melts and the pans are hot, about 5 minutes. Tilt the pans so the butter covers them evenly. Remove from the oven.

3. Place 5 or 6 slices of the soaked bread on each of the hot pans, spacing them evenly. Bake for 15 minutes. Take the pans out of the oven and turn each piece of bread over with a wide spatula. Return the pans to the oven, placing the one from the top rack on the bottom and the one from the bottom rack on the top, and bake until the bread is puffed and evenly browned, 15 to 20 minutes more.

4. Transfer to a platter, dust with confectioners' sugar and serve with maple syrup, if desired.

Makes 6 servings

My Favorite Breakfast

A Perfect Soft-Cooked Egg and Toast Fingers

 "And I wonder how she can say no to a soft-boiled egg when there's nothing in the world like it."—FRANK MCCOURT

I certainly share Frank McCourt's appreciation for an egg soft-cooked in the shell. But as a cooking teacher, I'd have to point out that it's a mistake to call it a "boiled" egg. The key to a perfect soft-cooked egg (and a delicious, nicely colored hard-cooked egg as well) is NOT TO BOIL IT— boiling an egg will cause the proteins to toughen. Whether you want your egg to be soft and drippy or completely firm, gentle cooking in barely simmering water is the key. To emphasize this point, I always refer to the eggs as "soft-cooked" and "hard-cooked."

There are two methods for soft-cooked eggs that work well. Precise timing is critical, since a few extra seconds in hot water will change the texture of both the yolk and the white. The times given here are for large eggs. Extra-large eggs will need 30 seconds more; small eggs will need 30 seconds less.

Before cooking, take the eggs from the refrigerator and quickly warm them to room temperature by placing them in a bowl and covering them with warm tap water. Let stand for about 5 minutes. For even cooking, do not try to soft-cook more than three eggs at one time, because using more eggs can lower the temperature of the water and affect the cooking time.

Cold-Water Method

♦ Place the eggs in a deep medium or small saucepan and add cold water to cover completely.

♦ Bring the water to a boil and immediately remove the pan from the heat.

♦ Cover the pan and let stand for 2 minutes for an egg with a runny yolk and a just-set, very tender white or 3 minutes for a soft yolk and a firm but tender white.

Boiling-Water Method

♦ Fill a deep medium or small saucepan with enough water to cover the eggs completely.

♦ Bring the water to a boil and, using a spoon, gently lower the eggs into the boiling water.

♦ Immediately reduce the heat to very low so that the water just stays hot.

♦ Cook for 4 minutes for an egg with a runny yolk and a just-set, very tender white or 5 minutes for an egg with a soft yolk and a firm but tender white.

Popover Pancake

Sometimes called a Dutch baby, this puffy pancake can be either sweet or savory (see the variations that follow).

4 large eggs

¾ cup milk

½ teaspoon kosher salt

¾ cup all-purpose flour

2 tablespoons unsalted butter

Warm maple syrup, honey or other sweet syrup

1. Preheat the oven to 400°F. Place an 8-to-10-inch cast-iron skillet or other heavy ovenproof skillet in the oven to heat for 5 minutes.

2. Combine the eggs, milk and salt in a large bowl and whisk to blend. Add the flour and whisk until the batter is smooth.

3. Using an oven mitt, remove the hot skillet from the oven. Add the butter and swirl the skillet to melt it and coat the skillet evenly. Add the batter all at once and return the skillet immediately to the oven. Bake until the pancake puffs up around the edges, about 18 to 20 minutes.

4. As soon as it is done, take the pancake to the table, before it falls. Cut it into wedges and serve with syrup or honey.

Makes 2 to 4 servings

Sweet Popover Pancake with Strawberries

Combine 1 pint strawberries, rinsed, hulled and sliced, 1 tablespoon sugar and ½ teaspoon pure vanilla extract in a medium bowl and toss to blend. Let stand at room temperature until ready to serve. As soon as you remove the pancake from the oven, cover it with a blanket of sifted confectioners' sugar. Spoon the berries into the center and serve.

Savory Popover Pancake with Sautéed Mushrooms and Pancetta

Add 2 tablespoons freshly grated Parmigiano-Reggiano cheese to the batter and freshly ground black pepper to taste. While the pancake bakes, make the filling: Heat 2 tablespoons extra-virgin olive oil in a large nonstick skillet. Add one slice (¼ inch thick) pancetta, diced, and cook over medium-high heat until lightly browned, about 5 minutes. Add 3 cups sliced fresh mushrooms and cook until browned and tender, about 5 minutes. If necessary, boil off any liquid in the skillet to concentrate the flavors. Add 1 tablespoon finely chopped fresh flat-leaf parsley, salt to taste and a grinding of pepper. To serve, cut the pancake into 4 wedges, place on plates and top with the mushroom mixture.

Matzoh Brei

Matzoh, unleavened bread, is eaten throughout the world by Jews celebrating Passover. Moistened with water and mixed with eggs, it becomes matzoh brei, the Jewish version of French toast. Although chicken fat or vegetable oil is traditional, I like matzoh brei best fried in butter and generously dusted with confectioners' sugar or, better yet, drizzled with maple syrup. It is the perfect breakfast food, whether it is Passover or not.

4 **unsalted matzoh**

3 **large eggs**

½ **teaspoon kosher salt**

4 **tablespoons (½ stick) unsalted butter or ¼ cup vegetable oil**

Confectioners' sugar or warm maple syrup

1. Place the matzoh in a baking dish, cover with cold water and let stand for 5 minutes. Drain off the water. Carefully turn them out onto a thick kitchen towel and press lightly to remove most of the excess water. Transfer to a bowl (they will have broken up into smaller pieces).

2. In a small bowl, whisk the eggs and salt until blended. Pour over the matzoh and fold together just until blended.

3. Preheat the oven to 200°F. Heat a large skillet, preferably nonstick, over medium-low heat. Add 2 tablespoons of the butter or oil. When it sizzles, pour half of the matzoh mixture into the skillet so that it forms a large, thin pancake. Cook, without disturbing, until the bottom is golden brown, 2 to 3 minutes. Use a spatula to cut the pancake into irregular pieces and turn to brown the other side. Transfer to a platter and keep warm in the oven. Add the remaining 2 tablespoons butter or oil to the pan and cook the remaining matzoh mixture.

4. Serve at once with confectioners' sugar or syrup.

Makes 4 servings

Eggcellent Sandwiches to Go

 You don't have to go to a drive-up window to get a great egg sandwich to enjoy on a trip. Try these:

♦ **Mom's Pepper and Egg Sandwich:** My mom used to make this sandwich for our road food, long before the days of fast-food chains. Fry long strips of Italian peppers in olive oil, add beaten eggs and cook until soft-scrambled. Pile into split hard rolls, cut in half and wrap in waxed paper.

♦ **Pan Bagnat:** A classic French Provençal sandwich, so drenched in superb olive oil that its name means "bathed bread." Take a long French roll, split lengthwise in half and drizzle the cut sides generously with extra-virgin olive oil. Layer with 2 or 3 flat anchovy fillets, 2 slices ripe tomato, 1 hard-cooked egg, cut into slices, a sprinkling of kosher salt and a grinding of black pepper on the bottom half; I also like to add a few leaves of fresh basil or arugula. Cover with the top of the roll and wrap tightly in foil. Let sit for at least 30 minutes or longer before eating so the oil and juices soak into the bread.

♦ **Marie's Fried Egg Sandwich on an English Muffin:** Here's my favorite midmorning pick-me-up when I have skipped breakfast and won't have time for lunch. Most days, I just carry this upstairs from my kitchen to my office. But you can wrap it in foil and tuck it in a bag. Fry an egg in melted butter. Toast and butter an English muffin. Place the egg on the muffin, add a slice of ripe tomato, a piece of prosciutto or Canadian bacon and a slice of Swiss, Teleme or other cheese, if desired, and enjoy.

Western Omelette Sandwich

Growing up in a small town in rural New York, I earned pocket money working the early-morning weekend shift at Joe's Diner, where one of the favorite menu items was a Western omelette sandwich. We served it on those squishy rolls that are called hard rolls but aren't hard at all.

1 tablespoon unsalted butter

2 tablespoons minced green bell pepper

2 tablespoons minced ham

1 tablespoon minced onion

2 large eggs

Kosher salt and freshly ground black pepper

1 hard roll, split

1. Melt the butter in a small nonstick skillet over medium heat. Add the bell pepper, ham and onion and cook, stirring, until the vegetables are tender, about 3 minutes.

2. Whisk the eggs, salt to taste and a grinding of pepper in a small bowl. Add to the skillet, reduce the heat to low and cook like a pancake, until the eggs are set, about 2 minutes. Turn and cook the other side, about 1 minute.

3. Transfer the omelette to the roll, folding in the edges; serve.

Makes 1 serving

Warm Egg Salad on Whole Wheat Toast

Egg salad made from freshly hard-cooked eggs that are cooled just enough so you can remove the shells without burning your fingers is the perfect egg salad for sandwiches. The bread is also important. Depending on my mood, I like squishy potato rolls or a good firm whole wheat or multigrain bread. You can add lettuce, but it isn't really necessary.

4   large eggs, hard-cooked (page 162), still warm, peeled and halved lengthwise

2   tablespoons finely chopped onion

2   tablespoons finely chopped celery

½   teaspoon prepared mustard
    Kosher salt and freshly ground black pepper

¼   cup mayonnaise

4   slices whole wheat or multigrain bread, toasted

2   large soft lettuce leaves (optional)

1. Cut the eggs into chunks; do not mash them. Place in a medium bowl and add the onion, celery, mustard, salt to taste and a grinding of pepper. Add the mayonnaise and gently stir until blended.

2. Place 2 slices of the toast on a work surface. Top each with a lettuce leaf, if using. Spoon the egg salad on top, cover with the remaining toast, cut in half and serve warm.

Makes 2 sandwiches

A Different Egg Salad Sandwich

Egg salad with warm hard-cooked eggs mixed with extra-virgin olive oil instead of mayonnaise seasoned with minced red onion and fresh basil then slathered on toasted Italian bread, makes a dynamic open-faced sandwich. For a more traditional sandwich, spread the egg salad on a crusty roll and add a few leaves of arugula or spinach and a slice of ripe tomato. This is the place to use your best fruity olive oil.

4   large eggs, hard-cooked (page 162), still warm, peeled and halved lengthwise

¼   cup finely chopped red onion

3   tablespoons extra-virgin olive oil

2   tablespoons julienned fresh basil (see box)

½   teaspoon kosher salt
    Freshly ground black pepper

4   slices Italian bread, toasted, or 2 rolls, split

1. Separate the egg yolks from the whites. Coarsely cut up the whites and place in a medium bowl. Coarsely crumble the yolks and add to the whites.

2. Add the onion, oil, basil (if serving immediately; if not, add just before serving), salt and a grinding of pepper. Stir with a fork. Some of the yolks will dissolve into the oil and the salad will become creamy.

3. Spread on the toast or rolls. Serve warm, or refrigerate and serve chilled, if desired.

Makes 2 sandwiches

TO JULIENNE BASIL LEAVES: *Stack 3 or 4 leaves, roll them tightly and cut across into thin slices. This technique bruises the leaves less than chopping. If you are making the salad ahead, don't add the basil until just before serving, or it will turn dark upon standing.*

Miriam's Egg Salad

Similar to a pâté, this delicious and unusual egg salad is excellent when spread on matzoh or bagels. In her book *Miriam's Kitchen, a Memoir*, Elizabeth Ehrlich describes in mouthwatering detail the ritual of her grandmother making a version of this salad, cooking the onions very slowly until they become caramelized.

2 tablespoons vegetable oil

1 cup chopped onions

2 cups coarsely chopped fresh mushrooms (about 8 ounces)

Kosher salt and freshly ground black pepper

4 large eggs, hard-cooked (page 162), peeled

¼ cup mayonnaise

2 tablespoons chopped fresh dill, or more to taste

4 matzohs or 4 bagels, halved and toasted

1. Heat the oil in a large skillet over medium heat. Add the onions and sauté for 2 minutes. Add the mushrooms and cook, stirring, until their moisture evaporates and the mushrooms and onions are golden, about 10 minutes. Season with salt to taste and a grinding of pepper. Remove from the heat and let cool to room temperature.

2. Place the eggs in a medium bowl and coarsely chop them. Add the mushroom mixture and the mayonnaise and continue chopping until the mixture is very fine. Add the dill; taste and add more dill or salt and pepper, if necessary.

3. Spread on the matzohs or bagels and serve open-faced.

Makes 4 servings

A good way to chop the eggs is to use a wooden chopping bowl and a curved steel chopping blade, also called a crescent cutter or mezzaluna. If you don't have a mezzaluna, use a pastry blender.

Broiled Egg Salad with Swiss Cheese on Rye Bread

Make the egg and Swiss cheese salad ahead of time, spread on the bread, cover and refrigerate and broil when ready to serve.

4   slices rye bread

4   large eggs, hard-cooked
    (page 162), peeled and
    coarsely chopped

½   cup minced celery

⅓   cup mayonnaise

¼   cup plus 4 rounded table-
    spoons grated Swiss cheese

¼   cup minced sweet onion

2   teaspoons prepared mustard

    Dash of Tabasco sauce

½   teaspoon kosher salt

    Freshly ground black pepper

8   thin slices ripe tomato
    (optional)

1. Preheat the broiler. Arrange the bread slices on the broiler pan and broil until toasted on one side. Turn and toast the other side. Set aside; leave the broiler on.

2. In a medium bowl, combine the eggs, celery, mayonnaise, ¼ cup of the cheese, onion, mustard, Tabasco, salt and a grinding of pepper. Fold gently to blend.

3. Arrange two overlapping slices of tomato, if using, on each slice of toast. Spoon about ½ cup of the egg mixture on top of each slice of toast, spreading it out to the edges of the bread. Sprinkle each sandwich with a rounded tablespoonful of the remaining cheese.

4. Broil 3 to 4 inches from the heat until the tops of the sandwiches are browned and bubbly. Serve at once.

Makes 2 sandwiches

Cheddar Scrambled Egg Sandwiches with Bacon, Lettuce and Tomato

This is my special version of a BLT, with cheddar scrambled eggs. Make the sandwiches on toast if you are a purist about your BLTs, but I like to use square focaccia rolls.

6 **large eggs**

  Freshly ground black pepper

1 **tablespoon extra-virgin olive oil**

½ **cup grated cheddar cheese**

4 **focaccia rolls, split**

8 **slices bacon, cooked until crisp and drained on paper towels**

8 **thin slices ripe tomato**

  About ¼ cup mayonnaise

4 **large soft lettuce leaves**

1. Whisk the eggs and a grinding of pepper in a medium bowl. Heat the oil in a large nonstick skillet over medium heat. Add the eggs and cook, stirring gently, until almost set, about 3 minutes. Stir in the cheese and cook for 30 seconds. Remove from the heat.

2. Place each split focaccia roll on a plate. Spoon the eggs on top, distributing them evenly. Top each sandwich with 2 slices bacon and 2 slices tomato. Place a generous spoonful of mayonnaise on each sandwich, add the lettuce and serve at once.

Makes 4 sandwiches

Open-Faced Mozzarella Sandwiches with Fried Eggs and Anchovy Butter

My sister and I used to make open-faced melted mozzarella sandwiches as an after-school meal. It wasn't until I was an adult that I decided to adorn my favorite snack with a fried egg and anchovy butter.

3 tablespoons unsalted butter

4 anchovy fillets, rinsed, patted dry and finely chopped

4 slices Italian bread

4 slices mozzarella cheese, cut to fit the bread

4 large eggs

1 tablespoon finely chopped fresh flat-leaf parsley

1. Melt 2 tablespoons of the butter in a small skillet over low heat. Add the anchovies and stir until they dissolve into the butter. Remove from the heat and keep warm.

2. Preheat the broiler. Place the bread on a broiler pan and broil until toasted on one side. Turn and toast the other side. Top each slice with a slice of the mozzarella and broil until the cheese is melted. Remove from the heat and place on individual plates.

3. Meanwhile, melt the remaining 1 tablespoon butter in a large nonstick skillet over medium-low heat. Break the eggs one at a time into a cup and slip into the skillet. Fry until the whites begin to set, about 1 minute. Cover and cook until the whites and yolks are set to the desired doneness, about 5 minutes more.

4. Place an egg on top of each sandwich and drizzle with a little of the warm anchovy butter. Sprinkle with the parsley and serve at once.

Makes 4 open-faced sandwiches

Eggs Cooked in Savory Toast
with Parmesan, Walnuts and Prosciutto

The best bread for this dish, an updated version of "toad in the hole," is a round or an oblong loaf that will make thick slices roughly 5 inches long and 3 inches wide. This is a great main course for brunch or lunch.

4   1¼-inch-thick slices bread cut from a large round or oblong loaf (see headnote)

1   cup milk

6   large eggs

½   teaspoon kosher salt
Freshly ground black pepper

¼   cup finely chopped walnuts

1   tablespoon unsalted butter

1   tablespoon extra-virgin olive oil

¼   cup freshly grated Parmigiano-Reggiano cheese

4   not-too-thin slices prosciutto di Parma or other air-dried cured ham

Look for an unusual bread, such as one with bits of olives, herbs, sun-dried tomatoes or cheese.

1. Cut an oval about 2 inches wide and 3 inches long out of the center of each bread slice with a small paring knife. (Reserve the cut-out ovals of bread for another use.) Place the bread slices in a 13-x-9-inch baking dish.

2. In a small bowl, whisk the milk, 2 of the eggs, the salt and a generous grinding of pepper until well blended. Pour the egg mixture over the bread and let stand, occasionally turning and pressing gently on the bread with a spatula, until the bread has absorbed all the egg mixture, about 10 minutes.

3. Place the walnuts in a small skillet over medium-low heat and cook, stirring often, until they begin to color, 3 to 5 minutes. Set aside.

4. Melt the butter with the oil in a large skillet over medium heat. Add the soaked bread. Cook, turning once, until golden brown, about 5 minutes per side. Break the eggs one at a time into a cup and slip into the cut-out sections in the slices of bread. Cover and cook over low heat until the whites are set and the yolks are soft-cooked, about 8 minutes. Sprinkle with the cheese and remove from the heat.

5. Place a a slice of prosciutto on each of four warm plates. With a spatula, transfer an egg-bread slice to each plate. Sprinkle with the walnuts and serve.

Makes 4 servings

Pizza with Eggs and Arugula Salad

I was first served pizza with an egg on the top at a wonderful little Italian trattoria called Manetta's in Long Island City, New York. I was delighted as much by the appearance and taste as I was by the name: Bull's-Eye Pizza or, in Italian, *Pizza Occhio di Bue*. This recipe makes four individual pizzas.

Pizza Dough

- ½ **cup warm water**
- 2 **teaspoons active dry yeast**
- 1¼ **cups all-purpose flour, plus more as needed**
- ¼ **cup whole wheat flour**
- 1 **tablespoon extra-virgin olive oil**
- 1 **teaspoon kosher salt**

Tomato Sauce

- 1 **28-ounce can plum tomatoes, with their juices**
- 1 **small leafy sprig fresh basil**
- 2 **tablespoons extra-virgin olive oil**
- 1 **garlic clove, bruised with the side of a knife**
- ½ **teaspoon kosher salt**

1. **Make the pizza dough:** Pour the water into a medium bowl and sprinkle with the yeast. Stir in ¼ cup of the all-purpose flour. Cover with plastic and set aside until foamy, about 20 minutes.

2. Add 1 cup all-purpose flour, the whole wheat flour, oil and salt to the yeast mixture. Stir with a wooden spoon until the dough is ropy. Stir in additional all-purpose flour, about 1 rounded tablespoon at a time, until the dough forms a sticky ball.

3. Transfer the dough to a lightly floured surface and knead, adding more flour as needed to prevent sticking, until it is smooth and no longer sticky but still soft, about 5 minutes.

4. Lightly oil a large bowl. Add the dough and turn to coat. Cover with plastic and set in a warm spot to rise until doubled in bulk, about 1½ hours. (If you want to use the dough later, refrigerate it to slow the rising. Remove it from the refrigerator about 1 hour before using and let it finish rising at room temperature.)

5. **Meanwhile, make the sauce:** Set a food mill over a wide saucepan or deep skillet and puree the tomatoes. (Or puree them in a food processor, then force through a strainer using a rubber spatula; discard the solids.) Add the basil, oil, garlic and salt and bring to a boil. Reduce the heat to low and cook until the sauce is thickened, about 20 minutes. Remove the basil and garlic. Reserve ¾ cup of the sauce for the pizza; freeze the remaining sauce (about half) for another use.

4 ounces mozzarella cheese, preferably fresh, thinly sliced

4 large eggs

Arugula Salad

½ garlic clove

1½ tablespoons extra-virgin olive oil

½ tablespoon red wine vinegar

Kosher salt and freshly ground black pepper

2 bunches arugula, rinsed and trimmed (about 4 cups packed)

2 tablespoons torn fresh basil leaves

Make 2 pizzas at a time if your oven isn't large enough to bake all 4 at once.

6. Position a rack in the bottom third of the oven and place a pizza stone or unglazed tiles on the rack, if using. Preheat the oven to 500°F. Divide the dough into 4 pieces. Roll into balls on a floured surface. Roll or stretch one piece at a time into an 8-inch circle. Place on a floured peel or a well-floured inverted baking sheet. Repeat with the remaining dough, using two baking sheets with 2 rounds of dough on each one. Let rest for 10 minutes.

7. Cover each pizza with about 3 tablespoons of the sauce, spreading it to within ½ inch of the edge. Arrange the mozzarella evenly on top. Bake the pizzas directly on the inverted baking sheets or transfer them by sliding off the peel or baking sheets directly onto the hot pizza stone or tiles in the oven, if using.

8. Break 1 of the eggs into a cup, open the oven door, slide the egg onto the center of a pizza and close the oven door. Repeat with the remaining 3 eggs and pizzas. Bake until the eggs are set and the dough is lightly browned on the edges, 8 to 10 minutes.

9. **Meanwhile, make the salad:** Rub the inside of a large bowl with the cut side of the garlic clove; discard the garlic. Add the oil, vinegar, a pinch of salt and a grinding of pepper; whisk to blend. Add the arugula and toss to coat.

10. To serve, slide the pizzas onto four dinner plates. Sprinkle with the basil and top each with a spoonful of the salad, dividing it evenly. Serve at once.

Makes 4 pizzas

Strata Strategies

 Think of strata as a savory bread pudding, a baked bread-and-custard dish that can have many different flavors and ingredients. It doesn't require lots of planning, because you can usually improvise with staples in your kitchen and fridge—bread, eggs, milk and cheese—plus all kinds of delicious leftovers. Another great convenience is that you can prepare a strata completely the night before you'll serve it. Just pop it into the oven 1 hour before the meal.

Here's a basic plan for constructing a strata from scratch:

♦ **Choose your bread:** You need to have six to eight ½-inch-thick slices of tasty bread. I use all kinds: plain white bread, multigrain, sourdough, even Italian semolina. I prefer to cut my own slices, but I do use *thick* commercially sliced bread if that's what I have on hand. A strata is the perfect way to use up day-old bread, but fresh bread works too. The important thing is having enough bread to make two layers to enclose the filling. While some cooks mix up small cubes of bread with other ingredients, like a traditional bread pudding, I always layer—"strata," after all, means layers.

♦ **Choose your pan:** You need a baking dish that is deep enough to hold two layers of bread, filling and custard. My favorite is about 9 inches square and 2½ inches deep, with a volume of exactly 8 cups. Any dish with an equivalent volume can be used, even a round casserole. Just trim the bread to fit the contours of the dish.

♦ **Choose your filling ingredients:** Almost any combination of ingredients can be used, as long as you have approximately 1 cup grated cheese, 1 to 2 cups of a flavorful vegetable (such as sautéed mushrooms, onions, garlic, red bell peppers, broccoli or spinach) and/or meat (such as crumbled cooked sausage, bacon or minced ham).

♦ **Make your custard:** The formula I use is 5 eggs to 2½ cups milk. But if you have only 4 eggs and 2 cups milk, don't worry; you can still make a delicious dish.

♦ **Assemble the strata:** Follow the technique of the recipes, layering half the bread in the bottom of the buttered or oiled dish, distributing all of the filling on top of that and then spreading half the cheese over it. Finish with a second layer of bread, then pour all the custard over the top and sprinkle with the remaining cheese. Refrigerate, covered, for at least 4 hours, or overnight, occasionally pressing down on the top layer of bread so the custard will seep through the layers evenly.

♦ **Bake the strata:** Bake the strata in a preheated 350°F oven for about 45 minutes, or until puffed and browned. Let stand for 10 minutes before serving.

Mushroom, Spinach and Cheese Strata

In the fall, the Ferry Plaza Farmers' Market in San Francisco has a remarkable assortment of fresh mushrooms. There I can find exotic chanterelles, black trumpets and pleurottes alongside the more familiar shiitakes, creminis, white buttons and portobellos. The cheese in this strata can vary according to what you have on hand—mozzarella, fontina, Gruyère and Monterey Jack all work well. You don't want the taste of the cheese to overwhelm the delicate flavor of the mushrooms, however, so avoid pungent varieties.

1 10-ounce bag fresh spinach, rinsed and trimmed, or one 10-ounce package frozen chopped spinach, thawed and squeezed dry

8 ounces mixed mushrooms (chanterelles, shiitakes, black trumpets, pleurottes, creminis, portobellos and/or white buttons)

3 tablespoons unsalted butter

1 garlic clove, minced

1½ teaspoons kosher salt
   Freshly ground black pepper

5 large eggs

2½ cups milk

2 teaspoons prepared mustard

6–8 thick (½-inch) slices firm white sandwich bread, preferably 1 day old

2 cups grated mild cheese (about 8 ounces)

1. If using fresh spinach, steam it in a steamer basket over boiling water until wilted, about 3 minutes. Transfer to a strainer and let cool; squeeze very dry with your hands. Transfer to a cutting board and coarsely chop; you should have about 1 cup. Set aside.

2. Trim the mushrooms; if using shiitakes, remove and discard the stems. Wipe the mushrooms clean and cut into ¼-inch-thick slices.

3. Use some of the butter to lightly coat a 2-quart shallow baking dish. Melt the remaining butter in a large skillet over high heat until it foams. Add the mushrooms and sauté, stirring, until lightly browned, about 3 minutes. Reduce the heat to medium and sauté, stirring, until tender, about 5 minutes. Add the garlic, ½ teaspoon of the salt and a grinding of pepper and cook for 1 minute. Add the spinach and cook, stirring, to evaporate any remaining moisture. Remove from the heat and set aside.

4. In a large bowl, whisk the eggs until foamy. Whisk in the milk and mustard until blended. Add the remaining 1 teaspoon salt. Set aside.

5. To assemble the strata, use half the bread slices to make a single layer in the prepared baking dish, cutting them, if necessary, to fit tightly. Spoon the mushroom mixture evenly over the bread. Sprinkle with 1 cup of the cheese. Use the remaining bread slices to make a second layer, once again cutting them to fit, if necessary.

6. Pour the egg mixture evenly over the top of the strata, using a spatula to press on the bread so the liquid is evenly absorbed. Top with the remaining 1 cup cheese. Cover with plastic and refrigerate for at least 4 hours, or overnight.

7. Preheat the oven to 350°F. Uncover the strata and bake until puffed and browned, about 45 minutes. Serve.

Makes 6 to 8 servings

Ricotta, Basil and Roasted Red Pepper Strata with Parmesan

The ricotta makes this strata almost puddinglike. For the best flavor, use your own roasted red peppers, but you can substitute store-bought. Just make sure to rinse them well and pat dry before using.

2 **red bell peppers, roasted (page 75) and cut into 1-inch-wide strips**

1 **tablespoon extra-virgin olive oil**

1 **small garlic clove, minced**
   Kosher salt and freshly ground black pepper

1 **15-ounce container ricotta cheese**

1 **cup freshly grated Parmigiano-Reggiano cheese (about 4 ounces)**

5 **large eggs**
   Freshly grated nutmeg

2½ **cups milk**

8 **½-inch-thick slices firm Italian bread, preferably 1 day old**

2 **tablespoons chopped fresh basil**

1. In a small bowl, combine the roasted peppers, oil, garlic, a pinch of salt and a grinding of pepper. Set aside.

2. In a medium bowl, whisk together the ricotta, ½ cup of the cheese, 1 of the eggs and nutmeg. Set aside.

3. In a separate medium bowl, whisk the remaining 4 eggs until blended. Whisk in the milk, the remaining ½ cup cheese, ½ teaspoon salt and a grinding of pepper.

4. To assemble the strata, lightly coat a 2-quart shallow baking dish with butter. Use half the bread slices to make a single layer in the baking dish, cutting them, if necessary, to fit tightly. Spread the ricotta mixture evenly over the bread. Sprinkle with the basil. Scatter the roasted-pepper mixture on top and drizzle with any juices left in the bowl. Use the remaining bread slices to make a second layer, once again cutting them to fit, if necessary.

5. Pour the egg mixture evenly over the top of the strata, using a spatula to press on the bread so the liquid is evenly absorbed. Cover with plastic and refrigerate for at least 4 hours, or overnight.

6. Preheat the oven to 350°F. Uncover the strata and bake until puffed and browned, about 45 minutes. Serve.

Makes 6 to 8 servings

From the Henhouse to the Store: Selected Terms

 Gathering: Very few farmers gather eggs by hand these days. In large production facilities, hens lay their eggs onto specially designed nests or sloping floors leading to conveyor belts, which take them immediately to refrigerated holding rooms.

Washing: Before they are packed, the eggs are washed and sanitized, as is required by law. During this process, the bloom—the natural protective layer that coats the shell—is removed. To restore that protection, many producers coat their eggs with an imperceptible layer of mineral oil before sending them to the market.

Candling: Long ago, egg producers checked the quality of each egg by holding a candle up behind the egg. Today the process is mechanized, with the eggs traveling on rollers over high-intensity lights, allowing inspectors to detect imperfections.

Breakout: For quality control, eggs are taken at random from production and broken on a surface to measure the height and the thickness of the albumen and the firmness, color and shape of the yolk. The thicker the white, the fresher the egg. Thin, runny whites indicate that the eggs were improperly cooled and refrigerated after gathering.

Grading: Eggs are graded as AA, A and B, determined by examining the interior (candling and breakout) and exterior quality of the eggs. Grades AA and A are similar in quality, with AA being slightly fresher. Grade B eggs are rarely available to consumers as whole eggs; most are used in egg products.

Sausage, Gruyère and Onion Strata

The flavoring in the sausage will greatly affect the taste of this strata. I like breakfast sausage well seasoned with sage and garlic or sweet Italian sausage seasoned with fennel, but almost any sausage will do.

8 ounces breakfast, sweet Italian or other sausage, casings removed

1 tablespoon extra-virgin olive oil

½ cup chopped onion

½ cup chopped red bell pepper

1 garlic clove, minced

2 tablespoons chopped fresh flat-leaf parsley

Kosher salt and freshly ground black pepper

5 large eggs

2½ cups milk

6–8 thick (½-inch) slices firm white sandwich, Italian or French bread, preferably 1 day old

1½ cups grated Gruyère cheese (about 6 ounces)

1. Crumble the sausage into a large skillet and cook, stirring, until lightly browned, breaking it up with a spatula, about 5 minutes. Transfer to a strainer set over a bowl to drain; discard any fat. Wipe out the skillet.

2. Add the oil to the skillet and heat over medium heat. Add the onion and bell pepper and cook, stirring, until golden, about 8 minutes. Add the garlic and cook for 1 minute. Stir in the parsley, a pinch of salt and a grinding of pepper. Add the sausage and stir to blend. Set aside.

3. In a large bowl, whisk the eggs until foamy. Whisk in the milk until blended. Add 1 teaspoon salt and a grinding of pepper.

4. To assemble the strata, lightly coat a 2-quart shallow baking dish with olive oil. Use half the bread slices to make a single layer in the baking dish, cutting them, if necessary, to fit tightly. Spoon the sausage mixture evenly over the bread. Sprinkle with 1 cup of the cheese. Use the remaining bread slices to make a second layer, once again cutting them to fit, if necessary.

If you prefer, use a chopped fully cooked smoked sausage. Although that kind of sausage needs no cooking, I like to sauté it with the onion to blend the flavors.

5. Pour the egg mixture evenly over the top of the strata, using a spatula to press on the bread so the liquid is evenly absorbed. Top with the remaining ½ cup cheese. Cover with plastic and refrigerate for at least 4 hours, or overnight.

6. Preheat the oven to 350°F. Uncover the strata and bake until puffed and browned, about 45 minutes. Serve.

Makes 6 to 8 servings

Leek, Sun-Dried Tomato and Brie Strata

Otherwise savvy cooks often neglect leeks. Related to both garlic and onions, leeks have a sweet, subtle but distinctive flavor.

1 pound leeks (3–5, depending on size)

3 tablespoons unsalted butter
Kosher salt and freshly ground black pepper

5 large eggs

2½ cups milk

½ cup freshly grated Parmigiano-Reggiano cheese

6–8 thick (½-inch) slices firm white sandwich, Italian or French bread, preferably 1 day old

12 oil-packed sun-dried tomato halves, drained, patted dry and quartered

8 ounces Brie cheese, rind removed, cut into ½-inch pieces

1. Trim the root ends from the leeks. Trim off the darkest green tops. Peel off and discard any wilted or discolored outer leaves. Halve or quarter the leeks lengthwise. Rinse the leeks well under cold water. Place in a bowl and fill with cold water. Repeat the process at least twice to remove any sand from between the layers; drain and pat dry. Cut into thin slices. You should have about 4 cups.

2. Lightly coat a 9-inch baking dish with some of the butter; set aside.

3. Melt the remaining butter in a large skillet over low heat. Add the leeks and cook, stirring, until tender but not browned, about 10 minutes. Sprinkle with salt to taste and a grinding of pepper; remove from the heat and set aside.

4. In a large bowl, whisk the eggs until foamy. Whisk in the milk until blended. Add the Parmigiano-Reggiano, ½ teaspoon salt and a grinding of pepper.

5. To assemble the strata, use half the bread slices to make a single layer in the prepared baking dish, cutting them, if necessary, to fit tightly. Spoon the leeks evenly over the bread. Distribute the sun-dried tomatoes evenly over the leeks and top with the Brie. Use the remaining bread slices to make a second layer, once again cutting them to fit, if necessary.

6. Pour the egg mixture evenly over the top of the strata, using a spatula to press on the bread so the liquid is evenly absorbed. Cover with plastic and refrigerate for at least 4 hours, or overnight.

7. Preheat the oven to 350°F. Uncover the strata and bake until puffed and browned, about 45 minutes. Serve.

Makes 6 to 8 servings

Popovers

Just five simple ingredients are needed to make popovers. High, hollow and steamy in the center, with a dark crusty outer layer, they literally pop up and over the rim of the pan as they bake. Popovers can be baked in muffin tins or custard cups. They are great served with soup, spread with jam and enjoyed with a mug of morning coffee or served with eggs instead of toast.

4 tablespoons (½ stick) unsalted butter, melted

3 large eggs, at room temperature

1¼ cups milk, at room temperature

1½ cups all-purpose flour

½ teaspoon kosher salt

1. Position a rack in the center of the oven and preheat the oven to 400°F. Generously coat a 12-cup muffin tin or 12 custard cups with the melted butter. Place the custard cups, if using, on a baking sheet.

2. Whisk the eggs in a large bowl (preferably one with a pouring spout) until well blended. Add the milk and whisk until blended. Add the flour and salt; whisk until thoroughly blended and the batter is smooth.

3. Pour the batter into the prepared muffin tin or custard cups, filling each cup two-thirds full. Place the tin or cups in the oven and immediately turn the heat up to 450°F. Bake for 10 minutes. Without opening the oven door, reduce the oven temperature to 350°F and bake for 20 minutes more. Remove from the oven and let cool in the tin or cups for a few minutes. Serve hot or warm. (To reheat leftover popovers, set on a baking sheet and heat in a preheated 350°F oven for 10 minutes.)

Makes 12 popovers

A few important guidelines:
Use room-temperature eggs and milk, preheat the oven and do not, under any circumstances, open the oven door until the popovers are done.

Parmesan Spoon Bread

Spoon bread is soft and fluffy, much like a soufflé, but sturdier and more filling. For a substantial vegetarian meal, serve hot with a mess of cooked greens (broccoli rabe, kale, collards, Swiss chard, dandelions or mustard greens are all good choices) and a ripe-tomato salad. Spoon bread is also delicious served with a mixture of sautéed mushrooms.

3 tablespoons unsalted butter

1 cup diced onions

1 garlic clove, minced

1 cup yellow cornmeal
  (the finer the cornmeal,
  the lighter the spoon bread)

3 cups cold water
  (or half water and half milk)

½ teaspoon kosher salt

½ cup freshly grated
  Parmigiano-Reggiano cheese,
  or more to taste

3 large eggs, separated
  Freshly ground black pepper
  (optional)

1. Melt the butter in a large, wide saucepan over medium heat. Add the onions and cook, stirring, until golden, about 15 minutes. Add the garlic; cook for 1 minute. Stir in the cornmeal until it is coated with the butter. Gradually add the water (or water and milk), stirring constantly, then add the salt and bring to a boil, stirring constantly. Reduce the heat to low and cook, stirring, until the cornmeal thickens and pulls away from the sides of the pan, 10 to 15 minutes. Remove from the heat and stir in the cheese. Let stand until warm, not hot.

2. Preheat the oven to 375°F. Lightly butter a 1½-quart soufflé dish or small, deep casserole.

3. Place the egg yolks in a large bowl; whisk to blend. Using a rubber spatula or wooden spoon, stir a little of the hot cornmeal mixture into the yolks, then stir in the remaining cornmeal. Add a grinding of pepper, if desired.

4. In a large clean bowl, beat the egg whites until soft peaks form. Gently but thoroughly fold the whites into the cornmeal mixture in three additions.

5. Spoon into the prepared dish and bake until the top is slightly puffed and browned, 35 to 40 minutes. Serve at once.

Makes 6 servings

I like this with Parmesan, but almost any flavorful cheese, such as cheddar, fontina or Gruyère, can be used.

Foolproof Pâte à Choux

 Gougère (page 157) is only one of many pastries that can be made from *pâte à choux,* or choux paste. Cream puffs, éclairs and other elaborate desserts are also made with this high-rising combination of water, butter, flour and eggs. Eggs are the only leavening agent in *pâte à choux.* Although choux paste isn't difficult to make, it does need to be prepared and baked with care. Follow these basic guidelines to ensure that your pastry will be puffed and golden.

♦ Dump the flour into the boiling-water mixture all at once and stir vigorously. The heat of the water swells the starch in the flour, giving the batter the strength to rise.

♦ Add the eggs one at a time to the flour mixture, beating after each addition, until the batter is very smooth.

♦ To pipe the batter, use a pastry bag fitted with a large (⅓-inch) plain or fluted tip.

♦ Bake on the lowest oven rack so the intense heat at the bottom of the oven will make the batter puff up before the top of the pastry sets.

♦ If you want the gougère to be extra crisp, let it sit in the turned-off oven for another 15 minutes after baking.

Gougère

Gougère, a glossy wreath of egg bread made from a paste of heated flour, water and butter (called *pâte à choux*), is one of the easiest savory pastries imaginable: all you do is beat eggs into the hot paste. You can flavor the dough with fresh herbs (rosemary and thyme) and other cheese, instead of the traditional Gruyère. Little bits of snipped prosciutto, sun-dried tomato or crisp bacon can be stirred into the dough or sprinkled on top before baking. Serve with a hearty soup on a chilly night.

1   cup water

4   tablespoons (½ stick) unsalted butter

1   cup sifted all-purpose flour

1   teaspoon kosher salt

3   large eggs, at room temperature

2   large egg whites, at room temperature

½   cup coarsely grated Gruyère, fontina, Parmigiano-Reggiano or Asiago cheese

Minced fresh rosemary, prosciutto or oil-packed sun-dried tomatoes (optional)

1. Position a rack in the lower third of the oven and preheat the oven to 400°F. Generously butter a large baking sheet. With the tip of a skewer, using a pot lid or a plate as a guide, draw a 10-inch circle in the center of the baking sheet.

2. In a medium saucepan, combine the water and butter and heat until the butter has melted and the liquid is boiling. Add the flour and salt all at once and beat with a wooden spoon until the mixture forms a ball, about 1 minute. Remove from the heat and let stand for about 5 minutes. The paste should be hot but not steaming when the eggs are added. Transfer the paste to a large mixer bowl for easier beating, or leave it in the saucepan if beating it by hand or with a hand-held mixer.

3. In a medium bowl, stir the whole eggs and egg whites together with a fork just until blended. Gradually add the eggs, ¼ cup at a time, to the paste, beating well after each addition with a wooden spoon or an electric mixer until thoroughly incorporated and the paste has a dull, smooth sheen.

4. Stir in the cheese and add any other seasonings, if using. Scoop up the paste by the heaping tablespoonful and place side by side on the circle on the prepared baking sheet.

5. Bake for 20 minutes. Without opening the oven door, reduce the temperature to 350°F and bake for 20 minutes more, or until the gougère is puffed and golden with a crisp crust. Cool on a rack, then transfer to a platter and serve warm or at room temperature. Slice with a serrated knife or pull apart into sections.

Makes 8 servings

VARIATION

For a gougère that is less crisp on the outside and moister inside, use 4 large eggs instead of the combination of eggs and egg whites.

CHAPTER 5 *Seductively Stuffed Eggs*

"Gentle heating is the real secret to cooking proteins, whether in eggs or in meat."

—SHIRLEY CORRIHER

When I was growing up, deviled eggs were a popular appetizer, turning up at every picnic and church supper. But, like so many egg dishes, these hors d'oeuvres fell out of favor for a decade or more. I am delighted to see that they are fashionable once again, as there are few finger foods as simple, pretty and irresistible as a hard-cooked egg half with a mound of soft, nicely seasoned egg yolk.

Of course, one has to start with a perfectly cooked egg. You notice that I use the term "hard-cooked" rather than "hard-boiled." The latter may be a good description for a tough guy, but it's a misnomer for eggs properly cooked in the shell until firm. Indeed, boiling eggs is a no-no according to food scientists, as the high temperature causes the protein structure in the egg to tighten, squeezing out the moisture that keeps the yolk tender. An egg that's been boiled is as hard and leathery as an old detective!

Instead, when you want a delicious egg cooked in the shell, whether soft-set or quite solid, you must gently heat it in water that is just a bit cooler than boiling. My method for hard-cooked eggs is to put them into a pan of cold water, bring it just to the verge of boiling and immediately remove the pan from the heat. The eggs will hard-cook in the hot water but remain tender—and the yolk will not turn green around the outside, another result of overheating.

While I still love old-fashioned deviled eggs—my version on page 165 is truly devilish, with hot sauce and mustard in the yolks—the recipes here demonstrate that stuffed eggs lend themselves to many other flavors. Nowadays I use olive oil more often than mayonnaise to soften the yolks, and I have made stuffings of everything from mashed potatoes with salmon and caviar to cream cheese and chutney. In this chapter, you will also find fascinating and delicious recipes from Sardinia and the Italian region of Abruzzi for hard-cooked eggs that are seasoned, cooked a second time in a skillet and served as a hot appetizer.

My Tried-and-True Method for Hard-Cooked Eggs

 ♦ Don't use absolutely fresh eggs, because they will be hard to peel. (See page 164.)

♦ NEVER boil the eggs.

♦ Time your eggs precisely while they are in the hot water and drain and chill them immediately when the time is up. This keeps them tender, facilitates peeling and prevents the formation of a green tinge around the yolk. (This tinge is iron sulfide and is a result of prolonged heat. It's perfectly safe to eat and doesn't affect the egg's flavor—but it is visually unappealing.)

Here's my method:

1. Place the eggs in a saucepan large enough to hold them in a single layer. Add tap water to cover by 1 inch. Set over medium-high heat and heat, uncovered, until the water is almost boiling. When you see one or two bubbles break on the surface, remove the pan from the heat and cover. Leave the eggs in the hot water for 10 to 15 minutes, depending on the size of your eggs and the consistency you like. I prefer a barely cooked yolk that is set but creamy and a very tender white that isn't at all rubbery. To achieve this, I set a timer and allow 10 minutes for medium eggs, 11 minutes for large eggs and 12 to 15 minutes for extra-large eggs. If you want a very firm yolk, you can leave the eggs in for 1 minute more.

2. When the time is up, I immediately tilt the pan over the sink and drain off the hot water. Set the pan in the sink, cover the eggs with cold water and add a handful of ice cubes. Carefully lift out each warm egg and break

the shell at the large, more rounded end by giving it a tap with a heavy spoon or hitting it against the side of the sink. Return the cracked egg to the pan and let cool completely.

3. When the eggs arc cool to the touch, remove them one at a time and crack the shell lightly all around by rolling it on the work surface. Carefully peel, removing the shell in small pieces, then dip the egg into the pan of water to remove any clinging bits of shell.

Tips for Easy Peeling

 ♦ Choose older eggs for hard-cooking. Fresh eggs are more acidic, scientists tell us, which makes them harder to peel; older eggs are more alkaline and easier to peel. In this case, I use eggs that have been in my refrigerator for a week or more.

♦ Immediately after cooking, make a small crack in the egg and submerge it in ice water. The water will seep between the membranes just inside the shell, allowing the egg white to separate more easily.

♦ Roll the cooled eggs on the work surface to make cracks all around and release the membranes from the white.

♦ Peel off the small pieces of shell while holding the egg under cold running water or dipping it in a pan of cool water.

Old-Fashioned Deviled Eggs

For most people, stuffed eggs mean deviled eggs. It's said that Washington Irving first used the word "deviled" to describe a spicy dish similar to a curry in his 1820 *Sketch Book*. Now, almost two centuries later, deviled dishes are newly popular. This is my idea of the perfect deviled egg.

4 large eggs, hard-cooked (page 162), peeled and halved lengthwise

2½ tablespoons mayonnaise

1½ teaspoons Dijon mustard

Tabasco or other hot pepper sauce

Kosher salt and freshly ground black pepper

2 tablespoons minced fresh chives

1. Carefully remove the yolks from the whites. Place the whites cut side up on a plate. With the back of a spoon, press the yolks through a sieve into a small bowl, or mash them in the bowl with a fork. Add the mayonnaise and mustard and mash with a fork until blended. Add hot pepper sauce, 2 or 3 dashes at a time, tasting as you go, until the heat is the level you like. Beat with a wooden spoon until smooth and fluffy, then add salt to taste and a grinding of pepper.

2. Using a teaspoon, carefully stuff the whites with the yolk mixture, mounding the tops. Garnish the stuffed eggs generously with the chives. Serve at room temperature or chilled.

Makes 4 servings

Tips for Successful Stuffed Eggs

 1. Halve the hard-cooked eggs lengthwise with a thin-bladed knife, wiping the blade clean after slicing each egg. Carefully remove the yolks from the whites.

2. Use the eggs as soon as they have cooled rather than refrigerating them for later. The still warm yolks will have a creamy texture and can be easily mashed with the seasonings. Chilled eggs tend to have crumbly yolks that are more difficult to combine with other ingredients. If you must use refrigerated hard-cooked eggs, press the yolks through a strainer with the back of a spoon or a rubber spatula. The sieved yolks will blend more easily with the other stuffing ingredients, producing a smoother mixture.

3. With the back of a fork, mash the yolks with the other ingredients until blended, then beat the mixture with a wooden spoon until fluffy.

4. Cut a thin slice off the underside of each white so that the egg won't tip over as you are filling or serving it.

5. To fill the eggs, scoop up a mound of stuffing in a small teaspoon and push the mound into the white with your fingertip or a small rubber spatula. Alternatively, fit a pastry bag with a round or fluted tip with a wide opening (about ½ inch), fill it with the stuffing and squeeze a mound into each white. If you don't have a bag and a tip, you can spoon the stuffing into a small clean plastic bag. Squeeze the stuffing into one corner of the bag. Snip off the corner with scissors to make an opening about ½ inch long and squeeze a mound of stuffing into each white.

6. Serve the stuffed eggs immediately if possible, as they will have the softest and most seductive texture. You can, however, cover and refrigerate stuffed eggs until ready to serve. If there's butter in the stuffing, it will harden when chilled, so take the eggs out of the refrigerator about 15 minutes before serving to allow the filling to come to room temperature and soften.

Italian Stuffed Eggs with Parsley and Olive Oil

Tim Biancalana, a talented cook and friend, suggested this recipe. The most important ingredient is the olive oil. It makes the yolks light and creamy, and the olive flavor comes through loud and clear.

4 **large eggs, hard-cooked (page 162), peeled and halved lengthwise**

¼ **cup extra-virgin olive oil**

2 **tablespoons minced fresh flat-leaf parsley**

¼ **teaspoon minced garlic**

¼ **teaspoon kosher salt, or more to taste**

Freshly ground black pepper

Paprika (optional)

1. Carefully remove the yolks from the whites. Place the whites cut side up on a plate. With the back of a spoon, press the yolks through a sieve into a small bowl, or mash them in the bowl with a fork. Add 2 tablespoons of the oil, 1 tablespoon of the parsley, the garlic, salt and a generous grinding of pepper. Mash with a fork until blended. Using a wooden spoon, gradually beat in the remaining 2 tablespoons oil until the yolk mixture is smooth and fluffy. Taste and add more salt or pepper, if desired.

2. Using a teaspoon, carefully stuff the whites with the yolk mixture, mounding the tops. Sprinkle the tops of the stuffed eggs with the remaining 1 tablespoon parsley and paprika, if desired. Serve at room temperature or chilled.

Makes 4 servings

Do add paprika along with the parsley, if you like; after all, red, green and white are the colors of the Italian flag.

Curried Stuffed Eggs

Curry powder is a mixture of many different spices, sometimes as many as 20. In Indian kitchens, the mixture varies from cook to cook and is ground fresh every day. Most Americans buy preblended curry powder. I like the Madras-style variety that comes in a yellow and gold tin and is available in many supermarkets. It is sweeter and less hot than many other curry powders, and it goes particularly well with eggs.

2 teaspoons curry powder, preferably Madras-style

4 large eggs, hard-cooked (page 162), peeled and halved lengthwise

¼ cup mayonnaise, yogurt or sour cream

1 tablespoon minced onion

2 teaspoons fresh lemon juice

½ garlic clove, minced

¼ teaspoon kosher salt
  Freshly ground black pepper

1 tablespoon minced fresh cilantro

1. Place the curry powder in a small dry skillet and toast over low heat until fragrant, about 30 seconds. Transfer to a small plate to cool.

2. Carefully remove the yolks from the whites. Place the whites cut side up on a plate. With the back of a spoon, press the yolks through a sieve into a small bowl, or mash them in the bowl with a fork. Add the mayonnaise, yogurt or sour cream, onion, curry powder, lemon juice, garlic, salt and a generous grinding of pepper. Mash with a fork until blended, then beat with a wooden spoon until smooth and fluffy.

3. Using a teaspoon, carefully stuff the whites with the yolk mixture, mounding the tops. Sprinkle with the cilantro and serve at room temperature or chilled.

Makes 4 servings

Parmesan Stuffed Eggs with Toasted Walnuts

These eggs are great for a summer picnic, with a platter of sliced tomatoes garnished with basil and drizzled with olive oil.

3 tablespoons chopped walnuts

4 large eggs, hard-cooked (page 162), peeled and halved lengthwise

5 tablespoons freshly grated Parmigiano-Reggiano cheese, plus more for garnish

4–5 tablespoons extra-virgin olive oil

Kosher salt and freshly ground black pepper

1. Place the walnuts in a small dry skillet and toast over medium-low heat, stirring, until golden and fragrant, about 3 minutes. Transfer the walnuts to a small plate to cool.

2. Carefully remove the yolks from the whites. Place the whites cut side up on a plate. With the back of a spoon, press the yolks through a sieve into a small bowl, or mash them in the bowl with a fork. Add the 5 tablespoons cheese and mash with a fork until blended. Using a wooden spoon, beat in the oil 1 tablespoon at a time, until the yolk mixture is smooth and fluffy. Add salt to taste and a grinding of pepper.

3. Using a teaspoon, carefully stuff the whites with the yolk mixture, mounding the tops. Sprinkle a few toasted walnuts and some cheese over each stuffed egg. Serve at room temperature or chilled.

Makes 4 servings

For the very best flavor and texture, be sure to use freshly grated real Parmigiano-Reggiano to make the stuffing for these eggs; it is moister and softer than pre-grated Parmesan cheese.

Sun-Dried Tomato Stuffed Eggs

Sun-dried tomatoes have a very concentrated tomato flavor and are generally used sparingly, but I like their intensity in these stuffed eggs. I prefer the tomatoes packed in olive oil, but you can use the dry-packed kind: simply soak them in boiling water until soft, drain and pat dry before using.

4 large eggs, hard-cooked (page 162), peeled and halved lengthwise

¼ cup oil-packed sun-dried tomatoes, blotted dry with paper towels and finely chopped

¼ cup extra-virgin olive oil

1 teaspoon red wine vinegar

½ garlic clove, minced

¼ teaspoon fresh thyme leaves or ⅛ teaspoon dried, crumbled

¼ teaspoon kosher salt, or to taste

Freshly ground black pepper

4 kalamata olives, pitted and halved

1. Carefully remove the yolks from the whites. Place the whites cut side up on a plate. With the back of a spoon, press the yolks through a sieve into a small bowl, or mash them in the bowl with a fork. Add the sun-dried tomatoes, 2 tablespoons of the oil, the vinegar, garlic, thyme, salt and a grinding of pepper. Mash with a fork until blended. Using a wooden spoon, gradually beat in the remaining 2 tablespoons oil until the mixture is smooth and fluffy.

2. Using a teaspoon, carefully stuff the whites with the yolk mixture, mounding the tops. Garnish each stuffed egg with an olive half. Serve at room temperature.

Makes 4 servings

You may want to make these eggs ahead of time. They improve as they stand, and the tomato flavor permeates the yolks. Just remove from the refrigerator about 15 minutes before serving so they won't be icy cold.

Avocado and Jalapeño Stuffed Eggs

In this guacamole-inspired rendition of stuffed eggs, the avocado stands in for mayonnaise, adding a creamy texture to the yolks.

4 **large eggs, hard-cooked (page 162), peeled and halved lengthwise**

⅓ **cup mashed ripe avocado**

1 **tablespoon minced fresh cilantro**

1 **tablespoon minced scallion (white and light green parts)**

1-2 **teaspoons minced, seeded jalapeño**

1-2 **teaspoons fresh lime juice**

¼ **teaspoon kosher salt, or more to taste**

Fresh cilantro sprigs for garnish

1. Carefully remove the yolks from the whites. Place the whites cut side up on a plate. With the back of a spoon, press the yolks through a sieve into a small bowl, or mash them in the bowl with a fork. Add the avocado, cilantro, scallion, 1 teaspoon of the jalapeño, 1 teaspoon of the lime juice and the salt. Mash with a fork until blended. Taste and add more jalapeño, lime juice and/or salt to taste.

2. Using a teaspoon, carefully stuff the whites with the yolk mixture, mounding the tops. Garnish each stuffed egg with a small cilantro sprig. Serve at room temperature or chilled.

Makes 4 servings

Serve as a side dish with black beans and tomato salsa.

Green Olive Stuffed Eggs with Roasted Red Peppers

I like to garnish these stuffed eggs with twirled strips of roasted red pepper.

4   large eggs, hard-cooked
    (page 162), peeled and
    halved lengthwise

¼   cup extra-virgin olive oil

2   teaspoons fresh lemon juice

½   garlic clove, minced

¼   cup rinsed, pitted and
    chopped green olives

1   tablespoon finely chopped
    roasted red pepper, plus
    ½ roasted red pepper
    (page 75), cut into thin strips

1. Carefully remove the yolks from the whites. Place the whites cut side up on a plate. With the back of a spoon, press the yolks through a sieve into a small bowl, or mash them in the bowl with a fork. Add the oil, lemon juice and garlic. Mash with a fork until blended, then beat with a wooden spoon until smooth and fluffy. Fold in the olives and chopped roasted pepper.

2. Using a teaspoon, carefully stuff the whites with the yolk mixture, mounding the tops. Garnish each stuffed egg with a strip of roasted pepper, shaped into a ring. Serve at room temperature or chilled.

Makes 4 servings

Chipotle Chile Stuffed Eggs

Chipotle chiles are smoked, dried jalapeños. They usually come in small cans packed in adobo sauce and can be purchased wherever Latino groceries are sold. They are fiery hot, so just one chile and one teaspoon of the adobo sauce add a terrific burst of flavor.

½ teaspoon ground cumin

4 large eggs, hard-cooked (page 162), peeled and halved lengthwise

3 tablespoons sour cream or mayonnaise

1 tablespoon minced scallion greens

2 teaspoons fresh lime juice

1 canned chipotle chile in adobo sauce, finely chopped

1 teaspoon adobo sauce

¼ teaspoon kosher salt

Coarsely chopped fresh cilantro for garnish

1. Place the cumin in a small dry skillet and toast over low heat until fragrant, about 10 seconds. Transfer to a small plate to cool.

2. Carefully remove the yolks from the whites. Place the whites cut side up on a plate. With the back of a spoon, press the yolks through a sieve into a small bowl, or mash them in the bowl with a fork. Add the sour cream or mayonnaise, scallion greens, lime juice, chipotle, adobo sauce and cumin. Mash with a fork until blended, then beat with a wooden spoon until the yolk mixture is smooth and fluffy. Add the salt.

3. Using a teaspoon, carefully stuff the whites with the yolk mixture, mounding the tops. Garnish each stuffed egg with a sprinkling of cilantro. Serve at room temperature or chilled.

Makes 4 servings

Transfer the rest of the can of chipotles to a plastic container and freeze for later use in stews, bean dishes or salad dressings.

Chèvre, Dill and Chive Stuffed Eggs

Chèvre is French goat cheese, which can be either creamy and mild or dry and pungent. For this recipe, choose a creamy fresh cheese. I like dill, but fresh thyme or a mixture of thyme and rosemary can be substituted.

4 large eggs, hard-cooked (page 162), peeled and halved lengthwise

2½ ounces mild, creamy goat cheese, at room temperature

2 tablespoons unsalted butter, at room temperature

1½ teaspoons minced fresh dill

1½ teaspoons minced fresh chives

Kosher salt and freshly ground black pepper

Fresh dill sprigs and/or minced fresh chives for garnish

1. Carefully remove the yolks from the whites. Place the whites cut side up on a plate. With the back of a spoon, press the yolks through a sieve into a small bowl, or mash them in the bowl with a fork. Add the goat cheese, butter, minced dill, 1½ teaspoons chives, a pinch of salt and a grinding of pepper. Mash with a fork until blended, then beat with a wooden spoon until the mixture is smooth and fluffy.

2. Using a teaspoon, carefully stuff the whites with the yolk mixture, mounding the tops. Garnish each stuffed egg with a tiny sprig of dill and/or a sprinkling of chives. Serve at room temperature or chilled.

Makes 4 servings

Tarragon and Honey Mustard Stuffed Eggs

Tarragon is widely used in classic French cooking. I love its delicate, aniselike taste paired with eggs.

4 large eggs, hard-cooked (page 162), peeled and halved lengthwise

3 tablespoons mayonnaise

1½ teaspoons honey mustard

½ teaspoon fresh lemon juice

2 tablespoons minced fresh tarragon

1 tablespoon minced sweet onion

Kosher salt and freshly ground black pepper

1. Carefully remove the yolks from the whites. Place the whites cut side up on a plate. With the back of a spoon, press the yolks through a sieve into a small bowl, or mash them in the bowl with a fork. Add the mayonnaise, mustard and lemon juice. Mash with a fork until blended, then beat with a wooden spoon until smooth and fluffy. Add 1 tablespoon of the tarragon and the onion and stir to blend. Add salt to taste and a grinding of pepper.

2. Using a teaspoon, carefully stuff the whites with the yolk mixture, mounding the tops. Garnish with the remaining 1 tablespoon tarragon. Serve at room temperature or chilled.

Makes 4 servings

Tofu, Scallion and Mustard Stuffed Eggs

The filling of these tofu-stuffed eggs is fluffy and abundant, making each half of an egg a rather overstuffed but pleasing mouthful.

4 hard-cooked large eggs (page 162), peeled and halved lengthwise

½ cup crumbled soft tofu

3 tablespoons mayonnaise

2 teaspoons Dijon mustard

2 tablespoons minced scallions (white and light green parts), plus 1 tablespoon finely sliced greens for garnish

Kosher salt and freshly ground black pepper

1. Carefully remove the yolks from the whites. Place the whites cut side up on a plate. With the back of a spoon, press the yolks through a sieve into a small bowl, or mash them in the bowl with a fork. Add the tofu, mayonnaise and mustard. Mash with a fork until blended, then beat with a wooden spoon until smooth and fluffy. Add the minced scallions and stir to blend. Add salt to taste and a grinding of pepper.

2. Using a teaspoon, carefully stuff the whites with the yolk mixture, mounding the tops. Garnish with the scallion greens. Serve at room temperature or chilled.

Makes 4 servings

Anchovy Stuffed Eggs with Capers

The world is divided between those who adore anchovies and those who don't. I'm an anchovy lover.

4 large eggs, hard-cooked (page 162), peeled and halved lengthwise

3 tablespoons extra-virgin olive oil

4 anchovy fillets, drained and rinsed; 3 finely chopped, 1 cut into 8 pieces

1 tablespoon finely chopped fresh flat-leaf parsley

2 teaspoons fresh lemon juice

¼ teaspoon minced garlic

Freshly ground black pepper

1 tablespoon capers, rinsed and drained

1. Carefully remove the yolks from the whites. Place the whites cut side up on a plate. With the back of a spoon, press the yolks through a sieve into a small bowl, or mash them in the bowl with a fork. Add the oil, finely chopped anchovies, parsley, lemon juice, garlic and a grinding of pepper. Mash with a fork until blended, then beat with a wooden spoon until smooth and fluffy.

2. Using a teaspoon, carefully stuff the whites with the yolk mixture, mounding the tops. Garnish each stuffed egg with a piece of anchovy and a few capers. Serve at room temperature or chilled.

Makes 4 servings

Smoked Salmon and Potato Stuffed Eggs with Caviar

I developed this recipe to make a sophisticated stuffed egg with fewer calories and a little less saturated fat. I use six eggs but just three yolks, substituting cooked potato for the missing yolks.

1 russet potato (8 ounces), peeled and cut into ½-inch cubes

6 large eggs, hard-cooked (page 162), peeled and halved lengthwise

2 tablespoons sour cream

1 tablespoon fresh lemon juice

2 teaspoons whole-grain Dijon mustard

3 tablespoons minced smoked salmon (about 1 ounce)

2 tablespoons finely chopped scallions (white and light green parts)

Kosher salt and freshly ground black pepper

2 tablespoons salmon caviar for garnish

1. Place the potato cubes in a medium saucepan, add water to cover and bring to a boil. Cover and cook over medium-low heat until the cubes are tender when pierced with a skewer, about 10 minutes. Drain and let cool.

2. Carefully remove the yolks from the whites; reserve 3 of the yolks (6 halves) for another use. Place the whites cut side up on a plate. With the back of a spoon, press the yolks through a sieve into a small bowl, or mash them in the bowl with a fork. Add the potato, sour cream, lemon juice and mustard. Mash with a fork until blended. Stir in the salmon and scallions and season with salt to taste and a grinding of pepper

3. Using a teaspoon, carefully stuff the whites with the yolk mixture, mounding the tops. Garnish the stuffed eggs with the caviar. Serve at room temperature or chilled.

Makes 6 servings

Sometimes I make these eggs without the smoked salmon and caviar, adding more mustard for extra flavor.

Italian Tuna Stuffed Eggs

Use imported canned Italian tuna in olive oil for the stuffing in these eggs. It has a soft texture and an assertive taste—perfect for blending with the yolks.

4 large eggs, hard-cooked (page 162), peeled and halved lengthwise

1 3½-ounce can Italian tuna in olive oil, drained

3 tablespoons mayonnaise

1 tablespoon minced sweet onion

1 tablespoon minced fresh flat-leaf parsley, plus whole leaves for garnish

Kosher salt and freshly ground black pepper

1. Carefully remove the yolks from the whites. Place the whites cut side up on a plate. With the back of a spoon, press the yolks through a sieve into a small bowl, or mash them in the bowl with a fork. Add the tuna, mayonnaise, onion, minced parsley, salt to taste and a grinding of pepper. Mash with a fork until blended.

2. Using a teaspoon, carefully stuff the whites with the yolk mixture, mounding the tops. Garnish with the parsley leaves. Serve at room temperature or chilled.

Makes 4 servings

Cream Cheese and Chutney Stuffed Eggs

There are many different types of chutney on the market; some are spicier than others, some are sweeter. Taste the egg-yolk mixture after you add the chutney, and add more, if desired. You might also want to balance the flavors by adding a teaspoon or so of fresh lemon or lime juice, some grated fresh ginger or ginger juice and/or just a pinch of salt. Let your palate be your guide.

4 large eggs, hard-cooked (page 162), peeled and halved lengthwise

2 ounces cream cheese, at room temperature (about ¼ cup)

3 tablespoons chutney

1–2 tablespoons milk

1–2 teaspoons fresh lemon or lime juice (optional)

1–2 teaspoons minced jalapeño (optional)

½ teaspoon grated ginger or a drop of ginger juice (optional)

Kosher salt

¼ cup finely chopped dry-roasted peanuts or cashews

1 tablespoon chopped fresh cilantro

1. Carefully remove the yolks from the whites. Place the whites cut side up on a plate. With the back of a spoon, press the yolks through a sieve into a small bowl, or mash them in the bowl with a fork. Add the cream cheese and mash with a fork until blended. Add the chutney, breaking up any large chunks with the fork, and stir to blend. Using a wooden spoon, gradually beat in enough milk, 1 teaspoon at a time, so the yolk mixture is smooth and fluffy. Taste and add lemon or lime juice, jalapeño and ginger or ginger juice to taste, if desired. Season with salt to taste.

2. Using a teaspoon, carefully stuff the whites with the yolk mixture, mounding the tops. Garnish each stuffed egg with a sprinkling of nuts and a pinch of cilantro. Serve at room temperature or chilled.

Makes 4 servings

Anna Teresa's Sensational Fried Stuffed Eggs

This is a fascinating recipe with a rich history. In *Food and Memories of Abruzzo*, Anna Teresa Callen includes a recipe called *Uova Delicate*, or delicate eggs. In *A Drizzle of Honey*, David M. Gitlitz and Linda Kay Davidson describe a similar dish from a thirteenth-century Arabic manuscript: "The [halved] cooked eggs are stuffed with yolks, cilantro, onion and cinnamon. The egg halves are then put back together, secured with sticks, covered with saffron, dusted with flour and fried."

This spectacular appetizer is well worth the effort. The yolks are mashed with béchamel sauce, then the whites are stuffed, chilled and deep-fried. The result is an egg with a soft creamy center and a golden crust on the outside.

8 large eggs, hard-cooked (page 162), peeled and halved lengthwise

3 tablespoons Béchamel Sauce (opposite page)

3 tablespoons freshly grated Parmigiano-Reggiano cheese

¼ teaspoon freshly grated nutmeg

Pinch of kosher salt

Freshly ground black pepper

About ½ cup all-purpose flour

About 1 cup fine dry bread crumbs

1 large egg

1 tablespoon milk

Vegetable oil for deep-frying

1. Carefully remove the yolks from the whites; reserve 2 of the yolks (4 halves) for another use. Place the 6 yolks in a bowl and mash with a fork. Add the béchamel sauce, cheese, nutmeg, salt and a grinding of pepper and mix well. Stuff half of the whites with the yolk mixture, then cover each stuffed half with one of the remaining whites to reassemble the eggs.

2. Spread the flour on one sheet of waxed paper and the bread crumbs on a separate sheet. Whisk the egg and milk in a shallow bowl. Roll each reassembled egg one at a time in the flour, shake off the excess, then dip into the beaten egg, letting the excess drip off, and roll in the bread crumbs. Set the eggs on a plate and refrigerate until the coating is set, about 30 minutes.

3. Heat 2 inches of oil in a deep frying pan or wide, heavy saucepan. When the oil is hot enough to brown a crust of bread, add the eggs and fry, turning, until golden brown, about 5 minutes. Halve the eggs crosswise and serve hot.

Makes 6 servings

Béchamel Sauce

2 tablespoons unsalted
butter

2 tablespoons
all-purpose flour

1¼ cups milk, warmed

½ teaspoon kosher salt,
or to taste

1. Melt the butter in a small saucepan over medium-low heat. Add the flour and cook, stirring, for 2 to 3 minutes. Remove from the heat and gradually add the milk, whisking constantly until smooth.

2. Return to low heat and cook, whisking constantly, for 5 to 8 minutes, or until the sauce thickens and boils. Add the salt. Let cool to room temperature.

Makes about 1¼ cups

TO USE LEFTOVER BÉCHAMEL SAUCE: Add 2 chopped hard-cooked eggs to the warm sauce. Place 1 slice of toasted bread in a gratin dish, and top with the sauce. Sprinkle with grated Parmesan or another cheese and broil until golden.

Makes 1 serving

Asian Tea Eggs

Tea eggs are just one of a variety of seasoned hard-cooked egg dishes that are popular in China. The shells of the cooked eggs are lightly cracked with a spoon, and the eggs are then simmered in an aromatic tea-based liquid, which leaves an attractive marbleized pattern on the whites when they are peeled. The eggs themselves take on the delicate flavors of soy and star anise.

8 **eggs, preferably medium**

½ **cup dark soy sauce**

½ **cup dry sherry**

4 **star anise**

1 **strip (½ x 2 inches) orange zest**

3 **cups water**

3 **Lapsang Souchong tea bags, strings removed**

Toasted sesame oil for rubbing the eggs (optional)

1. Place the eggs in a single layer in a saucepan. Cover with water and bring to a boil over medium heat. As soon as the water boils, remove the pan from the heat, cover and let stand for 10 minutes. Drain off the water, cover the eggs with cold water and let stand until cool enough to handle.

2. Meanwhile, combine the soy sauce, sherry, star anise, orange zest and water in the saucepan and bring to a simmer. Add the tea bags.

3. When the eggs are cool, gently tap them with the back of a tablespoon so the shells are evenly cracked. Do not peel. Using the spoon, carefully lower the eggs one at a time into the simmering liquid. If it does not cover the eggs entirely, add more water. Cover the pan and simmer for 1 hour.

4. Transfer the eggs to a bowl or small casserole with a lid. Cover with the hot liquid and cool to room temperature. Cover and refrigerate, preferably overnight.

5. Drain, peel and pat each egg dry. Rub with sesame oil, if desired. Serve halved or quartered.

Makes 4 servings

These eggs make a great snack or hors d'oeuvre, but they are also delicious cut up in a salad or a bowl of broth.

Ada Boni's Sardinian-Style Hard-Cooked Eggs

This dish of hard-cooked eggs simmered in olive oil and vinegar and seasoned with fresh herbs epitomizes simple yet sophisticated Italian cooking. I found this recipe in an out-of-print cookbook by Ada Boni called *Italian Regional Cooking*. Although I have increased the amount of bread crumbs and added rosemary, the concept is all hers.

¼ cup extra-virgin olive oil

4 teaspoons red wine vinegar

¼ teaspoon kosher salt

6 large eggs, hard-cooked (page 162), peeled and halved lengthwise

2 tablespoons finely chopped fresh flat-leaf parsley

½ teaspoon minced fresh rosemary

½ teaspoon minced fresh thyme

1 garlic clove, minced

⅓ cup fresh bread crumbs
   Freshly ground black pepper

1. Combine the oil, vinegar and salt in a large skillet. Add the eggs and cook over low heat, carefully turning the eggs once or twice, until the vinegar has evaporated, leaving just a film of oil in the pan. Transfer the eggs, cut side up, to a heated serving dish. Cover with foil to keep warm.

2. Add the parsley, rosemary, thyme and garlic to the skillet and cook over low heat, stirring, for 1 minute. Add the bread crumbs and cook, stirring, until golden, about 3 minutes more. Add the black pepper.

3. Carefully spoon the bread-crumb mixture over the eggs. Serve warm or at room temperature.

Makes 6 servings

Hard-Cooked Egg Pâté

The Polish Cookbook by Zofia Czerny, published in English in 1961, describes a mixture of hard-cooked eggs, sweet butter and chives that the author calls simply egg and chive paste. I especially like this pâté on small rounds of dark bread, topped with a bit of canned sardine and served as an appetizer. It is also good stuffed into celery stalks.

3 **large eggs, hard-cooked (page 162), peeled and halved lengthwise**

3 **tablespoons unsalted butter, at room temperature**

2 **tablespoons minced fresh chives**

¼ **teaspoon kosher salt, or more to taste**

Minced fresh chives or thin radish slices for garnish (optional)

12 **slices pumpernickel party bread or crackers**

1. Carefully remove the yolks from the whites and very finely chop the whites. With the back of a spoon, press the yolks through a sieve into a small bowl. Add the whites, butter, chives and salt and mash with a fork until blended. Taste and add more salt, if desired. Cover and refrigerate until ready to use.

2. Let the pâté come to room temperature before serving. If desired, garnish with chives or radish slices. Spread on bread or accompany with bread or toast and serve.

Makes about ¾ cup

CHAPTER 6 *Broths, Stews and Braises*

"An oeuf *can be as good as a feast."*
—MARION MAXWELL

S ome people need a hunk of meat or something similarly solid and chewy to make a meal, but I can be perfectly satisfied with a bowl of soup for supper, lunch or even breakfast on occasion. I think this is because I was nurtured on soup as a baby— specifically the eggy broth on page 191, which is known in our family as Nana's Baby Soup. My grandmother's creation is as simple as it is wonderful—fragrant chicken broth, thick with pastina (tiny pasta), rich with grated Parmesan and studded with soft golden bits of instantly cooked egg. It's fair to say that this soup has made me who I am—hale and hearty, with a culinary perspective shaped by my grandmother's Italian home cooking.

Almost since eggs were first gathered, they've been added to simple broths to lend nourishment, substance, texture and flavor—and as a means of stretching one or two among several diners. But what began as a frugal measure in peasant cultures evolved into a luxuriant style of cooking in which robust meat stews thickened with egg yolks boasted of their own richness—and of that of their creators! Cuisines of countries as diverse as Portugal, Italy, Greece and China all feature these egg-enriched brothy dishes. It wasn't easy to choose between them, because a whole book could be written about soup cookery with eggs.

In the simplest form of this type of soup, beaten eggs are drizzled or stirred into hot broth, where they form tender morsels as they cook almost instantaneously in the liquid. The effect is different, depending on whether the eggs are stirred or not as they are added. Stirring produces delicate threads throughout, as in Nana's soup and the somewhat more elegant Egg Thread Soup on page 194. In Italy, the eggs are often beaten with grated Parmesan or Romano cheese, then stirred into beef or chicken soup to form *stracciatella*, or "little rags." In Chinese egg drop soup, on the other hand, the eggs are added without stirring, creating ethereal puffs on top of the soup, which are then ladled into individual bowls.

Poached eggs make a wonderful soup enhancement; broth ladled over a piece of sturdy bread and a poached egg is traditional in many cuisines. My recipes are a little fancier: I've slipped poached eggs into savory tomato broth and into bowls of Asian chicken-and-rice porridge.

I also garnish my soups with eggs in more unusual ways, cutting thin pancakelike omelettes into strips to make flavorful "noodles." For a special first course, I make a luxurious custard with cream and Parmesan cheese, cut it into elegant diamond shapes and float it in crystal-clear chicken consommé (page 198).

Nothing, however, makes a soup, stew or sauce silkier than the addition of beaten egg yolks. The beguiling combination of egg yolks and lemon juice, called *avgolemono*, is the basis for many famous Greek dishes, including a lamb stew that satisfies the urges of soup lovers like me and all those who want more substantial "hunks" for dinner.

Nana's Baby Soup

I practically lived on this soup when I was a baby. A generation later, I fed the same soup to my own daughter. The recipe is from my grandmother Antoinette Abbruzzese, a fine cook who greatly influenced my cooking as I was growing up. Evidently, she influenced my palate in my earliest years of life as well.

1½ cups unsalted homemade chicken broth or canned reduced-sodium chicken broth, fat skimmed

3 tablespoons pastina

Kosher salt (optional)

1 large egg, beaten

Freshly grated Parmigiano-Reggiano cheese

1. Bring the broth to a boil in a small saucepan. Add the pastina and cook until it is soft and the soup has thickened. Taste and add salt, if needed.

2. Pour the egg into the simmering soup all at once and cook, stirring to break the egg into small clumps, about 1 minute.

3. Ladle into a bowl, sprinkle with cheese and serve.

Makes 1 serving

Egg Drop Soup

Egg Drop Soup, a classic recipe of beaten eggs stirred into hot chicken broth, is also known as egg flower soup. That's because the eggs form small "flowers," or clusters, as they are poured into the simmering soup. Garnished with slivered scallion greens, this is perfect served plain and simple.

4 cups unsalted homemade chicken broth or canned reduced-sodium chicken broth, fat skimmed

1 tablespoon light soy sauce

1 thin slice ginger (optional)

2–3 large eggs, beaten

2 tablespoons thinly sliced scallion greens

1. Combine the broth, soy sauce and ginger, if using, in a medium saucepan and bring to a boil. Reduce the heat to a gentle simmer. Ladle the eggs ¼ cup at a time into the simmering broth; do not stir. The eggs will rise to the surface and cook in a big cluster. Let simmer for about 1 minute, or until the eggs are cooked.

2. To serve, ladle some soup and a portion of the egg cluster into each of four deep bowls. Garnish with the scallion greens.

Makes 3 to 4 servings

A Soupçon of Egg

 You can add extra richness, texture and color to any broth or soup by stirring whole eggs, egg yolks or egg whites into the hot liquid.

Egg Drops: Using 1 or 2 eggs for every 2 cups of liquid, whisk the eggs until frothy in a bowl or measuring cup with a pouring spout. Slowly pour into the simmering or gently boiling soup; do not stir. As the stream of egg cooks, it will form fluffy clusters on top of the soup.

Egg Threads: Using 1 or 2 eggs for every 2 cups of liquid, whisk the eggs until frothy. Stirring constantly, slowly pour into the simmering or gently boiling soup. Slow stirring will produce large threads; rapid stirring will produce small pieces of scrambled egg.

Egg White Threads: Using the whites of 1 or 2 eggs for every 2 cups of liquid, whisk the whites just to liquefy. Stirring constantly and gently, slowly pour the whites into simmering or gently boiling soup to form thin threads.

Chicken, Broccoli and Egg Thread Soup with Parmesan Chips

I try to keep homemade chicken broth frozen in two-cup containers, but I often use it up before I have time to replenish it. When I run out, I resort to canned or aseptic-packaged store-bought broth. I prefer reduced-sodium broth, because it is a bit more natural tasting; I then add kosher salt to taste. With a loaf of warm bread, this soup can be a meal.

6 cups unsalted homemade chicken broth or canned reduced-sodium chicken broth, fat skimmed

2½ cups water

½ cup small pasta shapes, such as ditalini, orzo or riso

3 cups coarsely chopped broccoli florets and tender stems

1 small carrot, peeled and diced

1–2 cups shredded cooked chicken (optional)

3 large eggs

Kosher salt and freshly ground black pepper

Parmesan Chips (opposite page) or ¼–½ cup freshly grated Parmigiano-Reggiano cheese

1. Bring the broth and 2 cups of the water to a boil in a large saucepan. Add the pasta and boil until the pasta is half-cooked, about 5 minutes. Stir in the broccoli and carrot and simmer for 8 minutes more, or until the vegetables are tender. Add the chicken, if using.

2. In a measuring cup, beat the remaining ½ cup *cold* water and the eggs until frothy. Slowly drizzle the egg mixture into the simmering soup, stirring very slowly so the eggs cook into long threads. Add salt to taste and a grinding of pepper.

3. Ladle the soup into bowls and garnish each serving with a Parmesan Chip or a heaping spoonful of cheese.

Makes 4 servings

The Parmesan Chips are easy to make and can be kept crisp in an airtight container for up to 1 week.

Parmesan Chips

These tender, cheesy crisps are similar to the Italian delicacy called *frico*, from the region of Friuli in northeastern Italy, where they are made with a local cheese called Montasio. These are my simplified version, made with Parmigiano-Reggiano. Use only real Parmigiano-Reggiano, not the finely grated supermarket brands. You can substitute Pecorino Romano cheese. Serve the chips as a garnish or an accompaniment to soup or as a garnish for a green salad. (The recipe can be doubled or tripled.)

½ **cup freshly grated Parmigiano-Reggiano cheese (I use the shredding holes on the grater)**

1. Preheat the oven to 350°F. Using a level tablespoonful of cheese for each crisp, place 8 mounds of cheese on a nonstick baking sheet, leaving about 2 inches between each one.

2. Bake for 6 minutes, or until the cheese is melted and soft and the crisps are a light golden brown. Remove from the oven and let stand until completely cooled and firm to the touch, about 20 minutes.

3. Using a thin metal spatula, lift the crisps from the baking sheet and arrange on a plate.

Makes 8 crisps

Chicken Broth with Omelette "Noodles" and Escarole

Omelette "noodles" swimming in a clear chicken broth make a comforting light lunch, supper or even breakfast.

Omelette "Noodles"

- 4 **large eggs**
- ¼ **cup cold water**
- 1 **tablespoon freshly grated Parmigiano-Reggiano cheese**
- 1 **tablespoon chopped fresh flat-leaf parsley**
- 1 **teaspoon finely chopped fresh thyme**
- ½ **teaspoon finely chopped fresh rosemary**
- 1 **teaspoon kosher salt**
  Freshly ground black pepper
  Extra-virgin olive oil

1. **Make the omelette "noodles":** Whisk the eggs, water, cheese, parsley, thyme, rosemary, salt and a grinding of pepper in a medium bowl until blended.

2. Brush an 8-inch nonstick skillet lightly with the oil. Heat over medium heat until hot enough to sizzle a drop of water. Add about ⅓ cup of the egg mixture to the skillet, tilting the skillet so the egg makes a thin, even layer on the bottom of the skillet. Cook until set, about 1 minute. Using a heatproof rubber spatula, turn the omelette over and cook the other side for 20 seconds. Turn out onto a platter. Repeat with the remaining egg mixture, ⅓ cup at a time. There should be enough for 5 or 6 omelettes. (The omelettes can be made up to 1 day ahead and refrigerated uncut or made ahead to the end of this step.) Roll up the omelettes loosely and cut crosswise into ½-inch-wide slices to make "noodles." Cover and refrigerate until ready to serve.

Broth

2 cups packed coarsely
  chopped escarole

½ cup thinly sliced carrots

8 cups unsalted homemade
  chicken broth or canned
  reduced-sodium chicken
  broth, fat skimmed

  Kosher salt and freshly
  ground black pepper

  Freshly grated Parmigiano-
  Reggiano cheese

3. **Make the broth:** Just before serving, steam the escarole and carrots in a steamer basket set over boiling water until tender, about 10 minutes.

4. Bring the broth to a boil. Taste it and correct the seasonings, if necessary. Place a handful of "noodles" in the bottom of each of four soup bowls. Distribute the escarole and carrot evenly on top. Ladle the boiling broth into the bowls, sprinkle with cheese and serve.

Makes 4 servings

You can make an Asian version of this soup by seasoning the omelette with a dash of toasted sesame oil, sesame seeds and scallions and adding thin slices of bok choy to the broth instead of the escarole.

Chicken Consommé with Parmesan Custard Diamonds

Eggs are used two ways in this soup: the whites to clarify the broth and the yolks to make the Parmesan custards. The custards are easy to prepare. Serve as a first course for a special dinner.

8   cups cold homemade chicken broth or canned reduced-sodium chicken broth, fat skimmed

4   large egg whites

4   eggshells, crushed

Parmesan Custards

1   large egg

2   large egg yolks

½   cup heavy cream

3   tablespoons freshly grated Parmigiano-Reggiano cheese

½   teaspoon kosher salt

Freshly grated nutmeg, to taste

Finely chopped fresh chervil or flat-leaf parsley, to taste

1. Place the broth in a large saucepan and clarify it using the egg whites and shells, following the directions on the opposite page.

2. **Make the Parmesan custards:** Position a rack in the center of the oven and preheat the oven to 325°F. Lightly butter a shallow 1-quart baking dish and set it in a larger baking pan. Put a kettle of water on to boil.

3. In a medium bowl, whisk the egg and egg yolks until light. Whisk in the heavy cream, cheese, salt and nutmeg. Pour the egg mixture into the buttered baking dish.

4. Place the baking pan in the oven and add enough boiling water to the pan to come halfway up the sides of the baking dish. Bake until the custard is firm, 20 to 25 minutes. Remove from the oven and from the water bath and let cool to room temperature.

5. Cut the cooled custard into 1-inch diamond shapes or squares.

6. When ready to serve, heat the clarified broth until steaming. Ladle into warm shallow bowls. Distribute the custard diamonds evenly among the bowls. Sprinkle with chervil or parsley and serve at once.

Makes 6 servings

The custards can be made and the stock clarified one day ahead and refrigerated.

Bringing Clarity to Soup

 What do chefs, winemakers and cowboys have in common? They all take advantage of one of the most fascinating properties of egg whites: their ability to "clarify" cloudy liquids.

When cowboys boiled ground coffee over the campfire to make their strong and muddy coffee, they found that tossing in empty eggshells produced a clearer, more potable drink. Winemakers still add egg whites to vats of wine to make it clear, and classically trained chefs use egg whites to remove any tiny suspended particles in stock or broth to make crystal-clear consommé.

When the whites are added to soup and heated gently, the proteins in the whites coagulate, forming a solid mass that is called a "raft." As the stock gently simmers, this raft traps all the floating particles that would make the liquid murky.

To Clarify Stock with Egg Whites
Thoroughly chill the stock and lift all traces of fat from the surface. Transfer the stock to a large saucepan or stockpot. Beat 2 large egg whites per each pint of stock until foamy. Add the beaten whites to the cold stock. Bring it to a simmer over medium heat, stirring constantly. The whites will form a "raft" when the liquid is just below the boiling point. Stop stirring; reduce the heat to low and simmer the stock for 30 minutes without stirring. Do not let the stock boil. Line a large strainer with cheesecloth and set over a deep bowl. Remove the pot from the heat and ladle the egg-white raft into the strainer. Carefully ladle the clear stock through the raft. Let stand undisturbed while all the stock slowly drips through, about 15 minutes.

Beef and Tomato Broth with Cheese and Egg Balls

Anna Teresa Callen, a friend and colleague, introduced me to cheese and egg balls. A mixture of bread crumbs, cheese and eggs is shaped into balls and fried quickly in very hot oil, then added to soup. These are a little like meatballs, but much lighter and cheesier.

Cheese and Egg Balls

1¼ cups fine dry bread crumbs, or more as needed

⅔ cup freshly grated Parmigiano-Reggiano cheese

⅓ cup freshly grated Pecorino Romano cheese

2 tablespoons minced fresh flat-leaf parsley

2 garlic cloves, minced

Kosher salt and freshly ground black pepper

5 large eggs

Vegetable oil for frying

Beef and Tomato Broth

3 cups unsalted homemade beef broth or canned reduced-sodium beef broth, fat skimmed

1 28-ounce can plum tomatoes, with their juices

1 small sprig fresh basil

Kosher salt and freshly ground black pepper

1. **Make the cheese and egg balls:** Combine the bread crumbs, cheeses, parsley, garlic, salt to taste and a grinding of pepper in a large bowl. Whisk the eggs in a medium bowl, then add to the bread-crumb mixture. Stir gently to combine. If the mixture is too moist, add more bread crumbs, 1 tablespoon at a time. The mixture will stiffen as it stands.

2. With wet hands, shape the mixture into 20 to 24 balls, about 1 inch in diameter. Place the balls on a plate, cover and refrigerate for 20 minutes before frying.

3. Heat the oil in a large skillet over medium heat until hot enough to lightly brown a crust of bread. Add the cheese and egg balls, a few at a time, and fry until golden, turning often, about 5 minutes. Drain on paper towels, transfer to a baking pan and keep warm in the oven set to the lowest temperature.

4. **Make the broth:** In a large saucepan, bring the broth to a boil. Place a food mill over the saucepan and puree the tomatoes and their juices into the broth. (Or puree in a food processor. Then press through a strainer, using a rubber spatula; discard the solids.) Add the cheese and egg balls and simmer for 15 minutes. Add the basil, salt to taste and a grinding of pepper.

5. Ladle the soup into four soup bowls. Distribute the cheese and egg balls evenly among them and serve.

Makes 4 servings

Jean Anderson's Portuguese Bread, Garlic and Egg Soup

This is a classic soup of the Alentejo, a province in Portugal to the southeast of Lisbon. Throughout the Mediterranean region, there are many soups of this persuasion, some with less bread and more broth, all based on water and garlic and all with the ubiquitous poached egg floating in the middle of each bowl. Cilantro, the most widely used fresh herb in Portugal, adds character. This soup is adapted from one in Jean Anderson's *The Food of Portugal*. It's hearty enough to be served as a main dish, followed by a tomato salad, olives and perhaps some sliced meats.

4   **large garlic cloves, quartered**

2½   **cups loosely packed fresh cilantro leaves, plus chopped cilantro for optional garnish (from 1 large or 2 small bunches)**

2   **teaspoons kosher salt**

⅓   **cup extra-virgin olive oil**

7   **cups water**

6   **large eggs**

6   **cups 1½-inch cubes day-old Portuguese, French or Italian bread (from a 15-to-18-inch-long loaf)**

½   **teaspoon freshly ground black pepper**

The freshest ingredients are essential: good-quality bread, preferably from a Portuguese bakery, the fruitiest olive oil and, of course, impeccably fresh eggs.

1. Using a mortar and pestle or in a small food processor, grind the garlic, cilantro leaves and salt to a paste. Transfer to a large heatproof bowl or soup tureen. Blend in the oil. Set aside.

2. Put the water in a large, deep skillet and bring to a boil. Reduce the heat to a simmer. Break the eggs one at a time into a cup and slip them into the water. Cook for 2 minutes. With a slotted spoon, remove the eggs in the order you added them to the pan and place on a folded kitchen towel or paper towel. Keep the egg-poaching water at a gentle boil.

3. Add the bread and pepper to the cilantro paste and toss to mix. Add the reserved egg-poaching water, with any little bits of egg white remaining in it, and stir gently to mix. Carefully place the eggs on top of the soup. Sprinkle with chopped cilantro, if desired.

4. To serve, ladle the soup into warm bowls, placing one egg in each bowl.

Makes 6 servings

Tomato Soup with Poached Eggs and Crispy Croutons

Nourishing and quick to make, this one-pot meal is perfect for a workday supper. Make the tomato soup ahead, then reheat it and poach the eggs just before serving.

3 tablespoons extra-virgin olive oil

2 cups ½-inch cubes day-old Italian bread (crusts removed)

Kosher salt and freshly ground black pepper

2–3 slices thick-cut lean bacon, cut into ⅛-inch dice

½ cup minced onion

1 garlic clove, minced

¼–½ teaspoon crushed red pepper flakes

2 28-ounce cans plum tomatoes, with their juices

4 medium or large eggs

1 tablespoon minced fresh flat-leaf parsley

Freshly grated Parmigiano-Reggiano cheese

1. Heat the oil in a large, wide, heavy saucepan over medium heat. When the oil is hot enough to sizzle a bread cube, add all the bread cubes and sauté until golden, about 3 minutes. With a slotted spoon, transfer to a medium bowl. Sprinkle with salt and a grinding of pepper and set aside.

2. Discard the oil in the pan and wipe the pan dry with a paper towel. Add the bacon to the pan and cook, stirring, over medium heat for 2 minutes. Add the onion, reduce the heat to medium-low and sauté until golden, about 5 minutes. Stir in the garlic and red pepper flakes and sauté for 1 minute more.

3. Place a food mill over the saucepan and puree the tomatoes and their juices directly into the pan. (Or, if you do not have a food mill, puree in a food processor and press through a strainer, using a rubber spatula; discard the solids.) Bring to a boil, reduce the heat to low and simmer, stirring occasionally, until the liquid is slightly reduced, about 20 minutes. Season to taste. (The soup can be made up to 1 day ahead.)

For this dish, I like to use medium eggs or, for an even more special touch, quail eggs, if I can get them.

4. Just before serving, break the eggs one at a time into a cup and slip them into the simmering soup, distributing them evenly. Cover and cook until the whites are set and the yolks are cooked to the desired doneness, 8 to 10 minutes.

5. Distribute the croutons among four soup bowls. Carefully ladle the eggs into the bowls, then ladle the soup on top. Top each serving with some of the parsley and cheese and serve.

Makes 4 servings

Chinese-Style Rice in Chicken Broth with Poached Eggs

Throughout Asia, a thick porridgelike mixture of rice seasoned with bits of shrimp, chicken, sesame seeds, peanuts and eggs is a popular dish, especially for breakfast. Sometimes called *congee*, it is also known as *jook* or *juk*. With a poached egg served on top and an assortment of condiments set out to season each bowl to taste, this makes a very satisfying meal at any time of day.

4 cups unsalted homemade chicken broth or canned reduced-sodium chicken broth, fat skimmed, plus more if necessary

4 cups water

2 garlic cloves, minced

1 ¼-inch-thick slice ginger

2 boneless, skinless chicken thighs, fat trimmed, cut into 1-inch-long slivers

1⅓ cups medium-grain rice

2 teaspoons kosher salt, or more to taste

¼ cup white vinegar

4–6 large eggs

Toppings: Minced cilantro, thinly sliced scallions, soy sauce, toasted sesame oil, hot pepper oil, chopped peanuts and/or sesame seeds

1. Combine the broth, water, garlic and ginger in a large pot and bring to a boil. Stir in the chicken, rice and salt and return to a boil. Cover, reduce the heat to medium-low and cook until the rice is very soft, about 20 minutes. The soup will be very thick; thin with additional broth or water, if necessary. Taste and add more salt, if needed.

2. Meanwhile, just before serving, fill a deep skillet with water and bring to a boil. Add the vinegar and reduce the heat to a simmer. Break the eggs one at a time into a cup and slip them into the water. Cook for 3 minutes, depending on the desired doneness. With a slotted spoon, remove the eggs in the order you added them to the pan and place on a plate. Trim off any ragged whites.

3. Ladle the soup into four soup bowls. Top each with an egg. Sprinkle with cilantro and/or scallions. Pass the other condiments at the table.

Makes 4 servings

> *Instead of the poached eggs, you can serve this with Asian Tea Eggs (page 184) on top.*

Tomato and Black Bean Soup
with Poached Eggs and Crisp Corn Tortilla Chips

All of my favorite Southwest flavors — avocado, cumin, black beans, cilantro and lime — make this a festive soup.

3 tablespoons extra-virgin olive oil

2 corn tortillas, cut into ½-inch squares
Kosher salt and freshly ground black pepper

½ cup minced onion

1 garlic clove, minced

1 teaspoon chili powder

½ teaspoon ground cumin

2 28-ounce cans plum tomatoes, with their juices

1–1½ cups cooked black beans, rinsed and drained if canned

4 medium or large eggs

1 cup diced avocado (1 medium avocado)

2 tablespoons minced fresh cilantro

1 tablespoon fresh lime juice

1 teaspoon minced jalapeño, or more to taste

1. Heat the oil in a large, heavy saucepan over medium heat. When the oil is hot enough to sizzle a tortilla square, add all the tortilla squares to the pan and sauté until crisp, about 3 minutes. With a slotted spoon, transfer to a small bowl and sprinkle with salt and a grinding of pepper; set aside.

2. Discard all but a thin film of the oil from the pan and reduce the heat to medium-low. Add the onion and sauté until tender, about 5 minutes. Stir in the garlic and sauté for 1 minute more. Add the chili powder and cumin and stir until fragrant, about 20 seconds. Place a food mill over the saucepan and puree the tomatoes and their juices directly into the pan. (If you do not have a food mill, puree in a food processor and press through a strainer with a rubber spatula; discard the solids.) Bring to a boil, reduce the heat to low and simmer, stirring occasionally, until the liquid is slightly reduced, about 20 minutes.

3. Add the beans to the soup. Taste and correct the seasoning. Bring to a boil, then reduce the heat to a simmer.

4. Just before serving, break the eggs one at a time into a cup and slip them into the simmering soup, distributing evenly. Cover and cook until the whites are set and the yolks are cooked to the desired doneness, 8 to 10 minutes.

5. Meanwhile, combine the avocado, cilantro, lime juice and jalapeño in a small bowl.

6. Divide the tortilla squares among four soup bowls. Carefully ladle the eggs into the bowls, then ladle the soup on top. Top each serving with some of the avocado mixture.

Makes 4 servings

Diane Kochilas's Avgolemono Soup

At its simplest, avgolemono soup is chicken broth thickened with eggs beaten with lemon juice. This hearty, filling version of the Greek specialty is adapted from a recipe from the mother of Diane Kochilas, whose cookbook *The Food and Wines of Greece* is a classic reference about Greek food and culture.

1   **3-to-4-pound chicken, rinsed in salted water and drained**

10 **cups cold water**

1   **large onion, unpeeled, studded with 2 whole cloves**

    Kosher salt

1   **cup long-grain white rice or bulgur**

3   **large eggs, at room temperature**

½ **cup strained fresh lemon juice**

    Freshly ground black pepper

1. In a large pot, combine the chicken, water and onion and bring to a simmer. Skim off the foam and discard. Add salt to taste and simmer, covered, until the chicken is falling off the bones, 2 to 3 hours.

2. Remove from the heat and, using two large spoons, carefully transfer the chicken to a platter to cool slightly. Remove and discard the onion from the broth.

3. Remove the meat from the chicken and discard the skin and bones. Finely shred or chop the chicken meat and return it to the pot. Taste the broth and add salt, if needed. Stir in the rice or bulgur and cook at a simmer, uncovered, until tender, about 15 minutes.

4. In a medium bowl, whisk the eggs and lemon juice until frothy. Ladle in about 1 cup of the hot broth, whisking constantly to prevent the eggs from curdling. Turn off the heat under the pot and slowly whisk the egg mixture into the soup.

5. Serve the soup immediately. Pass the pepper mill at the table.

Makes 6 to 8 servings

Temper, Temper
Using Egg Yolks as a Thickener

Adding egg yolks gives soups and sauces a smooth, full-bodied richness that flour, cornstarch, arrowroot or other thickeners can never match. The secret to this smoothness is a process called "tempering," whereby a small amount of hot liquid is whisked into the egg yolks (or eggs) to warm them gradually, then the warmed egg mixture is stirred into the larger pot of hot liquid. This slow heating prevents the eggs from seizing into curdled pellets or scrambled eggs—not the effect you're looking for at all!

The technique is simple. Allow 1 yolk per ½ cup liquid for sauce or 1 yolk per 1 cup liquid for soup. Whisk the egg yolk(s) in a small bowl. Whisk in about ⅓ cup of gently simmering liquid per yolk to warm slightly. When the mixture is smooth, gradually pour it, while stirring, into the pot or pan of hot (but never boiling) liquid. Continue stirring gently over low heat until the eggs begin to thicken the liquid.

Lamb Stew with Artichokes and Avgolemono Sauce

Throughout Italy and Greece during the Easter season, lamb stews are often served in egg-thickened sauces flavored with lemon.

2 tablespoons unsalted butter

2 tablespoons olive oil

2½ pounds lamb shoulder, cut into 1-to-2-inch chunks, with some bone left in

1 ¼-inch-thick slice pancetta or thick-sliced bacon, diced

1 onion, halved lengthwise and cut lengthwise into thin slivers (about 1 cup)

Kosher salt and freshly ground black pepper

1 tablespoon all-purpose flour

1 cup dry white wine

1 cup water

1 bay leaf

1 8-ounce package frozen artichoke hearts or 4 cooked artichoke bottoms (see page 108), cut into ½-inch cubes

3 tablespoons fresh lemon juice

2 large egg yolks

2 tablespoons chopped fresh flat-leaf parsley

1 teaspoon minced fresh oregano

1. Heat the butter and oil in a large skillet over medium heat. Add the lamb, pancetta or bacon and onion. Sprinkle with salt to taste and a grinding of pepper and cook, turning the lamb occasionally, until it is lightly browned on all sides.

2. Stir in the flour, then add the wine and bring to a boil. Continue to boil, stirring, until reduced by slightly more than half, about 5 minutes. Add the water and bay leaf, reduce the heat to medium-low, cover and cook, stirring occasionally, until the lamb is tender, about 1½ hours; add small amounts of water as necessary and reduce the heat to low if the stew threatens to become dry. Stir in the artichokes, cover and cook for 5 minutes. Reduce the heat to low.

3. In a small bowl, whisk together the lemon juice, egg yolks, 1 tablespoon of the parsley and the oregano. Stir a spoonful of the hot stew juices into the egg mixture to temper it. Stir the egg mixture into the stew and cook, stirring constantly, until the sauce is slightly thickened, about 2 minutes; do not boil. Add salt to taste and a grinding of pepper, spoon into a warmed serving bowl and sprinkle with the remaining 1 tablespoon parsley.

Makes 4 servings

Braised Chicken Avgolemono with Oyster Mushrooms, Carrots and Zucchini

Egg yolks combine with the chicken juices, white wine and lemon juice to make a velvety sauce that naps the tender morsels of chicken. Once you have prepared the ingredients, the dish will be ready to serve in less than 30 minutes.

2 skinless, boneless chicken breast halves

4 skinless, boneless chicken thighs

Kosher salt and freshly ground black pepper

⅓ cup all-purpose flour

2 tablespoons unsalted butter

1 tablespoon extra-virgin olive oil

½ cup finely chopped shallots

6 ounces oyster mushrooms, cut into 2-inch pieces if large

1 tablespoon plus 1 teaspoon minced fresh tarragon

⅓ cup dry white wine

1 cup unsalted homemade chicken broth or canned reduced-sodium chicken broth, fat skimmed

1. Rinse the chicken pieces with cold water and dry with paper towels. Trim off and discard the fat. Cut the chicken into 1½-inch pieces. Sprinkle with salt and a grinding of pepper, dredge in the flour and shake off the excess.

2. Heat 1 tablespoon of the butter and the oil in a large nonstick skillet over medium-high heat. When the foam subsides, add the chicken, without crowding; brown in two batches, if necessary. Cook the chicken, turning, until lightly browned on all sides, about 5 minutes. Transfer to a plate.

3. Add the remaining 1 tablespoon butter to the skillet and reduce the heat to low. Add the shallots and cook, stirring, until tender, about 3 minutes. Add the mushrooms and 1 tablespoon of the tarragon and cook, stirring to coat the mushrooms with the butter, about 1 minute. Add the chicken and any juices to the skillet, then add the wine and boil until reduced by half, about 1 minute.

1 cup 1-inch pieces peeled slender carrots

1 small zucchini, trimmed, halved lengthwise and cut into ½-inch slices (about 1 cup)

2 large egg yolks

2 tablespoons fresh lemon juice

Hot cooked rice or noodles (optional)

4. Add the chicken broth and carrots and bring to a boil. Reduce the heat to low, cover and cook for 15 minutes. Add the zucchini, cover and cook for 3 minutes.

5. Whisk the egg yolks and lemon juice together in a small bowl. Stir a spoonful of the hot broth into the egg mixture. Reduce the heat to very low, stir the egg mixture into the broth and cook, stirring, until thickened, about 45 seconds; do not boil. Taste and add more salt and pepper, if needed.

6. Serve with buttered rice or noodles, if desired, to absorb the flavorful juices, and sprinkle with the remaining 1 teaspoon tarragon.

Makes 4 servings

Braised Brazilian Beef Rolls
with Hard-Cooked Eggs and Olives

The filling for these beef rolls is an intensely flavored mixture of sieved tender egg yolks, chopped whites, green olives and sharp cheese, all wrapped in a slice of prosciutto (which you can omit, if you like). This recipe is adapted from one in *Half a Can of Tomato Paste and Other Culinary Dilemmas* by Jean Anderson and Ruth Buchan.

1 garlic clove, minced

4 thin slices round steak
(about 1 pound total),
pounded thin (about 8 inches
long and 5 inches wide)

½ cup hearty red wine
(such as Chianti or cabernet
sauvignon or port)

Stuffing

2 tablespoons unsalted butter

½ cup finely chopped onion

¼ cup finely chopped pitted
green olives

¼ cup grated sharp cheese, such
as Asiago, aged provolone or
Pecorino Romano

2 tablespoons chopped
oil-packed sun-dried
tomatoes

¼ cup finely chopped fresh
flat-leaf parsley

1. Rub the garlic evenly over the slices of beef. Place on a deep platter or in a large baking dish and add the wine. Marinate for 2 hours at room temperature or for up to 4 hours in the refrigerator.

2. **Make the stuffing:** Melt 1 tablespoon of the butter in a medium skillet over medium heat. Add the onion and cook, stirring, until golden, about 5 minutes. Remove from the heat and add the olives, cheese, sun-dried tomatoes, 2 tablespoons of the parsley and a grinding of pepper.

3. Remove the yolks from the egg whites. Press the yolks through a sieve set over a bowl. Finely chop the whites. Stir both into the onion mixture.

4. Lift the meat from the marinade and blot dry with paper towels; reserve the marinade. Lay the beef slices on a work surface and top each with a slice of prosciutto, if using. Spread with the egg mixture, leaving a ¼-inch border around three sides and a 1-inch border at one narrow end. Roll up toward the narrow end and fasten closed with a toothpick.

5. Place the flour on a sheet of waxed paper and add the salt and a grinding of pepper. Coat the beef rolls with the flour and shake off the excess.

Freshly ground black pepper

3 large eggs, hard-cooked (page 162), peeled and halved lengthwise

4 thin slices prosciutto (optional)

¼ cup all-purpose flour

½ teaspoon kosher salt

1 cup canned reduced-sodium beef broth, fat skimmed

2 tablespoons tomato paste

6. Preheat the oven to 350°F. Melt the remaining 1 tablespoon butter in a large nonstick skillet over medium heat. Add the beef rolls and brown, turning to brown evenly on all sides, about 5 minutes. Transfer to a 4-quart Dutch oven.

7. Add the reserved marinade to the skillet and boil gently until reduced by half, about 2 minutes. Stir in the broth and tomato paste and bring to a boil. Pour over the beef rolls. Set the Dutch oven over medium-high heat and return the liquid to a boil. Cover and cook in the oven, basting the beef rolls once or twice with the juices, until tender, about 1 hour 15 minutes.

8. Transfer the beef rolls to a serving dish. Remove the toothpicks. Pour the sauce over the top, sprinkle with the remaining 2 tablespoons parsley and serve.

Makes 4 servings

Serve with rice or noodles.

Braised Veal Roulades Stuffed with Herb and Prosciutto Omelette

These roulades are stuffed with a thin omelette flavored with cheese, garlic and rosemary. Slowly braised on top of the stove, the veal takes on the seasonings from the omelette, and the juices in the pan thicken into a marvelous sauce. The recipe is loosely based on one in Anna Teresa Callen's *Food and Memories of Abruzzo*.

4 **large eggs**

2 **tablespoons freshly grated Parmigiano-Reggiano cheese**

2 **tablespoons chopped fresh flat-leaf parsley**

1 **teaspoon minced fresh rosemary**

1 **teaspoon minced garlic**

Kosher salt and freshly ground black pepper

2 **tablespoons extra-virgin olive oil**

2 **ounces prosciutto, fat trimmed, chopped**

¼ **cup all-purpose flour**

1 **pound veal cutlets (4–8), pounded thin**

1. Whisk the eggs in a medium bowl with the cheese, 1 tablespoon of the parsley, ½ teaspoon of the rosemary and ½ teaspoon of the garlic. Add a pinch of salt and a grinding of pepper. Heat 1 tablespoon of the oil in a 10-inch nonstick skillet over low heat. Add the eggs and cook just until set on the bottom, about 1 minute. Tilt the pan and lift the edges of the eggs with a spatula so that the runny egg runs under the edges. Sprinkle the prosciutto evenly over the omelette. When the eggs are almost set on top, slip the omelette out of the pan onto a plate. Let cool slightly.

2. Cut at least ten 10-inch lengths of kitchen twine and set aside. Combine the flour, ½ teaspoon salt and a grinding of pepper on a plate. Lay the veal cutlets on a work surface. Sprinkle them lightly with salt and a grinding of pepper. Cut the omelette into pieces almost large enough to cover the surface of the cutlets, leaving a ¼-inch border around the edges, and place on the cutlets. Tightly roll up each cutlet into a roulade and tie with at least two pieces of the twine, one at either end, with an additional one in the center, if necessary. Roll the roulades in the flour and shake off the excess.

1 tablespoon unsalted butter

4 ounces white button mushrooms, trimmed, wiped clean and quartered (about 1½ cups)

4 ounces cremini mushrooms, trimmed, wiped clean and quartered (about 1½ cups)

½ cup dry white wine

⅔ cup canned reduced-sodium chicken broth, fat skimmed

1 large egg yolk

1 tablespoon fresh lemon juice

3. Heat the remaining 1 tablespoon oil and the butter in a large, heavy skillet with a lid over medium heat. When the foam subsides, add the roulades. Cook, turning, until lightly browned on all sides, about 5 minutes. Transfer the roulades to a large plate. Add the mushrooms to the skillet and sauté, stirring, until golden, about 3 minutes. Add the remaining 1 table-spoon parsley, the remaining ½ teaspoon rosemary and the remaining ½ teaspoon garlic and cook, stirring, for 1 minute. Season with salt and a grinding of pepper and transfer to the plate with the roulades.

4. Add the wine to the skillet and bring to a boil, stir-ring. Boil until reduced by half, about 3 minutes. Add the broth and return the roulades, mushrooms and any juices on the plate to the skillet. Cover and simmer, turning the roulades once or twice, until tender when pierced with a fork, about 20 minutes.

5. Transfer the roulades to a cutting board and cover with foil to keep warm. Boil the broth mixture until slightly reduced, about 2 minutes. Reduce the heat to low.

6. Meanwhile, whisk the egg yolk and lemon juice together in a small bowl. Whisk some of the hot broth into the egg mixture. Stir the egg mixture into the skil-let; do not let boil.

7. Cut the strings from the roulades and cut the roulades into ½-inch-thick slices. Arrange the slices on a platter, spoon the sauce and mushrooms over the top and serve.

Makes 4 servings

Tomato-Braised Pork Braciole with Hard-Cooked Eggs

A braciola is a thin slice of meat rolled up around a savory stuffing. The meat can be pork, beef, lamb or veal. This is a version of a dish I remember eating as a child for Sunday dinner: thin slices of pork stuffed with bread crumbs, cheese, garlic, raisins and hard-cooked eggs and simmered in tomato sauce.

2 tablespoons extra-virgin olive oil

2 tablespoons minced onion

1 teaspoon minced garlic

⅔ cup fine dry bread crumbs

¼ cup freshly grated Parmigiano-Reggiano cheese

1 tablespoon minced fresh flat-leaf parsley

Kosher salt and freshly ground black pepper

4 ¼-inch-thick pork cutlets cut from the leg (about 12 ounces total), pounded thin

2 tablespoons minced pitted green olives

2 tablespoons dried currants or chopped raisins

4 medium eggs, hard-cooked (page 162), peeled

1 28-ounce can plum tomatoes, with their juices

1 sprig fresh basil

1. Combine 1 tablespoon of the oil and the onion in a medium nonstick skillet and cook, stirring, over medium-low heat until the onion is golden, about 3 minutes. Add the garlic and cook for 30 seconds. Add the bread crumbs and cheese and cook, stirring, for 1 minute. Add the parsley and cook, stirring, for 1 minute. Add a pinch of salt and a grinding of pepper and transfer to a small bowl. Rinse and dry the skillet; set aside.

2. Cut four 16-inch lengths of kitchen twine. Lay the cutlets on a work surface. Sprinkle lightly with salt and a grinding of pepper. Spread the bread-crumb mixture evenly over the surface of the cutlets. Sprinkle with the olives and currants or raisins. Place a hard-cooked egg across the narrow end of one of the cutlets. Roll up tightly, tucking in the edges of the cutlet as you roll. Tie lengthwise and crosswise with the twine, knot it and trim the excess. Repeat with the remaining eggs and cutlets.

3. Heat the remaining 1 tablespoon oil in the skillet over medium-low heat. Add the rolled cutlets and brown, turning to brown evenly on all sides, about 15 minutes. Transfer the braciole to a wide, heavy saucepan. Set the skillet aside.

4. Place a food mill over a medium bowl and puree the tomatoes and their juices into the bowl. (Or, if you do not have a food mill, puree in a food processor and press through a strainer with a rubber spatula; discard the solids.) Add the pureed tomatoes to the skillet with the drippings and bring to a boil over medium-high heat, scraping up the browned bits from the bottom of the skillet. Pour the sauce over the braciole in the saucepan and add the basil sprig. Cover and cook over low heat, turning the rolls occasionally with tongs, until the meat is tender when pierced with a fork, about 50 minutes.

5. Transfer the braciole to a shallow serving bowl. Cover with foil to keep warm. Simmer the sauce, uncovered, over medium heat until slightly thickened, about 10 minutes.

6. Snip the string from the braciole and discard. Carefully slice the meat and egg bundles in half. Taste the sauce and add salt and pepper, if needed. Pour over the braciole and serve.

Makes 4 servings

Serve with a small pasta like orzo or riso.

CHAPTER 7   *Beyond the Usual Egg Salad*

"An egg is always an adventure."
—OSCAR WILDE

There's a wonderful world of egg salads that most Americans never experience. It opened up for me one day in France, where my husband and I were driving the superhighway from Provence to Paris. We had stopped for lunch in a small local restaurant near Lyons, and I ordered a salad. After hours of driving, I'd almost forgotten I was in France until the waiter arrived with the meal. The plate set before me was a revelation: leaves of rough, bitter, pale green frisée lettuce and sweet chunks of lightly browned bacon tossed with a tangy red-wine-vinegar dressing, with a creamy poached egg on top. It changed my notions about "egg salad" forever and suggested all sorts of new possibilities.

Now I pair eggs with bitter greens like frisée or with arugula, dandelion greens or mesclun, or with vegetables such as artichokes and asparagus, or with sharp-tasting vinaigrettes, tangy cheeses, salty pancetta and cured bacon. Eggs are also marvelously companionable with fresh herbs, and you can add unexpected accents of dill, mint, basil, oregano, parsley, thyme or tarragon. The salads in this chapter feature not only eggs that are hard-cooked — whether cut in half, chopped, grated, mashed or minced—but also eggs that are scrambled, poached or made into omelettes and shredded.

I prefer to use vinaigrettes in these salads rather than mayonnaise, because the acidity balances the richness of the eggs. For the same reason, I often dress egg salads with a tangy yogurt sauce, piquant salsa verde or sharp green herb sauce with capers, garlic and lemon. When I do use mayonnaise, I prefer to give it a special kick with roasted garlic, curry or even canned tuna. (I do love conventional egg salad, though, and you'll find an olive-spiked version on page 222, as well as plenty of simple suggestions for taking that kind of egg salad out of the realm of the ordinary.)

You'll find salads for all seasons of the year in this chapter. Some are best when tomatoes and basil are fresh from the garden, while others, made with warm dressing, greens, potatoes or rice, are perfect even in the middle of winter. All will make your family and friends sit up and take notice.

Egg Salad
Basic Proportions and Simple Variations

 There are lots of possibilities for variety in good-old American egg salad. You can slice or mash the eggs or chop them coarse or fine. You can dress them with homemade mayonnaise (pages 340–344), all kinds of flavored mayonnaise (see page 228) or bottled mayonnaise. You can add one or more of the additional ingredients listed below. Finally, you can serve egg salad in a number of ways: spread in a sandwich, spooned onto a lettuce leaf or nestled in a hollowed-out tomato or an avocado half.

Here are suggested proportions for basic egg salad: for every 4 eggs, use ¼ cup mayonnaise for a drier mixture or ⅓ cup mayonnaise for a moist mixture. Then add any of the following (or a combination) to suit your palate—and what you have on hand.

- Prepared mustard (1–2 teaspoons)

- Horseradish (1 tablespoon, or to taste)

- Red wine vinegar (about 1 teaspoon)

- Grated onion (1 tablespoon, or to taste)

- Sweet pickle relish or chopped dill pickle (about 2 tablespoons)

- Chopped celery or fresh fennel (¼ cup)

- Diced red onion or sliced scallions (2 tablespoons, or to taste)

- Finely chopped fresh chervil, tarragon, basil, dill or flat-leaf parsley (about 1 tablespoon)

- A dash of Tabasco sauce

- Freshly ground black pepper

Green Olive, Celery and Egg Salad in Tomatoes

Adding green olives to a traditional salad of hard-cooked eggs, mayonnaise and celery creates an entirely new effect. I also like this salad spread on crusty bread as an open-faced sandwich.

8 **large eggs, hard-cooked (page 162), peeled and thinly sliced**

1 **cup pimiento-stuffed green olives, coarsely chopped if necessary (see box)**

1 **cup diced celery, plus ½ cup chopped celery leaves**

½ **cup mayonnaise**

 Kosher salt and freshly ground black pepper

4 **large tomatoes**

1. In a large bowl, combine the eggs, olives, celery, celery leaves, mayonnaise, salt to taste and a grinding of pepper and stir until well blended. Cover and refrigerate.

2. Cut off the tops of the tomatoes. With a soupspoon, scoop out and discard the centers. Place a paper towel on a plate and place the tomatoes on it, cut side down. Drain for at least 10 minutes or until ready to fill. If preparing an hour or two ahead, refrigerate, but allow to come to room temperature before serving.

3. Spoon the salad into the tomatoes and serve.

Makes 4 servings

You can use crushed, sliced or whole pimiento-stuffed olives. If they are whole, chop them; if they are crushed or sliced, just drain well.

Tomato and Egg Salad with Basil

During tomato and basil season, this salad makes a regular appearance on my dinner table. I serve it as a side dish with grilled seafood or as part of a vegetarian menu.

2 cups sliced plum tomatoes (about 4 medium)

½ cup chopped fresh basil

1 garlic clove, minced

Kosher salt

6 large eggs, hard-cooked (page 162), peeled and quartered

⅓ cup extra-virgin olive oil

Freshly ground black pepper

Romaine lettuce or other salad greens

1. Combine the tomatoes, basil, garlic and salt to taste in a large bowl and stir to blend. Add the eggs, oil and a generous grinding of pepper and gently fold in.

2. Serve spooned over a bed of salad greens.

Makes 4 to 6 servings

Vegetable Dyes for Easter Eggs

The colors traditionally used for dyeing eggs were symbolic: red for love and the color of Christ's blood; yellow for spirituality and sunlight; green for nature; blue for good health; pink for success; orange for desire; and black for remembrance.

1 cup water

Pink: ½ cup cranberries, beets, cut-up radishes or frozen raspberries

Yellow or orange: 1 tablespoon ground turmeric

Orange: 1 cup packed yellow onion skins

Pale green: 1 cup packed trimmed spinach

Blue: ½ cup canned or frozen blueberries or chopped red cabbage

Brown/gold: 2 tablespoons dill seeds plus ½ cup walnuts

1 tablespoon white vinegar

Hard-cooked eggs (page 162) or blown-out eggs

Combine the water with one of the color choices listed above in a small saucepan. Bring to a boil, reduce the heat to low, cover and simmer until the water is the desired color, 10 to 20 minutes. Strain into a deep bowl and add the vinegar. Using a tablespoon or wire egg holder, lower each egg into the hot liquid and let stand, turning gently, until it is the desired color. Transfer to a rack to dry.

Scarlet Egg and Beet Salad

This beet and egg salad is delicately seasoned with tarragon and garnished with crescent-shaped slivers of onion. Serve as an appetizer on lettuce leaves or as a side salad.

4–6 **small-to-medium beets (about 12 ounces)**

1 **fresh tarragon sprig, plus 1 tablespoon minced fresh tarragon**

4 **medium eggs, hard-cooked (page 162), peeled**

1 **cup red wine vinegar**

2 **tablespoons sugar**

1 **teaspoon kosher salt**

½ **cup slivered sweet onion for garnish**

Freshly ground black pepper

1. Simmer the beets in a saucepan of water to cover until tender when pierced with a skewer, about 20 minutes. Drain, saving about 1 cup of the cooking liquid. Peel the beets and halve or quarter them if they are larger than the eggs.

2. Place the tarragon sprig in a wide-mouth canning jar or other large jar. Add the eggs and beets alternately, packing them as tightly as possible.

3. Combine the reserved cooking liquid, the vinegar, sugar and salt in a saucepan and bring to a boil. Remove from the heat, stirring to dissolve the sugar and salt. Cool slightly, then pour over the beets and eggs. Seal and refrigerate for at least 2 days before serving.

4. Drain off the liquid. Halve or quarter the eggs. Arrange with the beets on a plate. Garnish with the onion, minced tarragon and a grinding of pepper.

Makes 4 servings

Plan ahead: the eggs must pickle for at least 48 hours before serving.

Green Bean and Egg Salad with Mint

It was cookbook author Paula Wolfert who introduced me to egg salad with mint. She also gave me the idea of grating the hard-cooked eggs by hand. The mint-infused egg mixture coats the warm green beans, making a deliciously rich salad.

1   **pound tender green beans, stem ends trimmed (leave the graceful blossom end intact)**

1   **garlic clove, halved**

3   **tablespoons chopped fresh mint, plus whole leaves for garnish**

3   **large eggs, hard-cooked (page 162), peeled**

3   **tablespoons extra-virgin olive oil**

½   **teaspoon kosher salt**
     Freshly ground black pepper

1. Cook the beans in a large pot of boiling salted water until tender, 6 to 8 minutes, depending on their size. Drain.

2. Rub the inside of a serving bowl with the cut sides of the garlic clove; discard the garlic. Add the warm beans and 1 tablespoon of the chopped mint; toss to coat.

3. Using the wide-shred side of a box grater, grate the eggs into a bowl. Add the oil, the remaining 2 tablespoons chopped mint, the salt and a grinding of pepper and stir to blend well.

4. Add the egg mixture to the beans and stir to coat evenly. Garnish with a few whole mint leaves and serve.

Makes 4 servings

Serve with sliced summer tomatoes topped with torn fresh basil leaves.

Egg White Salad

When you have leftover hard-cooked egg whites, this is a delicious way to use them. In fact, this salad is so good that I cook the eggs especially for it, then press some of the yolks through a sieve so they adorn the top of the salad like flecks of gold.

½ cup mayonnaise

1 tablespoon cider vinegar

8 large egg whites, hard-cooked (page 162), coarsely chopped

4 pale green inner celery ribs, thinly sliced (about 1 cup), plus ¼ cup chopped tender green celery leaves (from the inner ribs)

½ cup slivered red onion
Freshly ground black pepper

4 or more large curly lettuce leaves (optional)

1 cup small cherry tomatoes or 4–6 medium ripe tomatoes (optional)

1. In a large bowl, combine the mayonnaise and vinegar and whisk to blend. Add the egg whites, celery and celery leaves, onion and a grinding of pepper.

2. Line a platter with lettuce leaves, if desired, and spoon the salad on top. Garnish with the cherry tomatoes. Or, if preferred, cut off the tops of the regular tomatoes. With a soupspoon, scoop out and discard the centers. Place a paper towel on a plate and place the tomatoes on it, cut side down. Drain for at least 10 minutes or until ready to fill. If preparing an hour or two ahead, refrigerate, but allow to come to room temperature before serving. Spoon the salad into the tomatoes and serve.

Makes 4 to 6 servings

Gussying Up Mayonnaise for Egg Salads

 One of the easiest ways to create an extraordinary egg salad is to flavor the mayonnaise that dresses the eggs and other ingredients. These combinations can be used to embellish either jarred commercial mayonnaise or homemade mayo (page 340).

Basil Mayonnaise: Combine ½ cup mayonnaise, 1 cup loosely packed fresh basil leaves and 1 garlic clove, chopped, in a food processor and blend well until the basil and garlic are pureed.

Use egg salad made with Basil Mayonnaise in a sandwich with thin slices of tomato, or spoon it into scooped-out ripe tomatoes.

Chipotle Chile Mayonnaise: Toast 1 teaspoon ground cumin in a small dry skillet over low heat until fragrant, about 20 seconds. Combine ½ cup mayonnaise, 1 teaspoon canned chipotle chiles in adobo sauce and the cumin in a food processor and blend well.

Caution: Chipotle chiles are very hot: use less, or more, to taste. I like to accompany chipotle egg salad with sliced avocado and cilantro leaves, either on a plate or in a sandwich.

Enlightened Mustard Mayonnaise: Here's a tasty way to cut the calories and add flavor to jarred mayonnaise: In a bowl, whisk together ¼ cup jarred mayonnaise, ¼ cup plain low-fat yogurt, 2 tablespoons Dijon mustard and 1 small garlic clove, minced. Refrigerate, covered, for about 1 hour before using.

Spread egg salad made with Enlightened Mayonnaise on toasted rye bread for an open-faced sandwich, or serve on a salad plate accompanied by crisp crudités of celery, carrot and red bell pepper.

Sun-Dried Tomato Mayonnaise: Soak 4 dry-packed sun-dried tomato halves, cut into strips, in boiling water to cover until very soft; drain. Combine the tomatoes, 1 garlic clove, minced, and ½ cup mayonnaise in a food processor and blend well until the tomatoes and garlic are pureed.

Mix with chopped hard-cooked eggs and boiled potatoes, and garnish with chopped kalamata olives and minced fresh rosemary.

Ginger-Curried Mayonnaise: Sprinkle 1 tablespoon curry powder into a small dry skillet and warm over low heat until fragrant, about 20 seconds. Combine the curry powder, 1 teaspoon grated ginger and ½ cup mayonnaise in a bowl and blend well.

Mix with chopped hard-cooked eggs, diced apple, dried currants and chopped toasted walnuts.

Egg, Roasted Pepper and Black Olive Salad with Roasted Garlic Mayonnaise

This salad of eggs, roasted red peppers and black olives makes a perfect lunch with a loaf of crusty whole-grain bread.

Garlic Mayonnaise

- 6 **garlic cloves, lightly bruised with the side of a knife**
- 1 **tablespoon extra-virgin olive oil**
- 1 **cup jarred or homemade (page 340) mayonnaise**

- 4 **red bell peppers, roasted and quartered (page 75)**
- 4–6 **large eggs, hard-cooked (page 162), peeled and halved lengthwise**
- ⅓ **cup coarsely chopped pitted kalamata or other brine-cured black olives**
- 2 **tablespoons finely chopped fresh flat-leaf parsley**

1. **Make the garlic mayonnaise:** Preheat the oven to 325°F. Place the garlic in a custard cup and add the oil. Cover with foil and roast until the garlic is pale golden, about 30 minutes. Let cool in the oil.

2. Combine the garlic and oil with the mayonnaise in the bowl of a food processor and process until the garlic is pureed. Cover and refrigerate for at least 1 hour before serving. (The garlic mayonnaise will keep for 2 to 3 days.)

3. To serve, arrange the peppers around the edge of a platter. Arrange the egg halves on the platter and sprinkle with the olives and parsley. Serve with the garlic mayonnaise on the side.

Makes 4 servings

Make the garlic mayonnaise ahead and keep on hand for this simple salad, for egg salad or to spread on bread for sandwiches.

Dandelion Greens, Pancetta and Egg Salad

Tender young dandelion greens are often available in the produce section of my supermarket, but as a child, I picked the greens in the fields around my house. The small, pale green inner leaves went into the salad bowl, and the dark green outer leaves were boiled and served as a side dish. The richness of the eggs is the perfect counterpoint to the sassy greens.

1 large bunch tender young dandelion greens (about 1¼ pounds)

4 large eggs, hard-cooked (page 162), peeled and halved lengthwise

1 teaspoon Dijon mustard

1 small garlic clove, minced

½ teaspoon kosher salt

3 ¼-inch-thick slices pancetta or thick-sliced bacon, cut into ¼-inch dice

5 tablespoons extra-virgin olive oil

2 tablespoons red wine vinegar
Freshly ground black pepper

1. Wash the dandelion greens thoroughly. Cut off and discard the stems. Stack the leaves and cut them crosswise into ½-inch pieces. You should have about 6 cups lightly packed. Set aside.

2. Separate the egg yolks from the whites; reserve 2 whites for the salad and save the other whites for another use. Place the yolks in a small bowl, add the mustard, garlic and salt and mash with a fork until blended. Set aside. Finely chop the 2 reserved egg whites and set aside separately.

3. Combine the pancetta or bacon and 1 tablespoon of the oil in a medium skillet and cook, stirring, over medium-low heat until crisp and browned. With a slotted spoon, transfer to a small bowl and set aside. Discard the fat and wipe the skillet dry.

4. Add the remaining 4 tablespoons oil, vinegar and the egg-yolk mixture to the skillet and whisk over low heat until the dressing is creamy and warm, about 1 minute; do not boil. Remove from the heat, add the greens to the skillet and toss to coat.

5. Spoon the salad into a serving bowl. Sprinkle with the pancetta or bacon, the chopped egg whites and a grinding of pepper. Serve warm or at room temperature.

Makes 4 side-dish or 2 main-course servings

Egg, Tuna and Caper Salad

Tonnato, or tuna, sauce, is traditionally served on *vitello tonnato*, a classic dish of sliced braised veal topped with tuna sauce. Because I love the combination of canned tuna and hard-cooked eggs, I decided to serve the sauce over hard-cooked eggs.

¾ cup mayonnaise

1 3½-ounce can Italian tuna in olive oil, drained

1 small garlic clove, minced

1–2 teaspoons fresh lemon juice

Freshly ground black pepper

1 tablespoon capers, rinsed and drained

4–6 large eggs, hard-cooked (page 162), peeled and halved lengthwise

2 tablespoons very thinly sliced scallion greens

Small sprigs of fresh dill, flat-leaf parsley or basil for garnish (optional)

1. Combine the mayonnaise, tuna, garlic, lemon juice and a grinding of pepper in a food processor and process until very smooth. Spoon into a small serving bowl and top with the capers.

2. Place the dish in the center of a platter and arrange the egg halves around the edge. Sprinkle with the scallions and herbs, if using. To serve, spoon some of the sauce over each hard-cooked egg half at the table.

Makes 4 servings

> *For the best flavor, look for cans of imported Italian tuna. It's darker, richer and softer than American brands and makes a smoother, tastier sauce.*

Roasted Beet and Egg Salad
with Arugula and Sherry Vinaigrette

Roasted beets have an intense flavor that cannot be matched by boiled beets. Because the beets take 1 to 1½ hours to roast, I often prepare them a day or two ahead and store them, still wrapped in the foil in which they were cooked, in the refrigerator until I'm ready to use them.

4–6 **medium beets (1½–2 pounds total), leaves trimmed (see box) and scrubbed**

Dressing

6 **tablespoons extra-virgin olive oil**

2 **tablespoons sherry vinegar**

1 **teaspoon grated orange zest**

½ **teaspoon kosher salt**

Freshly ground black pepper

1–2 **bunches arugula, stems trimmed, washed and dried (4 cups)**

4 **large eggs, hard-cooked (page 162), peeled and quartered**

½ **sweet onion, cut into thin slivers**

1. Preheat the oven to 400°F. Wrap each beet tightly in a square of foil. Place the beets on a baking sheet and roast until tender when pierced with a skewer, 1 to 1½ hours. Let cool, then rub the loosened skins from the beets and cut into ½-inch-thick wedges.

2. **Make the dressing:** In a large bowl, whisk all the ingredients until blended.

3. Add the beets, arugula, eggs and onion to the dressing and gently toss to blend. Serve at room temperature or chilled.

Makes 4 servings

If the beet greens are fresh and tender, save them and serve warm beet greens vinaigrette at another meal. Wash the greens well, chop them and cook in boiling salted water until tender, about 10 minutes; drain. While they are still warm, season with the same vinaigrette as above and serve.

Artichoke, Egg and Potato Salad

Buttery-tasting artichoke bottoms, boiled potatoes and hard-cooked eggs make an elegant salad. Although it's special, it goes as well with a hamburger as it does with filet mignon.

4–5 **artichokes, preferably with long stems**

Kosher salt

1 **tablespoon extra-virgin olive oil**

1 **teaspoon fresh lemon juice**

1 **small garlic clove, minced**

1 **pound red-skinned or Yukon Gold potatoes**

1. Trim a thin slice from the stem of each artichoke. Pull off a few of the large outside leaves. Place each artichoke on its side and slice off about 1 inch from the top. Place the artichokes and 1 teaspoon salt in a large saucepan, cover with water and bring to a boil. Cover and simmer until the artichokes are tender when pierced with a skewer, 25 to 35 minutes, depending on the size. Drain and cool.

2. Carefully pull off all the artichoke leaves and reserve them for another use. Discard the soft inner core of leaves with prickly tops. With the tip of a spoon, scrape away the fuzzy center (choke) and discard. With a paring knife, cut the bottoms (hearts) into quarters through the stem, then cut into ½-inch cubes. In a medium bowl, combine the artichokes with the oil, lemon juice, garlic and a pinch of salt. Toss to blend and set aside.

3. Meanwhile, place the potatoes in a medium saucepan, add water to cover and bring to a boil. Cover and cook over medium-low heat until tender when pierced with a skewer, 20 to 25 minutes; drain and let cool. Peel the potatoes and cut into ½-inch cubes. Set aside.

Dressing

½ cup extra-virgin olive oil

¼ cup red wine vinegar

1 teaspoon Dijon mustard

½ teaspoon kosher salt

   Freshly ground black pepper

½ cup thinly sliced celery

4 large eggs, hard-cooked
   (page 162), peeled and
   quartered

2 tablespoons coarsely chopped
   fresh flat-leaf parsley

2 tablespoons finely chopped
   red onion

4. **Make the dressing:** In a large serving bowl, whisk all the ingredients together until blended.

5. Add the artichoke hearts, potatoes and celery to the dressing and stir to combine. Gently fold in the eggs. Sprinkle with the parsley and onion and serve.

Makes 4 to 6 servings

> ***Don't throw away the outer leaves of the artichoke; I save them and snack on them throughout the day.***

Hard-Cooked Eggs, Potatoes and Tomatoes with Yogurt Sauce

The success of this dish lies in the quality of the ingredients and the presentation. Buy the best-quality, purest (with no additives or other suspect ingredients) yogurt you can find. The eggs should be free-range with dark yellow yolks, if possible, the tomatoes ripe and juicy. The rest is a matter of selecting a pretty plate and arranging the ingredients in an attractive way.

2 cups plain low-fat yogurt

½–¾ cup whole or 2% milk

1 garlic clove, minced
   Kosher salt

4 large eggs, hard-cooked (page 162), still warm, peeled and halved lengthwise

4 Yukon Gold or red-skinned potatoes, boiled and quartered, still warm

2 ripe tomatoes, cored and cut into wedges

1 tablespoon chopped fresh mint

1 tablespoon chopped fresh dill

1 tablespoon chopped fresh flat-leaf parsley
   Freshly ground black pepper

1–2 tablespoons extra-virgin olive oil

1 jalapeño, stem trimmed and cut into thin rounds, seeded if desired

1. A day before serving, spoon the yogurt into a fine-mesh strainer or one lined with cheesecloth set over a deep bowl. Cover with plastic wrap and refrigerate for at least 12 or up to 24 hours, draining off the liquid in the bowl at least once halfway through the draining time.

2. Discard the liquid in the bowl and transfer the yogurt to the bowl. Gradually stir in enough milk, 1 tablespoon at a time, so the yogurt is thin enough to run off the spoon in a thin stream. Add the garlic and ½ teaspoon salt. (If not using right away, cover and refrigerate; let stand at room temperature for at least 30 minutes before serving to take the chill off.)

3. Arrange the egg halves around the edge of a large round platter. Place the potatoes in a circle inside the circle of the eggs, then fill the middle with the tomatoes. Sprinkle everything with the mint, dill, parsley, salt to taste and a grinding of pepper. Drizzle with the oil. Spoon some of the yogurt sauce over the top and sprinkle with the jalapeño slices. Serve immediately, with the remaining sauce on the side.

Makes 2 to 4 servings

**The yogurt must drain for at least
12 hours, so plan ahead.**

Warm Potato, Bacon and Egg Salad with Wilted Spinach

For best results, the potatoes, hard-cooked eggs and dressing should be combined and served when the potatoes and dressing are still very warm or even hot. The egg yolks dissolve into the warm vinaigrette and coat the potatoes along with the mustardy dressing. Of course, leftovers are fine served right from the refrigerator the next day.

1½ pounds Yukon Gold or other waxy potatoes, such as red-skinned or creamers

6 slices bacon

4 cups packed rinsed and trimmed spinach leaves

6 large eggs, hard-cooked (page 162), peeled and quartered, warm or at room temperature

1 red onion or sweet onion, cut lengthwise into slivers

½ cup plus 2 tablespoons vegetable oil

⅓ cup plus 2 tablespoons cider vinegar

1 tablespoon Dijon mustard
Kosher salt and freshly ground black pepper

You can substitute arugula or a mix of tender bitter greens for the spinach.

1. Place the potatoes in a medium saucepan, add water to cover and bring to a boil. Cover, reduce the heat to medium-low and simmer until the potatoes are tender when pierced with a skewer, about 25 minutes. Drain and let cool until they can be handled.

2. Meanwhile, cook the bacon in a large skillet over medium heat until crisp, about 8 minutes; drain on paper towels. Cut the bacon into ½-inch-wide pieces and place in a large serving bowl. Reserve 2 tablespoons of the bacon fat; discard the rest. Set the skillet with the reserved bacon fat aside.

3. Peel the potatoes and cut them into ½-inch pieces. Add the potatoes, spinach, eggs and onion to the serving bowl.

4. Add the oil, vinegar, mustard and 1 teaspoon salt to the skillet with the reserved bacon fat and cook over low heat, whisking, until very hot.

5. Pour the hot dressing over the salad and gently toss to blend. Taste and add more salt, if necessary, along with a generous grinding of pepper. Serve hot or warm.

Makes 4 to 6 servings

White Bean, Egg and Kalamata Olive Salad

I much prefer this salad made with dried beans that have been soaked and slowly cooked in the oven; canned beans just won't do. The idea for the recipe comes from Michele Schmidt, a colleague and friend from San Francisco. Serve as part of a buffet of salads for dinner or lunch.

3 cups cooked cannellini or Great Northern beans (opposite page)

4 large eggs, hard-cooked (page 162), peeled and chopped

⅓ cup extra-virgin olive oil

2 tablespoons fresh lemon juice, or more to taste

2 tablespoons chopped fresh oregano

1 small garlic clove, minced
  Kosher salt and freshly ground black pepper

¼ cup coarsely cut-up pitted kalamata olives

1. Combine the beans, eggs, oil, lemon juice, oregano and garlic in a large bowl. Sprinkle with salt to taste and add a grinding of pepper. Stir to blend.

2. Add the olives and gently fold to blend. Taste and add more lemon juice, salt and/or pepper, if needed, and serve.

Makes 4 servings

Oven-Baked Cannellini Beans

1 pound dried
cannellini (white
kidney) beans or
other dried white
beans

4 garlic cloves, peeled
and crushed with the
side of a knife

2 tablespoons extra-
virgin olive oil

1 small onion, halved,
or 1 thick slice onion

1 bay leaf, a few fresh
sage leaves or a small
fresh thyme or
rosemary sprig

2–3 cups water or
unsalted homemade
chicken broth

Kosher salt and
freshly ground black
pepper

1. Place the beans in a large bowl; add enough water to cover the beans by 2 inches. Let stand for up to 4 hours or overnight; drain.

2. Preheat the oven to 325°F. Combine the beans, garlic, oil, onion and herb of choice in a 3-quart casserole. Stir to blend. Add enough water or broth to cover the beans. Cover and bake until the beans are tender, 1½ to 2 hours. When they are tender, add salt to taste and a grinding of pepper. As the beans cool, they will absorb most of the liquid; drain any liquid that isn't absorbed. Remove the onion and bay leaf, if using, from the beans before using. Refrigerate unused beans for up to 4 days or freeze and use for soup or stew.

Makes about 6 cups

Shrimp, Potato and Egg Salad

The tiny peeled precooked shrimp (often called "shrimp meat") sold in many fish markets are convenient for this salad. It's not necessary to cook the peas, just rinse them with lukewarm water until thawed and drain well before adding to the salad.

1 **pound small yellow potatoes, such as Yukon Gold**

1 **12-ounce bag peeled precooked tiny shrimp, thawed if frozen**

4 **large eggs, hard-cooked (page 162), peeled and chopped**

1 **cup frozen tiny green peas, thawed (see headnote)**

½ **cup mayonnaise**

2 **tablespoons minced sweet onion**

2 **tablespoons finely chopped fresh dill, or more to taste**

2 **tablespoons fresh lemon juice**

½ **teaspoon kosher salt, or more to taste**

Freshly ground black pepper

Lettuce and cherry tomatoes (optional)

1. Place the potatoes in a medium saucepan, add water to cover and bring to a boil. Cover and cook over medium-low heat until the potatoes are tender when pierced with a skewer, about 20 minutes. Drain, rinse and cool, then peel and cut into ¼-inch dice.

2. In a large bowl, combine the potatoes, shrimp, eggs, peas, mayonnaise, onion, dill, lemon juice, salt and a grinding of pepper. Gently fold all the ingredients together. Taste and add more dill, salt and/or pepper, if necessary. Serve slightly chilled or at room temperature, on a bed of lettuce garnished with cherry tomatoes, if desired.

Makes 4 servings

Chicken and Egg Salad
with Curried Mayonnaise and Toasted Hazelnuts

Chicken salad with hard-cooked eggs, almonds and curried mayonnaise was a favorite combination in the days when ladies went out to lunch. I have updated the recipe by toasting the spices before adding them to the curried mayonnaise, which gives the dressing more depth of flavor, and by substituting hazelnuts for the almonds.

4 **teaspoons curry powder, preferably Madras-style**

1 **teaspoon ground cumin**

¾ **cup mayonnaise**

⅛ **teaspoon cayenne pepper (optional)**

2½–3 **cups 1-inch pieces cooked chicken**

4 **large eggs, hard-cooked (page 162), peeled and quartered**

½ **cup diced, peeled crisp apple**

½ **cup diced sweet onion**

2 **tablespoons dried currants**

½ **cup toasted, skinned and coarsely chopped hazelnuts (page 388)**

Salad greens, preferably Boston or Bibb lettuce

1. Sprinkle the curry powder and cumin into a small dry skillet and heat over low heat until the spices are fragrant, about 1 minute. Remove from the heat and transfer to a small bowl; add the mayonnaise and cayenne, if using, and stir until blended.

2. In a large bowl, combine the chicken, eggs, apple, onion and currants. Gently fold in the mayonnaise mixture. Sprinkle the hazelnuts over the top of the salad and stir just once. Serve at room temperature or chilled on salad greens.

Makes 4 servings

Use freshly roasted or boiled chicken. A supermarket deli-roasted chicken will also work well.

Basmati Rice, Asparagus and Egg Salad with Ginger Vinaigrette

The eggs in this salad are like an Asian-style omelette, an interesting alternative to the hard-cooked eggs typically added to salads.

1 cup basmati rice

¾ teaspoon kosher salt

4 large eggs

¼ teaspoon grated peeled ginger

¼ teaspoon minced garlic

Peanut or other vegetable oil

1. In a large saucepan, bring 2 cups water to a boil. Add the rice and ½ teaspoon of the salt, cover and cook over low heat until the water has been absorbed and the rice is tender, about 15 minutes. Remove from the heat; do not stir. Uncover and let cool to room temperature.

2. Meanwhile, break the eggs into a medium bowl. Add the ginger, garlic and the remaining ¼ teaspoon salt and whisk vigorously until blended. Pour about ¼ inch of peanut or other vegetable oil into a 6-inch skillet. Heat over medium heat until hot enough to sizzle a drop of egg. Add the eggs all at once; do not stir. Let cook until the eggs puff up around the edges, about 2 minutes, adjusting the heat as necessary to prevent overcooking; the eggs should sizzle gently. When the eggs are set on the bottom and around the sides, pull one edge toward the center with a spatula to allow the uncooked eggs to run under the cooked eggs. Cook for 1 minute more. Carefully turn the omelette over and cook for 30 seconds.

3. Set a strainer over a heat-resistant bowl and transfer the omelette to the strainer to drain. Turn the omelette out of the strainer onto a plate lined with a double thickness of paper towels and let cool to room temperature, then cut or tear the omelette into bite-sized pieces and set aside.

12 ounces asparagus, trimmed

2 teaspoons toasted sesame oil

Dressing

½ cup rice wine vinegar

6 tablespoons flavorless vegetable oil, such as canola

1 tablespoon toasted sesame oil

1 teaspoon sugar

½ teaspoon grated peeled ginger

½ teaspoon minced garlic

½ teaspoon kosher salt

1 tablespoon sesame seeds

½ cup thinly sliced scallions (white and light green parts)

4. Place a steamer basket over 1 inch of simmering water, add the asparagus, cover and steam until tender but still bright green, 3 to 4 minutes. Rinse the asparagus with cold water, drain and cool to room temperature.

5. Cut the asparagus diagonally into 1-inch lengths. Place in a large serving bowl, drizzle with the sesame oil and toss to coat. Set aside.

6. **Make the dressing:** Combine the vinegar, vegetable oil, sesame oil, sugar, ginger, garlic and salt in a small bowl and whisk until well blended. Set aside.

7. Place the sesame seeds in a small dry skillet and toast, stirring, over medium-low heat just until they begin to color, about 1 minute. Immediately pour the sesame seeds onto a small plate (or they will burn).

8. **Assemble the salad:** Add the rice and scallions to the asparagus, then add the dressing and toss to coat. Add the omelette pieces and stir to mix. Sprinkle with the sesame seeds and serve at room temperature.

Makes 4 to 6 servings

Arborio Rice, Green Bean and Egg Salad with Lemon Dressing

The eggs, rice and green beans in this salad taste best when they are freshly cooked and still warm. If you trim and cook the beans while the rice and eggs are cooking, all the ingredients will be ready at the same time.

2 **cups Arborio rice**

Kosher salt

1 **pound green beans, trimmed and cut into 1-inch lengths**

1. Bring a large saucepan of water to a boil. Add the rice and 1 teaspoon salt and cook, uncovered, until tender, 15 to 18 minutes. Drain and rinse with cold water; set aside.

2. Meanwhile, bring another large saucepan of water to a boil. Add the beans and 1 teaspoon salt and cook, uncovered, until tender, about 5 minutes. Drain and set aside.

If the salad sits for any length of time, be sure you taste and adjust the seasonings before serving.

Dressing

½ cup olive oil, preferably light
    in color and flavor

1 teaspoon grated lemon zest

5 tablespoons fresh lemon juice

2 tablespoons cold water

1 small garlic clove, minced

½ teaspoon kosher salt
    Freshly ground black pepper

½ cup thinly sliced scallions
    (white and light green parts)

¼ cup freshly grated
    Parmigiano-Reggiano cheese,
    or more to taste

6 large eggs, hard-cooked
    (page 162), peeled and
    quartered

¼ cup torn fresh basil leaves

2 tablespoons minced fresh
    flat-leaf parsley

2 tomatoes, cored and cut into
    thin wedges
    Fresh basil leaves for garnish

3. **Make the dressing:** In a large bowl, whisk the oil, lemon zest, lemon juice, water, garlic, salt and a grinding of pepper until blended.

4. Stir in the rice, beans, scallions and cheese. Gently fold in the eggs, basil and parsley.

5. Spoon the salad onto a large deep platter or into a shallow bowl and garnish with the tomato and basil. Serve.

Makes 6 servings

Parmesan Scrambled Egg and Rice Salad

The first time I ate a rice salad was in Tuscany. It contained, among many other things, little bits of scrambled egg, and I loved it. This is a simplified version. Be sure to cook the rice fresh and toss it with the vinaigrette while it is still warm. The oil-vinegar ratio may seem wrong, but the bland rice absorbs so much flavor that you need the extra hit of vinegar.

1 cup Arborio or other
   medium-grain rice
   Kosher salt

Dressing

6 tablespoons red wine vinegar

¼ cup extra-virgin olive oil

1 small garlic clove, minced

½ teaspoon kosher salt

4 large eggs

¼ cup freshly grated
   Parmigiano-Reggiano cheese
   Freshly ground black pepper
   Extra-virgin olive oil

¼ cup diced red onion

¼ cup pine nuts, toasted
   (page 271)

2 tablespoons chopped fresh
   flat-leaf parsley

1. Bring a large saucepan of water to a boil. Add the rice and 1 teaspoon salt and cook, uncovered, until tender, 15 to 18 minutes. Drain the rice in a strainer for 5 minutes, then transfer to a serving bowl and set aside.

2. **Meanwhile, make the dressing:** In a medium bowl, combine all the ingredients and whisk to blend. Add to the hot rice and toss to coat.

3. In a medium bowl, whisk the eggs and cheese until well blended. Add a grinding of pepper. Pour a thin film of oil into a medium skillet and heat over medium-low heat. When the oil is hot enough to sizzle a drop of egg, add the eggs all at once, reduce the heat to low and cook, stirring constantly, until set and creamy, 1 to 2 minutes. Transfer to a plate and cool slightly.

4. Using the side of a spoon, break the eggs into ½-inch pieces and add to the rice. Add the onion, pine nuts and parsley. Taste and add more salt or pepper, if necessary. Serve at room temperature.

Makes 4 to 6 servings

This salad is pretty with about ½ cup of cut-up cooked green beans or tiny green peas added. It's also wonderful with diced artichoke hearts.

French-Style Frisée, Bacon and Poached Egg Salad

Don't imagine that you can eliminate the eggs in this classic preparation. They're crucial to balance the rough flavors of the bitter greens and the vinegar.

2 slices thick-cut bacon, cut into ¼-inch dice

2 tablespoons extra-virgin olive oil

3 tablespoons red wine vinegar
Kosher salt and freshly ground black pepper

½ head frisée, trimmed, rinsed, dried and torn (about 3 cups packed)

2 tablespoons white vinegar

2 large eggs
Finely chopped fresh thyme, dill, chives and/or chervil (optional)

1. In a small skillet, fry the bacon until golden but still soft, not browned and crisp. With a slotted spoon, transfer to a paper towel to drain. Transfer 1 tablespoon of the bacon fat to a large bowl; discard the rest.

2. Add the oil, red wine vinegar, a pinch of salt and a grinding of pepper to the bacon fat and whisk together. Add the frisée and toss to coat. Divide the salad between two plates and top with the bacon.

3. Fill a large skillet with water, bring to a boil and add the white vinegar. Reduce the heat to a simmer. Break the eggs one at a time into a cup and slip them into the water. Cook for about 3 minutes, depending on the desired doneness. With a slotted spoon, remove the eggs and place on a folded kitchen towel or paper towel. Trim off any ragged whites.

4. Place an egg on top of each salad. Sprinkle with the chopped herbs, if desired, and serve.

Makes 2 servings

Poached Eggs and Baby Spinach Salad with Afghan-Style Yogurt and Garlic Sauce

I have been haunted by the tangy flavor of this yogurt and garlic sauce ever since I first tasted it at an Afghan restaurant in New York City, where it was served over noodles. I like it over poached eggs. Make sure that the garlic is very finely minced so that it will blend evenly with the yogurt. Serve for lunch, as a light dinner or as a first-course salad followed by grilled lamb, eggplant and red bell peppers.

2 cups plain low-fat yogurt

½–¾ cup whole or 2% milk

1 garlic clove, very finely minced or grated

Kosher salt

2 tablespoons white vinegar

4 large eggs

10–12 ounces baby spinach, washed and dried

Extra-virgin olive oil

¼ cup finely chopped fresh mint

Paprika

Cayenne pepper

1 tomato, cored, halved, seeded and chopped

1. A day before serving, spoon the yogurt into a strainer set over a deep bowl. Cover with plastic wrap and refrigerate for at least 12 or up to 24 hours, draining off the liquid in the bowl at least once halfway through the draining time.

2. Discard the liquid in the bowl and transfer the yogurt to the bowl. Gradually stir in enough milk, 1 tablespoon at a time, so the yogurt is thin enough to run off the spoon in a thin stream. Add the garlic and ½ teaspoon salt. (If not using right away, cover and refrigerate; let stand at room temperature for at least 30 minutes before serving to take the chill off.)

3. Fill a large skillet with water, bring to a boil and add the vinegar. Reduce the heat to a simmer. Break the eggs one at a time into a cup and slip them into the water. Cook for about 3 minutes, depending on the desired doneness. With a slotted spoon, remove the eggs in the order you added them to the pan and place on a folded kitchen towel or paper towel. Trim off any ragged whites.

The yogurt for this recipe must drain for at least 12 hours, so plan accordingly.

4. To serve, in a medium bowl, toss the spinach with 1 tablespoon oil and a pinch of salt. Divide the spinach among four large plates and place an egg in the center of each plate. Spoon a scant ½ cup of the yogurt sauce over each. Sprinkle with the mint, paprika and cayenne. Garnish with the tomato, drizzle with additional oil and serve immediately.

Makes 4 servings

Poached Eggs with Chopped Tomato Salad and Arugula

Serve with good bread that has been toasted or grilled, rubbed lightly with the cut side of a garlic clove and drizzled with your favorite extra-virgin olive oil. This salad is also excellent served with warm hard-cooked eggs instead of poached eggs.

2 **tomatoes, peeled if the skins are tough, cored, halved, seeded and diced (about 2 cups)**

5 **tablespoons extra-virgin olive oil**

2 **tablespoons chopped fresh basil**

1 **tablespoon chopped fresh mint**

1 **tablespoon minced red onion**

¼ **teaspoon minced garlic**

4 **teaspoons fresh lemon juice**
  Kosher salt and freshly ground black pepper

2 **bunches arugula, stems trimmed, washed, dried and leaves torn if large (about 4 cups)**

2 **tablespoons white vinegar**

4 **large eggs**

1. In a medium bowl, combine the tomatoes, 3 tablespoons of the oil, the basil, mint, onion, garlic, 1 teaspoon of the lemon juice, a pinch of salt and a grinding of pepper. Set aside.

2. In a large bowl, combine the arugula, the remaining 2 tablespoons oil, the remaining 1 tablespoon lemon juice, a pinch of salt and a grinding of pepper and toss to coat. Divide among four salad plates.

3. Fill a large skillet with water, bring to a boil and add the vinegar. Reduce the heat to a simmer. Break the eggs one at a time into a cup and slip them into the water. Cook for about 3 minutes, depending on the desired doneness. With a slotted spoon, remove the eggs in the order you added them to the pan and place on a folded kitchen towel or paper towel. Trim off any ragged whites.

4. Place an egg on top of each bed of arugula and spoon the tomato salad over the eggs, dividing it evenly. Serve at once.

Makes 4 servings

CHAPTER 8 *Pasta and Eggs*

"Nonna never bought her eggs in cartons; she bought them from the chicken man. I always thought they were her special secret. I now know . . . that the wonder is in the Italian imagination and the ability to make so much from so little."

—NANCY VERDE BARR

We've come a long way from the days when "spaghetti" automatically meant meatballs and a puddle of bright red tomato sauce. In the past decade or so, Americans have become vastly more sophisticated about pasta in its many forms and the varied ways it can be prepared. Yet most of us still don't think of "pasta" and "eggs" at the same time. And that's a shame, because both are home-cooking essentials: nutritious, inexpensive, always available and quick and easy to cook. Put them together, and you can have a scrumptious meal on the table in no time.

Take Spaghetti alla Carbonara, the classic Roman dish popular throughout Italy. It combines three of our favorite foods — spaghetti, bacon and eggs — in an amazingly artful dish. And it's also incredibly easy: you just fry the bacon bits, beat the eggs and boil the spaghetti until al dente, then toss them all together in a big bowl with a heap of freshly grated cheese. The steaming spaghetti cooks the eggs and cheese into a lush custardy sauce that coats each strand. In an instant, you've created a hot dish of wonderfully balanced tastes and textures — in less time than it takes to heat up a jar of commercial spaghetti sauce. This is my kind of cooking!

The recipes in this chapter use eggs as a sauce, a filling or an enrichment for different kinds of pasta. Inspired by carbonara, I've created variations on the theme of beaten eggs as a sauce. In one recipe, I scramble eggs just until they start to thicken, then add orecchiette and heavy cream to the pan. The pasta absorbs some of the cream as the eggs continue to cook into the softest of curds (I slip some baby shrimp and tiny peas in there too). In a similar preparation, fresh fettuccine and a flavorful mix of eggs, herbs and cheese are all slowly scrambled together, creating a dish that's as satisfying for breakfast as it is for supper. Comfort food at its best, this recipe — which I've adapted from one of my favorite restaurants in Los Angeles — is aptly named Hugo's Pasta Mama.

Though more unusual, fried eggs also prove to be a fine accompaniment for pasta.

When fried carefully so the whites are soft-set and the yolks are hot but still fluid, they can be tossed with cooked long pasta like spaghetti or with tubular pasta like penne, along with such flavorful ingredients as caramelized onions, roasted peppers, sausage, prosciutto and various cheeses. The eggs break up, the runny yolks forming a natural sauce that clings to the pasta and the shredded whites adding flavor and texture.

Soft whole poached eggs or sliced hard-cooked eggs can be layered between lasagna noodles, along with cheese and sauce, replacing meat. The eggs add substance to the dish and can be complemented by a range of sauces such as pesto, tomato or custardy béchamel. And since baking is such an appealing way to reheat leftover pasta, I often make small indentations in the top of the pasta after I've layered it in a casserole and crack an egg into each hollow. The eggs bake as the noodles reheat and add richness, flavor and a bright look, transforming an old dish into a new one.

Hugo's Pasta Mama

Many years ago, I discovered Hugo's, a favorite hangout for breakfast and brunch in Los Angeles. Hugo's dedicates an entire section of its menu to pasta-and-egg dishes. This dish, one of my favorites, is a medley of soft-scrambled eggs and homemade fettuccine, fragrant with fresh herbs and garlic. I like to make it with butter, but extra-virgin olive oil can be used, if you prefer.

4 tablespoons (½ stick) unsalted butter

1 garlic clove, minced

6 large eggs

¼ cup freshly grated Parmigiano-Reggiano cheese, plus more for serving

2 tablespoons finely chopped fresh flat-leaf parsley

1 teaspoon minced fresh oregano

½ teaspoon kosher salt

Freshly ground black pepper

12 ounces fresh fettuccine

Chopped fresh basil for garnish

1. Melt the butter in a large skillet over medium heat; add the garlic and cook until sizzling, about 1 minute. Remove from the heat and set aside.

2. Whisk together the eggs, cheese, parsley, oregano, salt and a grinding of pepper in a medium bowl. Set aside.

3. Cook the fettuccine in a large pot of boiling salted water until tender, about 5 minutes. Drain and add to the skillet

4. Pour the egg mixture over the fettuccine and cook over medium heat, stirring gently, until the eggs are beginning to set and very hot.

5. Transfer to a serving bowl and sprinkle with more cheese and basil. Serve at once.

Makes 4 servings

You can add sautéed mushrooms, crumbled crisp bacon, strips of cooked chicken, steamed broccoli, browned crumbled Italian sausage or roasted red peppers.

Spaghetti alla Carbonara

Carbonara is a classic Roman dish of steaming-hot spaghetti, bits of crisp cooked pancetta (salt-cured unsmoked Italian bacon) and a delicate custardy coating of egg and cream. American bacon can be used, but because it is smoked, it will give the carbonara a different flavor. The traditional cheese for carbonara is Pecorino Romano, a sharp sheep's milk cheese from the region around Rome and the island of Sardinia. Parmigiano-Reggiano, a cow's milk cheese with a milder flavor, can be used, if preferred. Whatever way you make it, this is an especially easy dish for a quick supper.

1 tablespoon extra-virgin olive oil

4 slices pancetta or thick-cut bacon, cut into ¼-inch pieces

5 large eggs, at room temperature

2 tablespoons heavy cream, at room temperature

1 pound spaghetti

½ cup freshly grated Pecorino Romano cheese, plus extra for serving

Freshly ground black pepper

Finely chopped fresh flat-leaf parsley (optional)

Instead of the cream, you can use milk or the pasta water. If you have fewer than 5 eggs, see the opposite page for guidelines for the proper ratio of pasta to eggs.

1. Heat the oil in a large skillet. Add the pancetta or bacon and cook, stirring, until golden and crisp. Remove to a double layer of paper towels to drain.

2. Meanwhile, whisk the eggs and cream in a medium bowl until well blended. Set aside. Set a large colander in a serving bowl in the sink.

3. Cook the spaghetti in a large pot of boiling salted water until al dente, 10 to 12 minutes. Drain the pasta in the colander and immediately lift it out of the bowl to drain off almost, but not quite, all the water.

4. Dump out the water from the warm bowl; blot dry. Immediately add the spaghetti, the egg mixture and cheese and toss vigorously so that the eggs cook through in the heat from the steaming pasta but do not scramble. Add a liberal grinding of pepper and top with the reserved pancetta or bacon and parsley, if desired. Serve at once with more cheese.

Makes 4 to 6 servings

Spaghetti alla Carbonara
Getting It Right

 The trick to a luscious carbonara is to make sure that you have enough hot spaghetti—and that it's really hot!—to cook the eggs to a custardlike consistency so they cling to the strands. You don't want too much pasta, which may hard-scramble the eggs, nor do you want so many eggs that the pasta is swimming in liquid. (Don't worry, though; even if you goof and your eggs do scramble a bit, the flavor will still be fine.)

First, use these guidelines for the proper proportion of pasta to eggs:

- ♦ For 1 pound spaghetti, use 5 eggs.

- ♦ For 12 ounces spaghetti, use 4 eggs.

- ♦ For 8 ounces spaghetti, use 3 eggs.

Second, have the eggs at room temperature. Beat them with 2 tablespoons heavy cream or milk for extra creaminess. If you have no cream or milk on hand, substitute 2 tablespoons of the hot pasta cooking liquid. (Ladle it out of the pot before you drain the spaghetti.)

Third, have all your ingredients and equipment (serving bowl, etc.) ready before you put the spaghetti into the pot, so you can toss the pasta with the eggs when it is still piping hot.

Spaghetti and Vegetables, Carbonara-Style

This recipe substitutes three popular vegetables—carrots, cauliflower and green beans—for the meat in traditional spaghetti carbonara. Wine, not usually an ingredient in carbonara, adds flavor that is lost when the bacon is omitted.

2 tablespoons unsalted butter

2 garlic cloves, bruised with the side of a knife

¼ cup dry white wine

1 pound spaghetti
  Kosher salt

2 cups 2-inch lengths green beans

1 cup small cauliflower florets

1 cup slender carrot sticks (about ¼ x 2 inches)

5 large eggs, at room temperature

2 tablespoons milk or heavy cream, at room temperature (or use the pasta cooking liquid)

½ cup freshly grated Pecorino Romano cheese, plus extra for serving
  Freshly ground black pepper

1. In a deep skillet that is large enough to contain the cooked spaghetti and vegetables, melt the butter over low heat. Add the garlic and cook, stirring, until golden. Stir in the wine, bring to a boil and boil until reduced by half. Set aside.

2. Meanwhile, cook the spaghetti in a large pot of boiling salted water for 5 minutes. Add the vegetables and boil until spaghetti is al dente and the vegetables are tender, 4 to 6 minutes more.

3. While the pasta and vegetables are cooking, whisk the eggs and milk or cream in a bowl until well blended. Set a colander in a serving bowl in the sink.

4. Drain the pasta and vegetables in the colander and immediately lift out of the bowl to drain off almost, but not quite, all the water. Add the pasta and the vegetables to the skillet. Stir in the egg mixture and the grated cheese and toss vigorously so that the eggs cook through in the heat from the steaming pasta but do not scramble.

5. Dump out the water from the warm bowl; blot dry. Immediately add the spaghetti mixture. Add a liberal grinding of pepper and serve at once with more cheese.

Makes 4 to 6 servings

Spaghetti with Bacon, Soft-Scrambled Eggs and Cream

Adding heavy cream to softly scrambled eggs turns them into a sauce that coats the pasta.

4 slices bacon, cut into ½-inch pieces

6 large eggs

2 tablespoons freshly grated Parmigiano-Reggiano cheese, plus more for serving

2 tablespoons chopped fresh flat-leaf parsley

Kosher salt and freshly ground black pepper

1 pound linguine or spaghetti

2 tablespoons extra-virgin olive oil

1 garlic clove, minced

½ cup heavy cream, or more as needed

1. Cook the bacon in a large skillet until crisp. Drain on paper towels. Discard the bacon fat and wipe out the skillet; reserve the skillet for the eggs and sauce.

2. Whisk together the eggs, cheese, parsley, a pinch of salt and a grinding of pepper in a medium bowl. Set aside.

3. Cook the pasta in a large pot of boiling salted water until al dente, about 12 minutes. Drain.

4. Meanwhile, combine the oil and garlic in the reserved skillet and heat over medium heat just until the garlic begins to sizzle. Reduce the heat to low, add the egg mixture all at once and cook, stirring, just until creamy, about 1 minute. Do not overcook.

5. Add the linguine and cream to the eggs and stir until the cream coats the pasta. Add the bacon, sprinkle with more cheese and serve at once.

Makes 4 servings

VARIATION

For a vegetarian version, substitute 2 cups broccoli florets for the bacon, adding it to the pasta in the water for the last 4 minutes of cooking. Or, for another variation, use both.

Orecchiette with Peas, Baby Shrimp and Scrambled Eggs

Tiny green peas and baby shrimp are a favorite combination of mine, especially with pasta. But perhaps the thing I like best about this dish is that I almost always have the ingredients to make it on hand. All I need to do is boil the water.

12 ounces orecchiette or medium shells

8 ounces cooked baby shrimp, partially thawed if frozen

1 cup tiny green peas, partially thawed if frozen

4 large eggs

½ teaspoon kosher salt
Freshly ground black pepper

2 tablespoons unsalted butter

½–1 cup heavy cream (to taste)

¼ cup freshly grated Parmigiano-Reggiano cheese

2 tablespoons minced fresh chives

1. Cook the pasta in a large pot of boiling salted water until almost al dente, 10 to 15 minutes, depending on the pasta shape. Stir in the shrimp and peas and cook for 1 minute more; drain.

2. Whisk together the eggs, salt and a grinding of pepper in a medium bowl. In a large skillet, melt the butter over low heat. When the foam subsides, add the eggs and cook, stirring, until creamy but not quite cooked, about 3 minutes. Add the pasta mixture, cream, cheese and chives. Heat, stirring, until the pasta absorbs some of the cream. Spoon into a serving bowl and serve at once.

Makes 4 servings

Matching the Egg to the Pasta

 ♦ For chunky pastas like penne, shells or orecchiette (little ears), choose hard-cooked eggs that have been quartered or cut up.

♦ For long, thin pastas like spaghetti or fettuccine, choose fried eggs. As the eggs and pasta are mixed together, the liquid yolk becomes a sauce for the strands and the egg white is torn into thin shreds, matching the shape of the noodles.

♦ For tubular pastas or pastas that have hollows, such as orecchiette, shells or penne rigate, choose scrambled eggs. The crevices will hold bits of the egg, so you'll get a morsel with every bite.

♦ For layered pasta dishes like lasagna, choose hard-cooked eggs cut into thin slices or whole fried or poached eggs.

Spaghetti with Tomato Sauce, Fried Eggs and Prosciutto

Fried eggs sprinkled with a mixture of finely chopped garlic and parsley make a delectable addition to spaghetti with tomato sauce. I've added prosciutto for good measure.

¼ cup extra-virgin olive oil

4 large eggs

¼ cup packed fresh flat-leaf parsley

1 garlic clove

Kosher salt and freshly ground black pepper

½ cup chopped prosciutto (2–3 thin slices)

1 pound spaghetti

1½ cups Simple Tomato Sauce (opposite page)

Freshly grated Parmigiano-Reggiano cheese for serving

1. Heat the oil in a medium skillet over medium-low heat. Add the eggs and fry until the whites are set and the yolks are warm, about 6 minutes.

2. Meanwhile, finely chop the parsley and garlic together. Sprinkle the mixture over the hot eggs. Add a sprinkling of salt and a grinding of pepper, then add the prosciutto and set aside.

3. Cook the spaghetti in a large pot of boiling salted water until al dente, 10 to 12 minutes; drain.

4. Add the tomato sauce to the pasta-cooking pot and bring to a boil. Add the drained spaghetti and the contents of the skillet, including the oil. Immediately toss to coat the spaghetti with the egg yolks and break the whites into small bits. Sprinkle with cheese and serve at once.

Makes 4 servings

Crisp bacon or bits of cooked ham can be substituted for the prosciutto.

Simple Tomato Sauce

2 tablespoons extra-virgin olive oil

¼ cup finely chopped onion

1 garlic clove, minced

1 28-ounce can plum tomatoes, with their juices

Kosher salt and freshly ground black pepper

1. Heat the oil in a large skillet over medium low heat. Add the onion and cook, stirring, until tender. Add the garlic and cook for 1 minute. Add the tomatoes and their juices, breaking up the tomatoes with the side of a spoon, and bring to a boil. Reduce the heat to low and cook, uncovered, until thickened, 15 to 20 minutes. Season with salt to taste and a grinding of pepper and remove from the heat.

2. When the sauce is cool, pass through a food mill or puree in a food processor. You can keep the sauce in the refrigerator for 3 or 4 days or freeze it for later use.

Makes about 2 cups

Spaghetti with Caramelized Onions and Fried Eggs

Fried eggs and pasta are delicious together. The soft-cooked yolks form a sauce that coats the pasta, while the tender whites, torn into shreds, mix with the caramelized onions and crushed red pepper flakes. This dish was inspired by a recipe called Spaghetti Salerno-Style that appears in *Naples at Table*, an excellent cookbook by Arthur Schwartz.

¼ cup extra-virgin olive oil

2 onions, halved and cut into thin slices (about 2 cups)

1 garlic clove, minced

¼ teaspoon crushed red pepper flakes

Kosher salt and freshly ground black pepper

1 pound spaghetti

2 cups small broccoli florets (optional)

4 large eggs

½ cup freshly grated Parmigiano-Reggiano or Pecorino Romano cheese, plus extra for serving

1. Heat the oil in a large skillet over medium-low heat. Add the onions, reduce the heat to low and cook, stirring occasionally, until golden, about 15 minutes. Stir in the garlic, red pepper flakes, salt to taste and a grinding of pepper. Set aside.

2. Cook the spaghetti in a large pot of boiling salted water until al dente, 10 to 12 minutes. If using the broccoli, add it during the last 4 minutes of cooking.

3. Meanwhile, reheat the onions in the skillet over medium-low heat. Break the eggs on top of the onions, spacing them evenly, and cook until the whites are set but the yolks are still runny, about 5 minutes. Sprinkle with salt and pepper.

4. Drain the spaghetti and broccoli, if using, and immediately return to the cooking pot. Add the egg-and-onion mixture and the cheese and stir thoroughly until the yolks coat the spaghetti and the whites break up into pieces. Serve at once, with additional cheese on the side.

Makes 4 servings

Penne with Sausage, Peppers, Eggs and Ricotta Salata

My mother's sweet Italian sausage and green peppers and scrambled eggs were a favorite Sunday-morning ritual when I was a child. I've combined these elements with pasta and cheese. Ricotta salata, a dried salted ricotta, is becoming more readily available, but any dry, crumbly cheese, such as an aged goat cheese or a very mild feta, can be used instead.

6 links sweet Italian sausage, removed from the casings and broken into ½-inch lumps

5 tablespoons extra-virgin olive oil

2 large green bell peppers, cored, seeded and ribs removed, cut into thin strips

1 garlic clove, minced
  Kosher salt and freshly ground black pepper

4 large eggs

2 tablespoons finely chopped fresh flat-leaf parsley
  Pinch of crushed red pepper flakes

1 pound penne

8 ounces ricotta salata, crumbled

1. In a large, preferably nonstick skillet, cook the sausage over medium heat until lightly browned. With a slotted spoon, transfer to a large serving bowl.

2. Discard any fat from the pan and add 1 tablespoon of the oil to the skillet. Add the bell peppers and fry over medium-high heat until the edges begin to char, about 10 minutes. Reduce the heat to low, add the garlic and cook for about 1 minute; do not brown the garlic. Remove from the heat, sprinkle with salt to taste and a grinding of pepper and add to the bowl with the sausage.

3. Add the remaining ¼ cup oil to the skillet and heat over medium-low heat. Break the eggs one at a time into a cup, and add to the skillet. Fry until the whites are set, spooning the hot oil over the yolks. Sprinkle with the parsley and red pepper flakes. Slide into the bowl with the sausage and peppers. (It's OK if the yolks break, because all the ingredients will eventually be tossed together.)

4. Meanwhile, cook the penne in a large pot of boiling salted water until al dente, 10 to 12 minutes; drain.

5. Add the pasta to the bowl with the sausage, add the cheese and toss to break up the eggs. Serve at once.

Makes 4 servings

Macaroni with Tomato Sauce, Baked Eggs and Ricotta

Mixing pasta with tomato sauce, topping it with cheese and baking it is a convenient way to use up leftover pasta or to simplify preparation by making a dish ahead of time. Tucking eggs into the pasta adds richness.

12 ounces (about 6 cups leftover cooked) elbow macaroni

2–2½ cups Simple Tomato Sauce (page 263)

1 cup ricotta cheese

2 tablespoons finely chopped fresh flat-leaf parsley

4 large eggs

½ cup freshly grated Parmigiano-Reggiano cheese

1. Preheat the oven to 350°F. If using uncooked macaroni, cook in a large pot of boiling salted water until al dente, 8 to 10 minutes; drain.

2. Combine the macaroni with half of the tomato sauce, the ricotta and parsley. Spread in a 1½-quart (6-x-10-inch) baking dish. (The macaroni can be prepared to this point up to 1 day ahead. Refrigerate, covered, until 20 minutes before baking.)

3. Make 4 evenly spaced indentations in the macaroni and break an egg into each. Pour the remaining sauce over the top. Sprinkle with the cheese.

4. Bake until the eggs are set and the cheese is golden, 20 to 25 minutes. Serve immediately.

Makes 4 servings

I like to use elbow macaroni for this dish, but any shape will do.

Making Great Pasta Dishes from What's on Hand

 ♦ To 1 pound of hot spaghetti add 4 sunny-side-up eggs (page 24) and 2 garlic cloves, chopped, sautéed in ¼ cup olive oil until softened. Season with crushed red pepper flakes. Dust with freshly grated Pecorino Romano, provolone or Asiago cheese.

♦ To 1 pound of shells, add 2 cups cut-up broccoli rabe or broccoli or cauliflower florets during the last 4 minutes of cooking. Drain, reserving ⅓ cup of the cooking water, and add 3 or 4 eggs, scrambled in butter, the reserved pasta water, 1 cup diced ripe tomatoes and freshly grated Parmigiano-Reggiano to taste.

♦ To 1 pound of hot linguine, add 5 room-temperature eggs, whisked with 2 tablespoons heavy cream or milk, along with 1 bag (8 ounces) baby spinach, rinsed, or 2 cups thin strips zucchini and carrot, sautéed in butter until tender, and freshly grated Parmigiano-Reggiano to taste.

Spring Pasta with Eggs, Asparagus and Ham

Hard-cooked eggs, asparagus and ham make a pleasant springtime pasta. You can assemble this dish ahead of time and bake just before serving. Serve as a first course, followed by roast meat and vegetables, or as a main dish.

2 tablespoons unsalted butter

2 tablespoons finely chopped onion

2 tablespoons all-purpose flour

2½ cups milk

⅓ cup freshly grated Parmigiano-Reggiano cheese

8 ounces pasta, such as penne, penne rigate, conchiglie or gemelli

8 ounces asparagus, trimmed and cut into ½-inch diagonal pieces

½ cup tiny green peas, thawed if frozen

½ cup coarsely chopped carrots

1 cup shredded smoked ham

4 large eggs, hard-cooked (page 162), peeled and coarsely chopped

1 cup grated fontina cheese (about 4 ounces)

1. Preheat the oven to 350°F. Melt the butter in a large saucepan over medium heat. Add the onion and cook, stirring, until golden, about 5 minutes. Whisk in the flour until smooth and cook, stirring, for 2 minutes. Gradually whisk in the milk, bring to a boil, stirring, and cook until thickened, about 10 minutes. Stir in the Parmigiano-Reggiano and remove from the heat. Set aside.

2. Cook the pasta in a large pot of boiling salted water for 6 minutes. Add the asparagus, peas and carrots and cook until the pasta is firm to the bite, 2 to 3 minutes more. Drain.

3. Add the pasta and vegetables and the ham to the cheese sauce. Transfer half the mixture to a 2-quart baking dish. Top with half the hard-cooked eggs. Spoon the remaining pasta on top. Add the remaining eggs and sprinkle with the fontina.

4. Bake until the top is golden, about 25 minutes. Serve immediately.

Makes 4 servings

> *Vary the vegetables according to the season, or omit the ham to make this a meatless entrée for two.*

Fresh Pasta with Poached Eggs, Toasted Walnuts and Parmesan

At the Restaurant San Domenico in New York City, I ate a memorable raviolo encasing a soft-cooked egg yolk. The pasta square was large enough to fill the bottom of a shallow bowl and was smothered in melted butter, grated Parmigiano-Reggiano and finely chopped walnuts. My version is simple to prepare, and when I served it to friends, they were wowed.

8 tablespoons (1 stick) unsalted butter

2 tablespoons white vinegar

4 large eggs

8 4-inch squares fresh pasta (only fresh will do)

¼ cup freshly grated Parmigiano-Reggiano cheese

½ cup broken walnuts, lightly toasted (page 56) and finely chopped

It takes some kitchen acrobatics to coordinate the assembly of this dish, so don't try to make more than 4 servings at a time.

1. Bring a large saucepan of salted water to a boil.

2. Meanwhile, melt the butter in a small saucepan. Set aside over very low heat to keep warm.

3. Heat the oven to the lowest setting and place four shallow bowls in it to heat.

4. Line a plate with a double layer of paper towels. Fill a deep skillet with water, bring to a boil and add the vinegar. Reduce the heat to a simmer. Break the eggs one at a time into a cup, slip them into the water and cook for 3 minutes. When you have added the last egg to the pan, add the pasta to the boiling salted water and stir gently. When the eggs are ready, with a slotted spoon, remove them from the pan in the order you added them and place on the paper towels. Trim off any ragged whites. Cover with foil to keep warm.

5. When the pasta is cooked to taste, 3 to 5 minutes, drain it. Immediately set out the warm bowls and spoon about 1 tablespoon of the melted butter into each dish. Top with a square of pasta, place an egg in the center of each pasta square and top with a second square of pasta. Drizzle with the remaining butter, sprinkle each serving with 1 tablespoon of the cheese and scatter the walnuts over the top. Serve immediately.

Makes 4 servings

Lasagna with Pesto and Poached Eggs in Parmesan Custard

Pesto, the Ligurian specialty of pureed basil, pine nuts, garlic and Parmigiano-Reggiano, is delicious served over poached or fried eggs. It also makes a superb sauce for lasagna layered with poached eggs and a rich Parmesan custard.

Pesto

- 1 **cup pine nuts, lightly toasted (see box)**
- 2 **garlic cloves, chopped**
- 2 **cups tightly packed fresh basil leaves**
- 1 **teaspoon kosher salt**
- ⅔ **cup extra-virgin olive oil**
- ½ **cup freshly grated Parmigiano-Reggiano cheese**

Parmesan Custard

- 4 **tablespoons (½ stick) unsalted butter**
- ¼ **cup all-purpose flour**
- 2 **cups milk**
- 1 **cup canned reduced-sodium chicken broth, fat skimmed**
- 3 **large eggs**
- ½ **cup freshly grated Parmigiano-Reggiano cheese**
- ½ **teaspoon kosher salt, or to taste**
  Pinch of cayenne pepper
  Pinch of freshly grated nutmeg

1. **Make the pesto:** Finely chop the pine nuts and garlic in a food processor. Add the basil and salt and finely chop. With the motor running, add the oil in a slow, steady stream until incorporated. Scrape the mixture into a small bowl and stir in the cheese. Set aside. (The pesto can be made 1 to 2 days ahead and stored, tightly covered, in the refrigerator.)

2. **Make the custard:** Melt the butter in a medium saucepan over medium heat. Whisk in the flour until smooth and cook, whisking, for 2 minutes. Gradually whisk in the milk until smooth and bring to a boil. Add the broth and cook, whisking, until thick and smooth, about 10 minutes.

3. Meanwhile, beat the 3 eggs in a medium bowl. Whisk a spoonful of the sauce into the eggs, then whisk the eggs into the sauce. Remove from the heat and stir in the cheese, salt, cayenne and nutmeg. Set aside.

4. Cook the lasagna noodles in a large pot of boiling salted water until al dente, about 10 minutes. Drain and place in a large bowl of cold water until ready to use.

5. Fill a deep skillet with water, bring to a boil and add the vinegar. Reduce the heat to a simmer. Break 4 of the eggs one at a time into a cup and slip them into the water. Cook until the whites are set and the yolks are still runny, about 3 minutes. With a slotted spoon, remove the eggs in the order you added them to the

12 lasagna noodles

2 tablespoons white vinegar

8 large eggs

1½ cups ricotta cheese

½ cup freshly grated
Parmigiano-Reggiano cheese

2 cups grated fontina or
mozzarella cheese
(about 8 ounces)

3–5 fresh basil leaves

pan and place on a folded kitchen towel or paper towel; cover lightly with plastic wrap. Repeat with the remaining 4 eggs.

6. Preheat the oven to 350°F. Stir the ricotta and Parmigiano-Reggiano until blended; set aside. Spread 1 cup of the custard in the bottom of a 13-x-9-inch baking dish. Lift the lasagna noodles from the water and blot dry. Arrange 4 noodles, slightly overlapping, in the bottom of the dish. Spread with half of the pesto. Arrange 4 of the eggs evenly on top of the pesto. Drop half of the ricotta, by the tablespoon, between the eggs. Sprinkle with one-third of the fontina or mozzarella. Repeat the layers with 4 more noodles, the remaining pesto, the remaining 4 eggs, the remaining ricotta and another one-third of the fontina or mozzarella. Top with the remaining 4 noodles. Spoon the remaining custard on top of the noodles, pulling the noodles away from the edges of the dish so the sauce can seep to the bottom. Place the basil leaves on top. Sprinkle with the remaining fontina or mozzarella.

7. Bake until the lasagna is bubbly and golden, about 30 minutes. Let stand for 10 minutes before serving.

Makes 6 to 8 servings

TO TOAST PINE NUTS: *Spread in a dry skillet and toast over low heat, stirring constantly, just until they begin to color, 3 to 5 minutes. Do not leave unattended, as they burn easily. Transfer to a plate to cool.*

Lasagna with Eggs, Artichokes and Mushrooms

Hard-cooked egg slices add richness to this vegetarian lasagna. The tomato sauce can be a good-quality store-bought one or homemade.

4 medium or 2 large artichokes
  Kosher salt

6 lasagna noodles

3 tablespoons extra-virgin olive oil

12 ounces large white mushrooms, trimmed, wiped clean and thinly sliced (about 3 cups)

¼ cup packed chopped fresh flat-leaf parsley

1 ½-x-2-inch strip lemon zest, chopped

1 garlic clove, minced
  Freshly ground black pepper

2 cups tomato sauce, store-bought or homemade (page 263)

8 large eggs, hard-cooked (page 162), peeled and thinly sliced

2 cups grated mozzarella or fontina cheese (about 8 ounces) or 1 cup of each

¼ cup freshly grated Parmigiano-Reggiano cheese

1. Slice off the stem and remove a few of the outside leaves from each artichoke. Turn each artichoke on its side and cut off about 1 inch of the top. Place in a large saucepan with the salt, add water and bring to a boil. Cover and simmer until the artichokes are very tender when pierced with a skewer, 25 to 35 minutes, depending on the size. Remove the artichokes from the water, turn them cut side down to drain and let cool.

2. Pull off all the leaves from each artichoke and remove and discard the sharp purple-edged center core of leaves. Using a teaspoon, scrape away the fuzzy center (choke). With a paring knife, trim the bottoms (hearts) neatly. Thinly slice the bottoms and set aside. (The artichokes can be prepared ahead to this point; cover and refrigerate until ready to use.)

3. Cook the lasagna noodles in a large pot of boiling salted water until al dente, about 10 minutes; drain. Place in a bowl of cold water until ready to use.

4. Heat the oil in a large skillet over medium heat. Add the mushrooms and cook, stirring, until golden brown, about 8 minutes. Add the parsley, lemon zest and garlic and cook for 1 minute. Add the artichokes and sprinkle with salt to taste and a grinding of pepper. Cook, stirring gently, until heated through. Set aside.

Cook the artichokes up to 1 day ahead, remove the leaves and save for snacks. Children especially love to scrape the soft sweet artichoke flesh from each leaf with their teeth.

5. Preheat the oven to 350°F. Spread 1 cup of the tomato sauce in the bottom of a 13-x-9-inch baking dish. Arrange 2 lasagna noodles, side by side, in the bottom of the dish. Top with half of the artichoke mixture. Layer half of the egg slices over the top and sprinkle with one-third of the mozzarella and/or fontina and half of the Parmigiano-Reggiano. Repeat the layers with 2 more lasagna noodles, the remaining artichoke mixture, the remaining eggs, another one-third of the mozzarella and/or fontina and the remaining Parmigiano-Reggiano. Top with the remaining 2 lasagna noodles. Spread the remaining 1 cup tomato sauce over the top and sprinkle with the remaining mozzarella and/or fontina.

6. Bake until the top is melted and bubbly, about 30 minutes. Let stand for 10 minutes or more before serving.

Makes 4 to 6 servings

Gnocchi with Butter and Herbs

These gnocchi are made with semolina and egg yolks, giving them richness and a smooth texture. Serve them layered with the herb-and-butter sauce below or a light tomato sauce. When you have the time to make an especially memorable meal, this is it.

4 **cups whole milk**

4 **tablespoons (½ stick) unsalted butter**

1 **teaspoon kosher salt**

¼ **teaspoon freshly grated nutmeg**

1¼ **cups semolina flour**

4 **large egg yolks**

1½ **cups freshly grated Parmigiano-Reggiano cheese (about 6 ounces)**

Sauce

4 **tablespoons (½ stick) unsalted butter**

2 **tablespoons minced fresh flat-leaf parsley**

1 **teaspoon fresh thyme leaves**

½ **teaspoon minced fresh rosemary**

Freshly ground black pepper

1. Heat the milk, butter, salt and nutmeg in a large, wide saucepan over medium heat until very hot, but do not allow to boil. Gradually add the semolina, shaking it from a large cup while stirring constantly with a whisk, and whisk until the mixture boils and is smooth. Reduce the heat to low and cook, stirring constantly with a flat-bottomed wooden spoon, for 10 minutes, or until the mixture is extremely thick. Remove from the heat and let cool for 10 minutes, stirring occasionally.

2. Place the egg yolks in a small bowl and whisk to blend. Add a couple of big spoonfuls of the cooled semolina mixture to the yolks, stirring until well blended. Add the egg-yolk mixture to the semolina in the pan, then add 1 cup of the cheese and stir until blended.

3. Lightly brush a 14-x-10½-inch baking sheet with olive oil. Pour the semolina mixture onto the pan and spread in an even layer with a rubber spatula. Let stand at room temperature for 1 hour, or until the semolina has set enough to cut into shapes.

4. **Meanwhile, make the sauce:** Melt the butter in a small saucepan. Add the parsley, thyme, rosemary and a grinding of pepper. Remove from the heat.

5. Preheat the oven to 400°F. Lightly butter a 13-x-9-inch baking dish.

6. Cut the semolina into 2-x-3-inch squares (four across and five down). Arrange the squares in rows in the baking dish, slightly overlapping them. Drizzle with the butter sauce. Sprinkle with ¼ cup of the remaining cheese.

7. Bake the gnocchi until the top is golden brown, 25 to 30 minutes. Serve hot, sprinkling the remaining ¼ cup cheese on top.

Makes 4 servings

Semolina, coarsely ground durum wheat, is available in the grain section of health-food stores, Italian markets and some supermarkets. The semolina mixture can be made up to 24 hours ahead and refrigerated. You may need to bake it for about 10 minutes more, or as needed, to heat it through.

CHAPTER 9 *Quiches, Savory Pies and Side Dish Custards*

"Bring back the quiche."

—JULIA CHILD

B ack in the '70s, during my early days in the food business, quiche was on the culinary cutting edge—so unfamiliar that most people didn't even know how to pronounce its name. When I was managing the food service at the Brooklyn Academy of Music, one of New York's premier performing arts theaters, one of our most popular items was classic quiche Lorraine, cut into small squares. I'll never forget how high-class operagoers and ballet aficionados would crowd our counter, clamoring for a piece of "keetchy."

They learned to say "keesh" pretty quickly, though, because it soon appeared on every restaurant menu, from organic vegetarian cafés to swank dinner spots. But after a few years of gastronomic stardom, quiche lost its luster. Perhaps it was a victim of its own popularity. Maybe some guys got scared off by the best-selling humor book of the era, *Real Men Don't Eat Quiche*. (I can attest that this is a falsehood, judging from the hearty appetites of the men in my life.) Certainly, the fear of egg consumption that arose about the same time didn't help quiche's reputation either.

But when quiche disappeared from the food scene, I missed it!—and I started making it at home again. I went back to the traditional quiche Lorraine, named for the region of Alsace-Lorraine where this savory pastry was first created. With its rich flavor and delightful textural contrasts—creamy custard, crisp bits of bacon and flaky pastry crust—this must be the finest form that mere bacon-and-eggs can assume.

Many cooks, I know, are discouraged from spur-of-the-moment quiche making because they've no pie dough on hand and find it a difficult procedure. Not me. I am one of the happy few who actually enjoy producing homemade piecrusts. I admit that mixing the dough, then rolling, forming and prebaking the pastry shell so it will be crisp and flaky when served are humble, time-consuming tasks—but they're pleasing to me. And it's the only way to get a really delicious crust. My favorite piecrust recipe and techniques are outlined on page 282, and I guarantee the results are worth the effort.

I use this same crust for the savory pies and tortas in this chapter, double-crusted pastries that enclose beaten or hard-cooked eggs and a host of other tasty ingredients. These can be a hot main course for dinner or just a cold snack at a picnic. And if you'd just rather not bother with piecrust at all, you can make "crustless" quiches (page 280) and use store-bought filo pastry for the egg pies.

The base for all my quiche fillings is the same simple custard, a hand-beaten mixture of eggs and cream. But in this chapter you'll also find elegant cousins to the quiche: more refined and sophisticated savory custards, baked in individual ramekins or molds (sometimes called timbales). Each variation has a dramatically silky texture and subtle flavor derived from steeping herbs, spices and aromatic vegetables in the milk before baking. Unmolded and garnished, they make a beautiful first course or small entrée.

The Perfect Pan for Quiche

 A Pyrex pie plate has the perfect capacity for the fillings in all my quiche recipes. The widely available heavy tin or porcelain quiche dishes with fluted sides look fancier, but prebaking crusts in them is tricky.

Making Quiche Without a Crust

 Any quiche filling can be baked without a crust. Preheat the oven to 350°F. Lightly butter a 9-inch Pyrex pie plate or an 8-inch square baking dish and add the filling and cheese. Pour the cream-and-egg mixture over top. Bake until golden and puffed, 25 to 30 minutes. Serve warm or at room temperature, cut into wedges or small squares.

Mushroom, Onion and Bacon Quiche with Gruyère

The true quiche Lorraine is made with bits of bacon but without cheese. Although I love the purity of the classic recipe, I can't imagine quiche without cheese, so this variation incorporates Gruyère. Other quiches may sound more exotic, but this version is still my favorite.

4 slices bacon

1 tablespoon extra-virgin olive oil

12 ounces mushrooms (one kind or a mixture of white button, shiitakes and creminis), trimmed (if using shiitakes, discard the stems), wiped clean and thinly sliced

½ cup finely chopped onion

1 tablespoon finely chopped fresh flat-leaf parsley

1 garlic clove, minced

Kosher salt and freshly ground black pepper

3 large eggs

1 cup half-and-half

2 teaspoons prepared mustard

1 9-inch pie shell (page 282), baked

¾ cup grated Gruyère cheese

1. Preheat the oven to 375°F. Cook the bacon in a large skillet until semicrisp; drain on paper towels.

2. Discard all but 1 tablespoon of the bacon fat from the pan. Add the oil to the skillet and heat over medium heat. Add the mushrooms and onion and cook, stirring, until the mushrooms are lightly browned and the onion is tender, about 5 minutes. Add the parsley and garlic and cook for 1 minute more. Season with salt to taste and a grinding of pepper. Remove from the heat.

3. Snip the bacon into ¼-inch pieces and add to the mushroom mixture.

4. In a large bowl, whisk the eggs until light. Stir in the half-and-half and mustard. Spoon the mushroom mixture evenly into the pie shell. Sprinkle with the cheese and add the egg mixture.

5. Bake the quiche until puffed and golden brown, about 35 minutes. Serve warm or at room temperature, cut into wedges.

Makes 6 servings

Piecrust for Quiche

The crust for quiche must be prebaked to prevent it from becoming soggy when it is filled with the custard and baked again. Prebaking a pie shell is sometimes called "blind" baking (presumably because lining the formed shell with foil or parchment paper prevents the cook from seeing it). Dried beans or rice or store-bought weights designed especially for this technique hold the foil in place and prevent the crust from puffing up or slipping down into the pan as it bakes. In this crust, I use solid vegetable shortening for extra flakiness and a small amount of butter for flavor. The recipe can be doubled to make 2 crusts.

1½ **cups all-purpose flour**

1 **teaspoon kosher salt**

⅓ **cup solid vegetable shortening**

3 **tablespoons cold unsalted butter, cut into small dice**

About ½ cup ice water

1. Stir the flour and salt together in a mixing bowl. Using a pastry cutter, cut in the shortening and butter until evenly distributed in coarse crumbs throughout the mixture.

2. Sprinkle 2 tablespoons of the ice water over the crumbs and toss the mixture with a fork to incorporate and moisten it evenly. Repeat, adding 1 tablespoon water at a time, until the mixture begins to hold together in a ball. (You probably won't use all the water.) The dough should be moist but not wet. Press into a disk, wrap in foil and refrigerate for at least 20 minutes, but preferably 1 hour or longer.

3. Preheat the oven to 375°F. Place the dough on a lightly floured board or a pastry cloth sprinkled with flour. Dust a rolling pin with flour or cover with a rolling pin "stocking."

Roll the dough from the center out to the edges, changing the direction with every roll, making a circle about 13 inches in diameter; occasionally lift the dough to turn it a quarter turn or turn it over.

4. Fold the dough in half or in quarters and transfer to a 9-inch Pyrex pie plate. Ease the dough into the plate. Fold the edges under to make a generous rim around the edges of the pan. Using your thumb and index finger held at an angle, flute the crust into a high rim.

5. Cut a square of foil (or parchment paper) large enough to cover the bottom and sides of the pie shell. Line the pie shell with the foil and weight the foil with 1 cup of dried beans or rice (or pie weights), spread in an even layer.

6. Bake for 20 minutes. Remove from the oven. Lift the foil and weights from the pie shell. Prick any bubbles in the shell with the tip of a knife and bake for 5 minutes more. Transfer to a rack to cool.

Makes one 9-inch piecrust

Yellow Tomato and Ham Quiche with Two Cheeses

Almost any tomato can be used in this quiche, although I like the appearance and taste of the yellow tomatoes, which have less acid and are just a little sweeter than red tomatoes. Today, especially if you live near a tomato farm, you can select from dozens of types of tomatoes. They come in green (yes, these are ripe and sweet even though they are green), red, green or yellow striped (called zebra) and purple, in plum shapes or small globes and many more. One of my favorites is a yellow tomato called the pineapple tomato, and it does taste just a little like pineapple.

2 tablespoons extra-virgin olive oil

2 cups wedges yellow tomatoes (about 2 medium), seeds removed

1 garlic clove, minced

¼ cup torn fresh basil leaves

½ teaspoon kosher salt
Freshly ground black pepper

3 large eggs

1 cup half-and-half

1 9-inch pie shell (page 282), baked

½ cup chopped ham

½ cup freshly grated Parmigiano-Reggiano cheese

½ cup grated mozzarella cheese

1. Preheat the oven to 375°F. Heat the oil in a large skillet. Add the tomatoes and garlic and sauté, stirring gently, just until the tomatoes are heated through, about 2 minutes. Sprinkle with the basil, salt and a grinding of pepper. Set aside to cool. Spoon off any excess liquid.

2. In a large bowl, whisk the eggs until light. Stir in the half-and-half. Spoon the tomato mixture into the pie shell. Scatter the ham over it and sprinkle evenly with the cheeses. Pour in the egg mixture.

3. Bake the quiche until puffed and golden brown, about 35 minutes. Serve warm or at room temperature, cut into wedges.

Makes 6 servings

Sausage, Caramelized Onion and Roasted Red Pepper Quiche

I prefer Italian sausage with fennel seeds in this quiche, but if it isn't available, you can add ½ teaspoon fennel seeds, crushed in a mortar and pestle or with the side of a heavy knife, to the sautéed onion.

8   ounces sweet Italian sausage, casings removed, broken into small lumps

2   tablespoons extra-virgin olive oil

1   large onion, halved length-wise and cut lengthwise into thin slivers (about 2 cups)

1   garlic clove, minced

1   red bell pepper, roasted (page 75) and diced (about ⅓ cup)

   Kosher salt and freshly ground black pepper

3   large eggs

1   cup half-and-half

1   9-inch pie shell (page 282), baked

½   cup grated mozzarella cheese

½   cup freshly grated Parmigiano-Reggiano cheese

1. Preheat the oven to 375°F. Cook the sausage in a large skillet over high heat, breaking it up with a spatula, until lightly browned. Transfer to a small bowl and set aside.

2. Discard any fat in the skillet and wipe it clean with a paper towel. Add the oil to the skillet and heat over medium-low heat. Add the onion and cook, stirring, until golden and soft, about 10 minutes. Add the garlic and cook for 1 minute more. Stir in the roasted pepper, sausage, a pinch of salt and a generous grinding of pepper.

3. In a large bowl, whisk the eggs until light. Stir in the half-and-half. Spoon the sausage mixture evenly into the pie shell. Sprinkle with the cheeses and pour in the egg mixture.

4. Bake the quiche until puffed and golden brown, about 35 minutes. Serve warm or at room temperature, cut into wedges.

Makes 6 servings

Caramelized Tomato and Corn Quiche with Basil and Cheddar

This quiche combines three of my favorite summer flavors: tomatoes, corn and basil. Browning tomatoes in oil on top of the stove or in a hot oven concentrates their sugars and gives them an added depth of flavor.

2 tablespoons extra-virgin olive oil

4–5 plum tomatoes, cored and halved lengthwise

Kosher salt and freshly ground black pepper

1 garlic clove, minced

1 9-inch pie shell (page 282), baked

1 cup fresh corn kernels (cut from 1½ ears) or frozen corn, thawed

¼ cup loosely packed chopped fresh basil

1 jalapeño or other chile (optional), seeded and finely chopped (about 1 tablespoon), or more to taste

1 cup grated sharp cheddar cheese (about 4 ounces)

3 large eggs

1 cup half-and-half

1. Preheat the oven to 375°F. Heat the oil in a large nonstick skillet over high heat. Add the tomatoes, cut side down, and cook, without turning, until the bottoms begin to brown, about 10 minutes. Sprinkle with salt and a grinding of pepper and add the garlic. Gently turn the tomatoes so they don't fall apart and cook for 3 minutes more. Remove from the heat and let cool.

2. Arrange the tomatoes, cut side up, in the pie shell; reserve the juices in the pan. Top the tomatoes with the corn, basil and chile, if using. Sprinkle with the cheese.

3. In a large bowl, whisk the eggs until light. Stir in the half-and-half and the reserved juices. Pour into the pie shell.

4. Bake the quiche until puffed and golden brown, about 35 minutes. Serve warm or at room temperature, cut into wedges.

Makes 6 servings

Broccoli and Provolone Quiche

Provolone, a southern Italian cow's milk cheese, was a staple at home when I was a child. It came in a fat pear shape, tied with a string for hanging. My father's favorite snack before dinner was a piece of bread and a slice of provolone cheese. At the time, I thought it was smelly and strong-tasting, but as an adult, I have learned to appreciate its firm, chewy texture, salty edge and slightly smoky flavor. Provolone works very well in this quiche with the assertive flavors of broccoli, red onion and crushed red pepper flakes.

3 cups coarsely chopped broccoli florets and tender stems

2 tablespoons extra-virgin olive oil

1 garlic clove, minced

Pinch of crushed red pepper flakes

¼ cup minced red onion

½ teaspoon kosher salt

Freshly ground black pepper

3 large eggs

1 cup half-and-half

1 9-inch pie shell (page 282), baked

1 cup grated moderately sharp provolone cheese (about 4 ounces)

1. Preheat the oven to 375°F. Place the broccoli in a steamer basket and steam over boiling water until tender, about 4 minutes. Remove the steamer basket from the saucepan and set aside.

2. Combine the oil, garlic and red pepper flakes in a large skillet and cook, stirring, over medium-low heat just until the garlic begins to sizzle. Add the broccoli and cook for 1 minute more. Remove from the heat. Stir in the onion and sprinkle with the salt and a grinding of pepper.

3. In a large bowl, whisk the eggs until light. Stir in the half-and-half. Spoon the broccoli mixture evenly into the pie shell. Sprinkle with the cheese and pour in the egg mixture.

4. Bake the quiche until puffed and golden brown, about 35 minutes. Serve warm or at room temperature, cut into wedges.

Makes 6 servings

> **Be sure to use imported Italian provolone, not American sandwich provolone, which is a pale imitation.**

Spinach and Mushroom Quiche with Pine Nuts and Blue Cheese

The toasted pine nuts are delicious in this quiche, but coarsely chopped pecans or hazelnuts would be good too. I like the salty, sharp taste of American Maytag blue cheese, but Gorgonzola or Stilton can be used.

1 10- or 12-ounce bag spinach, stems trimmed, rinsed, with water still clinging to the leaves

2 tablespoons extra-virgin olive oil

2 cups chopped mushrooms

1 garlic clove, minced
  Kosher salt and freshly ground black pepper

3 large eggs

1 cup half-and-half

1 9-inch pie shell (page 282), baked

1 cup crumbled blue cheese (about 3 ounces)

3 tablespoons pine nuts, lightly toasted (page 271)

1. Preheat the oven to 375°F. Place the spinach in a large pot, cover and cook over medium-low heat just until wilted, about 3 minutes. Remove from the heat and spoon into a strainer set over a bowl. Let cool.

2. Press hard on the spinach in the strainer with the back of a spoon to remove most of the moisture, then squeeze in your hands to remove more. Turn out onto a cutting board and coarsely chop. Place between two layers of paper towels or wrap in a clean kitchen towel and press to remove more moisture. You should have about 1 cup packed spinach. Set aside.

3. Heat the oil in a large skillet over medium heat. Add the mushrooms and cook, stirring, until tender, about 5 minutes. Add the garlic and cook for 1 minute more. Add the spinach and cook, stirring, until any remaining moisture has evaporated, about 2 minutes. Remove from the heat. Add a pinch of salt (the blue cheese is salty, so you won't need much) and a grinding of pepper.

4. In a large bowl, whisk the eggs until light. Stir in the half-and-half. Spoon the spinach mixture evenly into the pie shell. Sprinkle with the cheese and pine nuts. Pour in the egg mixture.

5. Bake the quiche until puffed and golden brown, about 35 minutes. Serve warm or at room temperature, cut into wedges.

Makes 6 servings

Lemon, Leek and Dill Quiche with Feta Cheese

Feta is a zesty addition to creamy quiche, and it balances the sweetness of the leeks in this filling.

2 tablespoons unsalted butter

2 medium leeks, roots and green tops trimmed, thoroughly washed and chopped (about 2 cups)

¼ cup water

3 tablespoons chopped fresh dill

½ teaspoon kosher salt
Freshly ground black pepper

3 large eggs

1 cup half-and-half

1 teaspoon grated lemon zest

1 9-inch pie shell (page 282), baked

1 cup crumbled feta cheese (about 4 ounces)

1. Preheat the oven to 375°F. Melt the butter in a large skillet over low heat. Add the leeks and water, cover and cook for 5 minutes, or until the leeks are very tender. Add the dill and cook, uncovered, stirring, to evaporate the excess moisture. Add the salt and a grinding of pepper. Remove from the heat.

2. In a large bowl, whisk the eggs until light. Stir in the half-and-half and lemon zest. Spoon the leek mixture evenly into the pie shell. Sprinkle with the feta and pour in the egg mixture.

3. Bake the quiche until puffed and golden brown, about 35 minutes. Serve warm or at room temperature, cut into wedges.

Makes 6 servings

Artichoke and Goat Cheese Quiche with Roasted Red Peppers

If you live where artichokes are fresh, inexpensive and plentiful, cook them and use the tender, fleshy hearts in the filling of this quiche. I often cook artichokes when I have the time and reserve them for pasta dishes, frittatas and quiches for upcoming meals. They keep for several days and can also be frozen, tightly wrapped.

2 **large artichokes, stems trimmed, or one 8-ounce package frozen artichoke hearts, cooked according to package directions, drained, patted dry and cut into ½-inch pieces**

Kosher salt

1 **tablespoon extra-virgin olive oil**

1 **garlic clove, minced**

1 **red bell pepper, roasted (page 75) and diced (or use a good-quality store-bought roasted pepper, rinsed)**

1 **teaspoon fresh thyme leaves**

Freshly ground black pepper

3 **large eggs**

1 **cup half-and-half**

1 **9-inch pie shell (page 282), baked**

¾ **cup crumbled goat cheese (about 3 ounces)**

1. Preheat the oven to 375°F. If using fresh artichokes, rinse and place in a saucepan large enough to hold them tightly, add water to cover and 1 teaspoon salt and bring to a boil. Cover and simmer until tender when pierced with a skewer, 25 to 35 minutes, depending on their size. Drain and let cool.

2. Remove the outer leaves from each artichoke. Remove and discard the thorny-tipped center core of leaves. Scoop out the fuzzy centers (chokes). Cut the bottoms (hearts) into ½-inch dice. You should have about 1½ cups.

3. Heat the oil in a large skillet over medium-low heat. Add the artichokes and garlic and cook, stirring, until the artichokes are coated with the oil and garlic, about 3 minutes. Remove from the heat. Add the roasted pepper, thyme, a sprinkling of salt and a generous grinding of pepper.

4. In a large bowl, whisk the eggs until light. Stir in the half-and-half. Spoon the artichoke mixture evenly into the pie shell. Sprinkle with the cheese and pour in the egg mixture.

5. Bake the quiche until puffed and golden brown, about 35 minutes. Serve warm or at room temperature, cut into wedges.

Makes 6 servings

Fresh Salmon and Asparagus Quiche with Parmesan

I like to herald the arrival of spring by serving salmon and asparagus—often in this quiche —followed by fresh strawberries for dessert.

1 garlic clove, crushed with the side of a knife

1 fresh dill sprig

Kosher salt

1 8-ounce salmon fillet

12 ounces asparagus, trimmed and cut into ½-inch diagonal slices

1 tablespoon unsalted butter

¼ cup minced shallots

1 teaspoon minced fresh thyme

½ teaspoon grated lemon zest

Freshly ground black pepper

3 large eggs

1 cup half-and-half

1 9-inch pie shell (page 282), baked

¼ cup freshly grated Parmigiano-Reggiano cheese

You can use leftover poached, grilled or baked salmon for this quiche.

1. Preheat the oven to 375°F. Combine 1 inch of water, the garlic, dill and ½ teaspoon salt in a shallow saucepan and bring to a boil. Add the salmon, cover and cook over medium low heat until cooked through, about 10 minutes. Remove the salmon from the water and let cool. Remove and discard the skin and any bones and flake the salmon. You should have about 1 cup.

2. Set a steamer basket over 1 inch of boiling water in a saucepan or deep skillet. Add the asparagus, cover and steam until very tender, about 5 minutes. Remove the steamer basket and let cool.

3. Melt the butter in a large skillet over low heat. Add the shallots and cook, stirring, until tender but not browned, about 3 minutes. Remove from the heat and add the salmon, asparagus, thyme, lemon zest, salt to taste and a generous grinding of pepper.

4. In a large bowl, whisk the eggs until light. Stir in the half-and-half. Spoon the salmon mixture evenly into the pie shell. Sprinkle with the cheese and pour in the egg mixture.

5. Bake the quiche until puffed and golden brown, about 35 minutes. Serve warm or at room temperature, cut into wedges.

Makes 6 servings

Improvising Quiche from Your Refrigerator

 Like omelettes and stratas, a quiche can be improvised from ingredients you have on hand in your refrigerator and pantry. Here's my basic formula for creating a quiche on the spur of the moment:

♦ 1 cup milk, half-and-half or heavy cream

♦ 3 large eggs

♦ 1 cup grated, diced or crumbled cheese

♦ 1–2 cups solid ingredients, such as cooked vegetables, shredded or diced meats or seafood

It's best to limit yourself to three basic filling ingredients, compatible vegetables, meats or seafood and herbs. Incorporating more than a few muddles the flavors. Here are some good combinations:

♦ sausage, onions and mushrooms

♦ broccoli, roasted garlic and red bell pepper

♦ corn, tomatoes and jalapeño

♦ baby shrimp, scallions and dill

♦ smoked salmon, spinach and onion

Have fun creating your own quiche "combo" from these suggestions, choosing an appropriate seasoning for the other two ingredients you pick:

♦ Raw corn, tomatoes, green or red pepper or scallions

♦ Sautéed mushrooms, onions, celery, spinach, eggplant or red bell peppers

♦ Cooked carrots, broccoli, leeks, cauliflower, cabbage or kale

♦ Diced or shredded ham, chicken, prosciutto, salami, salmon or other fish

♦ Cooked and crumbled sausage

♦ Cooked baby shrimp, crabmeat or lobster

♦ Smoked salmon, mussels or oysters

♦ Seasonings: dry or prepared mustard; dried tomatoes; chipotle chiles in adobo; Tabasco or other hot sauce; fresh herbs (dill, cilantro, basil, thyme, chervil) or dried (oregano, rosemary, thyme); grated lemon or orange zest; or roasted garlic.

Escarole, Ricotta and Egg Pie

Vegetable pies are popular in Italy, especially in the south, where they are called *tortas*. Tortas are often made with Swiss chard, but I prefer the taste of escarole, which is a type of endive. Serve this pie warm or at room temperature as a first course at dinner or as a main course for lunch. Chilled, it is great as a snack or taken along on a picnic.

Kosher salt

1 pound escarole, trimmed and rinsed

1 tablespoon extra-virgin olive oil

½ cup chopped onion

3 garlic cloves, minced

Freshly ground black pepper

2 large eggs

1 cup ricotta cheese

½ cup freshly grated Parmigiano-Reggiano cheese

½ cup finely chopped fresh flat-leaf parsley

Pastry for a double-crust 9-inch pie (recipe follows), chilled

2 large eggs, hard-cooked (page 162), peeled and quartered

1 large egg yolk, beaten with 2 tablespoons milk

1. Bring a large pot of water to a boil. Add 1 teaspoon salt, stir in the escarole and cook until tender, 5 to 6 minutes. Drain and rinse with cold water. Place in a strainer set over a bowl and press with the back of a large spoon until most of the water is squeezed out, then squeeze with your hands to remove more. Turn out onto a folded kitchen towel and blot dry. Chop the escarole. You should have about 1 cup packed escarole.

2. Heat the oil in a large skillet over low heat. Add the onion and cook, stirring, until golden. Stir in the garlic and cook for 1 minute. Add the escarole and cook, stirring, until heated through and any moisture has evaporated; the mixture should be very dry. Season with salt to taste and a grinding of pepper and remove from the heat.

3. In a large bowl, whisk the eggs until blended. Add the cheeses, parsley and ½ teaspoon salt. Add the escarole mixture and stir to combine. Set aside.

4. Position a rack in the lower third of the oven and preheat the oven to 400°F. On a lightly floured surface, roll out one half of the chilled pastry to a 12-inch round. Fit the pastry into a 9-inch fluted tart pan with a removable bottom and trim the edges, leaving a ½-inch overhang. Spoon the filling into the pan. Place the egg quarters cut side down in the filling, spacing them evenly.

5. Roll out the remaining pastry to a 10-inch round. Drape over the top of the filled pie and trim the edges, leaving a ½-inch overhang. Fold the edges under to seal. Brush the top of the pie with the beaten egg yolk.

6. Place the pie on a baking sheet and bake for 15 minutes. Reduce the heat to 350°F and bake until golden, 25 to 30 minutes. Cool on a rack. Serve warm or at room temperature, cut into wedges.

Makes 6 to 8 servings

Pastry for a Double-Crust Pie

2½ **cups all-purpose flour**

1½ **teaspoons kosher salt**

¾ **cup solid vegetable shortening or ½ cup shortening plus 4 tablespoons (½ stick) unsalted butter, cut into small dice**

About 1 cup ice water

1. Stir the flour and salt together in a large bowl. Using a pastry blender, cut the shortening and/or butter into the flour until evenly distributed in coarse crumbs throughout the mixture.

2. Sprinkle with 3 tablespoons of the water and stir lightly with a fork to blend. Continue adding water 1 tablespoon at a time and tossing the mixture lightly until it comes together in a moist (not wet) ball. Divide in half and wrap each half in foil. Refrigerate for at least 30 minutes before rolling out.

Makes enough pastry for 1 double-crust 9-inch pie

Rice, Prosciutto and Egg Torta

I like to make this torta with Asiago fresco, which is a semisoft young Asiago. If it isn't available, use Muenster or Bel Paese.

4 **large eggs, beaten**

2 **cups cooked Arborio or other medium-grain rice**

1 **cup grated Asiago fresco, Muenster, Bel Paese or other semisoft, flavorful cheese (about 4 ounces)**

¾ **cup half-and-half**

2½ **ounces prosciutto, fat trimmed, cut into ¼-inch dice**

Freshly ground black pepper

Pastry for a double-crust 9-inch pie (page 295), chilled

2 **large eggs, hard-cooked (page 162), peeled and quartered**

1 **large egg yolk, beaten with 2 tablespoons milk**

1. In a large bowl, whisk the eggs until blended. Add the rice, cheese, half-and-half, prosciutto and a generous grinding of pepper. Set aside.

2. Position a rack in the lower third of the oven and preheat the oven to 400°F. On a lightly floured surface, roll out one half of the chilled pastry to a 12-inch round. Fit the pastry into a 9-inch fluted tart pan with a removable bottom and trim the edges, leaving a ½-inch overhang. Spoon the filling into the pan. Place the egg quarters, cut side down, in the filling, spacing them evenly.

3. Roll out the remaining pastry to a 10-inch round. Drape over the top of the filled pie and trim the edges, leaving a ½-inch overhang. Fold the edges under to seal. Brush the top of the pie with the beaten egg yolk.

4. Place the tart pan on a baking sheet and bake for 15 minutes. Reduce the heat to 350°F and bake until golden, 25 to 30 minutes. Cool on a rack. Serve warm or at room temperature, cut into wedges.

Makes 6 to 8 servings

About ¾ cup raw rice will yield 2 cups cooked.

Fried Filo Packets with Egg, Onion and Cilantro (Brik)

Simply described, *brik* is a pocket of flaky fried pastry with an egg cooked inside. Sometimes a spoonful of spicy meat mixture is added to the egg. In Tunisia, *brik* is a popular street food and is made with *ouarka*, the paper-thin pastry of the region. I substitute filo pastry. I like *brik* best plain, with the egg and a drizzle of harissa, a spicy condiment made from chiles, caraway, cumin, coriander and olive oil. Serve as a snack or a light meal.

This recipe is adapted from a recipe from friend and cookbook author Kitty Morse, who advised me that there is no graceful way to eat *brik*. "It is meant to be eaten with the fingers," she said. "The egg yolk is sure to dribble down your chin. That's all part of the fun."

12 **sheets filo dough, thawed according to the package directions**

6 **tablespoons finely chopped onion**

6 **tablespoons finely chopped fresh cilantro**

Vegetable oil

6 **large eggs**

Kosher salt

Harissa (optional)

Harissa can be purchased in jars at specialty Middle Eastern shops.

1. Unroll the filo and cut into two stacks of 8-inch squares; discard the trimmings. Stack the squares and cover with a sheet of plastic wrap and a dampened towel to keep them from drying out.

2. Line up the onion, cilantro, a saucer, a small bowl of cold water and a pastry brush near your stovetop. Heat 1 inch of oil in a large, deep skillet. Stack 4 squares of filo on the saucer. Break 1 egg into a cup and pour it into the center of the filo. Brush a ½-inch border of water around the edges of the filo. Top the egg with 1 tablespoon each of the onion and cilantro and a few grains of salt. Fold over the sides of the filo and then the top and bottom, being careful not to press on the yolk, overlapping the dampened edges to seal.

3. Slip the *brik* into the hot oil and fry, turning, until golden on both sides, about 2 minutes per side. Don't overcook; the egg yolk should be runny. Drain on paper towels. Continue with the remaining ingredients, assembling and cooking the *brik* one at a time.

4. Serve at once, with harissa on the side, if using.

Makes 6 servings

Spinach, Egg and Feta Pie in Filo Crust

Although it is called a pie, this special dish contains layers of flaky filo filled with spinach, eggs and cheese. Working with filo can be a little tricky, but if you follow the simple guidelines in this recipe, you should be fine. My advice is to forge ahead no matter how the filo may be misbehaving. This is a great dish for serving a crowd, and it is so filling, all it needs on the side is a plate of roasted red peppers or a tomato and cucumber salad. Serve warm or at room temperature.

2 10-ounce packages frozen chopped spinach (to use fresh spinach, see page 90)

10 tablespoons (1 stick plus 2 tablespoons) unsalted butter

1½ cups chopped onions

1 tablespoon minced garlic

½ cup chopped scallions (white and light green parts)

½ cup chopped fresh flat-leaf parsley

¼ cup chopped fresh dill

1 teaspoon kosher salt
Freshly ground black pepper

4 large eggs

2 cups crumbled feta cheese (about 8 ounces)

½ cup freshly grated Parmigiano-Reggiano cheese

1. Place the frozen spinach in a large saucepan, add ¼ cup water and cook, covered, over medium-low heat until thawed and partially cooked, about 8 minutes. Remove from the heat, transfer to a strainer set over a bowl and let cool.

2. When the spinach is cool enough to handle, press down on it with the back of a spoon to release excess moisture, then squeeze with your hands to remove more. Place between two layers of paper towels or wrap in a kitchen towel and squeeze hard until the spinach is fairly dry. You should have about 2 cups. Set aside.

3. In a large skillet, melt 2 tablespoons of the butter. Add the onions and cook over medium heat until golden, about 10 minutes. Add the garlic and cook for 2 minutes. Add the spinach, scallions, parsley and dill and cook, stirring, just until the spinach is heated through and any remaining moisture has evaporated. Add the salt and a generous grinding of pepper. Remove from the heat.

4. In a large bowl, whisk the eggs until blended. Stir in the cheeses. Add the spinach mixture and stir until blended. Set aside.

9 sheets filo dough, thawed according to the package directions

4 large eggs, hard-cooked (page 162), peeled and halved lengthwise

You can bake the pie in advance and reheat before serving: cover with foil and bake in a preheated 350°F oven for 15 minutes.

5. Soak a large kitchen towel with water and squeeze dry. Unroll the filo and place on a large baking sheet. Cover with plastic wrap and then with the dampened towel. (Do not let the towel come in direct contact with the filo, or all the layers will melt into one.)

6. Preheat the oven to 350°F. Melt the remaining 8 tablespoons butter in a small saucepan. Remove from the heat. Use a wide pastry brush to lightly coat the bottom and sides of a 13-x-9-inch baking dish with butter. Remove 1 sheet of filo, keeping the remaining filo covered, and brush with a thin layer of butter. Line the baking dish with the filo, leaving a 2-inch overhang on each of the long sides. Repeat with 5 more sheets of filo, brushing each with butter.

7. Spoon half of the spinach filling into the lined pan, spreading it evenly. Arrange the eggs cut side down evenly on the filling. Top with the remaining filling, spreading it to the edges. Fold the overhanging filo over the filling. Uncover the remaining 3 filo sheets and cut them crosswise in half (forming a stack of 6 approximately 13-x-9-inch sheets). Brush each sheet with butter and layer them on top of the spinach filling. With a sharp knife, cut through the top of the pie about ½ inch deep, making 8 or 12 squares (2 or 3 across and 4 lengthwise); this will make cutting and serving the pie after baking much neater, as the filo becomes very flaky when baked.

8. Bake the pie until golden brown, about 1 hour. Cool for at least 15 minutes before cutting into squares and serving. The pie is also excellent served at room temperature or slightly chilled.

Makes 8 main-course or 12 appetizer servings

Basic Cheese Custards with Variations

A roasted tomato sauce (page 88) or Simple Tomato Sauce (page 263) is the perfect accompaniment to cheese custards, especially when served surrounded by a wreath of cooked escarole or spinach. Or simply turn the custards out onto a bed of salad greens that have been tossed with a light lemon-and-olive oil dressing.

2 **large eggs**

2 **large egg yolks**

1 **cup milk**

1 **cup heavy cream**

1 **teaspoon kosher salt**

   Freshly ground black pepper

¾ **cup freshly grated Gruyère or Parmigiano-Reggiano cheese**

1. Preheat the oven to 350°F. Brush six 5-ounce custard cups lightly with butter. Place in a 13-x-9-inch baking pan. Set a kettle of water on to boil.

2. In a large bowl, whisk the eggs and egg yolks until blended. Whisk in the milk and cream until blended. Strain into a large glass measuring cup. Add the salt and a grinding of pepper. Stir in the cheese. Pour the mixture into the custard cups.

3. Place the baking pan in the oven and carefully pour enough hot water into the pan to come halfway up the sides of the cups. Bake until the custards are set, about 25 minutes. Remove the pan from the oven and, using a spatula and protecting your hand with an oven mitt, transfer the cups to a rack.

4. Serve warm, directly from the custard cups, or run a thin knife around the edge of each cup and invert the warm custards onto plates.

Makes 6 servings

You can make these custards ahead and reheat in the microwave, a few at a time, or wrap them in foil and reheat in a preheated 300°F oven for 15 minutes.

Sun-Dried Tomato and Basil Custards

Prepare the custard as directed, using Parmigiano-Reggiano cheese. Place 1 tablespoon chopped oil-packed sun-dried tomatoes and 1 teaspoon torn fresh basil leaves in each buttered custard cup before filling.

Feta, Scallion and Sun-Dried Tomato Custards

Prepare the custard as directed, but omit the cheese. Place 2 tablespoons crumbled feta cheese, 1 tablespoon chopped oil-packed sun-dried tomatoes and 1 tablespoon thinly sliced scallion greens in each buttered custard cup before filling.

Roquefort and Tarragon Custards

Prepare the custard as directed, but omit the cheese. Place 2 tablespoons crumbled Roquefort cheese and 1 teaspoon minced fresh tarragon in each buttered custard cup before filling.

Parmesan and Nutmeg Custards

Prepare the custard as directed, using Parmigiano-Reggiano cheese. Place an additional 1 tablespoon cheese in each buttered custard cup, and grate a generous amount of nutmeg over the cheese before filling.

Bacon, Corn and Gruyère Custards

This recipe can be easily adapted to whatever vegetables you have on hand. Yellow onions can be used in place of the scallions, green bell pepper instead of red, ham in place of bacon. Or, if you prefer, omit the meat altogether.

2 slices bacon

3 tablespoons finely chopped red bell pepper

3 tablespoons thinly sliced scallions (white and light green parts)

½ cup fresh or frozen corn kernels, thawed if frozen

1 teaspoon minced seeded jalapeño (optional)

Kosher salt and freshly ground black pepper

1½ cups milk

½ cup heavy cream

2 large eggs

2 large egg yolks

½ cup grated Gruyère cheese

1. Preheat the oven to 350°F. Brush six 5-ounce custard cups lightly with butter. Place in a 13-x-9-inch baking pan. Set a kettle of water on to boil.

2. Cook the bacon in a medium skillet until crisp; transfer to paper towels to drain. Discard all but 1 tablespoon of the bacon fat from the pan. Add the bell pepper to the skillet and cook, stirring, over medium heat until tender, about 2 minutes. Add the scallions; cook for 1 minute. Stir in the corn and remove from the heat.

3. Finely chop the bacon and add the bacon and jalapeño, if using, to the corn mixture. Sprinkle with salt to taste and a grinding of pepper.

4. Combine the milk and cream in a small saucepan. Heat until small bubbles appear around the edges of the pan. Remove from the heat.

5. In a medium bowl, whisk the eggs and egg yolks until blended. Whisk in the hot milk mixture. Strain into a large glass measuring cup. Stir in the cheese and ½ teaspoon salt. Distribute the corn mixture evenly among the prepared custard cups. Pour the cheese mixture into the cups.

6. Place the baking pan in the oven and carefully pour enough hot water into the pan to come halfway up the sides of the cups. Bake until the custards are set, about 25 minutes. Remove the pan from the oven and, using a spatula and protecting your hand with an oven mitt, transfer the custard cups to a rack.

7. Serve warm, directly from the custard cups, or run a thin knife around the edge of each cup and invert the warm custards onto plates.

Makes 6 servings

Cheddar, fontina and Parmigiano-Reggiano can be used instead of Gruyère.

Porcini Custards

I like to serve these custards with grilled fish or poultry and wild rice or as the centerpiece of a vegetarian supper. Unmolded onto lightly dressed salad greens, they are also nice as a salad course.

2 cups milk

½ cup heavy cream

1 cup dried porcini mushrooms (about 1 ounce)

1 thick slice onion

1 garlic clove, bruised with the side of a knife

1 bay leaf

1 teaspoon kosher salt

¼ cup freshly grated Parmigiano-Reggiano cheese

2 large eggs

2 large egg yolks

Freshly ground black pepper

1. Combine the milk, cream, mushrooms, onion, garlic, bay leaf and salt in a medium saucepan. Heat, stirring, until small bubbles appear around the edges of the pan. Remove from the heat, cover and let stand for 1 hour.

2. Set a strainer over a bowl and strain the mushrooms; reserve the milk mixture. Discard the bay leaf, onion and garlic. Rinse the mushrooms in the strainer, lightly with cold water. Transfer to a paper towel and blot dry. Finely chop enough mushrooms to measure ½ cup. Save any remaining mushrooms for another use.

3. Preheat the oven to 350°F. Brush six 5-ounce custard cups generously with butter. Sprinkle 1 teaspoon of the cheese in each cup, shaking to coat the bottoms and sides evenly. Place the cups in a 13-x-9-inch baking pan. Set a kettle of water on to boil.

4. In a large bowl, whisk the eggs and egg yolks together until blended. Add the reserved milk mixture and whisk to blend. Strain into a large glass measuring cup. Stir in the chopped mushrooms, the remaining 2 tablespoons cheese and a grinding of pepper. Pour the mixture into the custard cups, stirring the custard as necessary to evenly distribute the mushrooms.

5. Place the baking pan in the oven and carefully pour enough hot water into the pan to come halfway up the sides of the cups. Bake until lightly browned and set, about 25 minutes. Remove the pan from the oven and, using a spatula and protecting your hand with an oven mitt, transfer the custard cups to a rack.

6. Serve warm or at room temperature, directly from the custard cups, or run a knife around the edge of each cup and invert the custards onto plates.

Makes 6 servings

You can make the custards in advance and reheat in the microwave, a few at a time, or wrap them in foil and reheat in a preheated 300°F oven for 15 minutes.

Roasted Red Pepper and Basil Custards

I like to serve these tender custards as a light main dish on a bed of greens, with pieces of roasted peppers surrounding the salad, or as a side dish (instead of the more usual potatoes) with Italian sausage.

1   **cup milk**

½   **cup heavy cream**

¼   **cup loosely packed torn fresh basil, plus whole leaves for garnish**

1   **teaspoon minced garlic**

1   **teaspoon kosher salt**

2   **red bell peppers, roasted (page 75), with 2 tablespoons of their juices**

2   **large eggs**

2   **large egg yolks**

1   **tablespoon all-purpose flour Freshly ground black pepper**

1. Combine the milk, cream, ¼ cup basil, garlic and salt in a medium saucepan and heat, stirring, until small bubbles appear around the edges of the pan. Remove from the heat, cover and let stand for 30 minutes.

2. Place the roasted peppers and juices in a food processor and process until pureed. Measure out ½ cup plus 2 tablespoons of the puree; reserve any remaining puree for another use.

3. Preheat the oven to 350°F. Brush six 5-ounce custard cups lightly with butter. Place the cups in a 13-x-9-inch baking pan. Set a kettle of water on to boil.

4. In a large bowl, whisk the eggs, egg yolks and flour until well blended. Stir the roasted pepper puree into the milk mixture, then gradually stir the milk mixture into the egg mixture until well blended. Strain into a large glass measuring cup, pressing down hard to release all the flavors in the solids. Scrape the puree from the outside of the strainer into the measuring cup. Discard the solids. Add a grinding of pepper and pour the mixture into the custard cups.

5. Place the baking pan in the oven and carefully pour enough hot water into the pan to come halfway up the sides of the cups. Bake until the custards are set, about 25 minutes. Remove the pan from the oven and, using a spatula and protecting your hand with an oven mitt, transfer the custard cups to a rack.

6. Serve warm or at room temperature, directly from the custard cups, or run a knife around the edge of each cup and invert the custards onto plates. Garnish the custards with basil leaves.

Makes 6 servings

The custards can be made ahead and reheated, a few at a time, in the microwave or, wrapped in foil, in a preheated 300°F oven for 15 minutes.

CHAPTER 10 *Souﬄés and Roulades*

"A soufflé is an egg that takes a deep breath and holds it."
— PAULA HAMILTON

For any of my readers who suffer from soufflé anxiety — the fear of making one of the world's most delicious dishes — I offer, as reassurance and encouragement, the following tale.

During a visit to my daughter Stephanie's house to help take care of my granddaughter, Seraphina, I was called upon to make supper. What was in the refrigerator? Milk, eggs and cheddar cheese. Omelette? Something more special was needed. I remembered that I had given Stephanie a soufflé dish, and I decided to wow Seraphina by putting it to use.

Once I had located the dish in the back of a cabinet, I found that Stephanie's kitchen lacked a few other tools that I'd previously regarded as essential to soufflé making: a free-standing electric mixer for beating the whites, a rubber spatula for folding the batter together and a reliable oven. In this soufflé-challenged environment, I set to work.

Calling on the ability to improvise, born of years in the kitchen, I made do. Somewhat to my surprise, Steph's sputtering old electric mixer did a commendable job of beating the egg whites into a firm and glossy mound, and I used my cupped hand to gently fold the whites into the soufflé base. Despite my trepidation about the oven thermostat, the batter puffed gloriously. While I want to say that I triumphed, it's more accurate to say that the eggs triumphed — again. Seraphina was suitably impressed with the dinner, which was as lofty as it was tasty.

If a soufflé can succeed under such discouraging conditions, I guarantee that the recipes and technique tips in this chapter will work for you. Despite all the mythology that surrounds it, a soufflé doesn't demand enormous skill in the kitchen. You can also take heart from the knowledge that it's the eggs, not you, that make it succeed or not. If you follow the simple steps to handle the soufflé properly, you will be rewarded with a dramatic golden puff, a texture at once light and airy, moist and rich — and with the flavor of all the good things you've incorporated, whether it's just good cheddar or a tantalizing combination of smoked salmon, cream cheese and dill. The soufflé mixtures in this chapter can even be prepared in advance, leaving only the baking until the last minute.

Anatomy of a Soufflé

 The typical savory soufflé is essentially a mixture of three components:

1. **A base**, consisting of thick white sauce and egg yolks. White sauce, also known as béchamel, is milk or cream thickened with a paste of butter and flour. The base provides richness, moisture, structure and flavor.

2. **A primary flavoring component**, such as a vegetable puree, cheese or seafood, along with seasonings.

3. **Egg whites**, beaten to many times their original volume. The whites and the air they contain provide the rise and light texture of the soufflé.

But if the prospect of attempting a high rise in front of guests still makes you nervous, then meet the roulade, an easy variation on the soufflé that is more practical to serve for a group. Think of a roulade as a savory jelly roll. First you spread the soufflé batter in a shallow rimmed baking pan and bake it. It will rise nicely but not dramatically. Then you remove it from the pan and smother it with your choice of any tasty mixture—from sautéed wild mushrooms to chopped fresh tomatoes with watercress—and roll it up just like a jelly roll. Served warm or cold, slices of roulade make a pretty, festive, do-ahead meal for eight, with no last-minute anxieties.

Egg White Basics

Follow these pointers for dramatic rises:

♦ Use room-temperature eggs. Although eggs separate more easily when cold, warm egg whites will whip up to a greater volume. If you take the eggs directly from the refrigerator, heat them gently in a bowl of hot tap water for 10 minutes before separating.

♦ When separating eggs, be very careful that no yolk gets into the whites. The yolk contains fat, which will inhibit the foaming of the beaten whites.

♦ Make sure the mixing bowl and beaters are free of fats, oil or grease. Wash the bowl and beaters in warm soapy water and rinse and dry them well before beating the whites.

♦ Add a pinch of cream of tartar to the egg whites. This adds acid, which helps to stabilize the whites so they will not lose their volume and smooth texture if slightly overbeaten.

♦ Use an electric mixer to beat the egg whites. Beat them first on low to medium speed until they are foamy throughout. Then increase the speed to high. Watch them carefully: if they are either underbeaten or overbeaten, your soufflé will not rise properly. Underbeaten egg whites have a dull, airy look, while overbeaten egg whites are curdled and clumpy. Perfectly beaten egg whites form stiff peaks with a smooth, satiny sheen.

♦ Fold the egg whites carefully into the soufflé base. Don't spoon the base on top of them, which would deflate them. The best tool for folding is a large rubber spatula, freshly washed and free of fat. Add about one-third of the whites to the soufflé base and gently fold down through the center, across the bottom and up the side, then start over. When the first addition is evenly incorporated, fold in the remaining whites.

Baking Basics

Prepare the soufflé mixture in advance: The savory soufflé mixtures here are sturdy enough to make ahead and keep, refrigerated, for up to 2 hours before baking.

Find the right soufflé dish: Traditionally, a soufflé is made in a special ceramic dish, but almost any straight-sided baking dish will do. Generally, a 4-egg soufflé needs a 6-to-8-cup dish and a 5- or 6-egg soufflé needs an 8-to-10-cup dish. Individual soufflés can be made in ramekins or custard cups. The baking dishes can be filled to within ½ inch of the top; the soufflés will puff up without running over the edges.

Prepare the dish: Some experts say not to butter the soufflé dish because the eggs need to cling to the sides as they rise. But I prefer to butter the dish and provide traction by dusting it with a thin layer of grated Parmesan, yellow cornmeal or fine dry bread crumbs. This method gives the soufflé a nice outer crust and adds a little extra flavor.

If your dish is too small, make a collar to contain the mixture, since a soufflé can puff up to more than 1½ times its original volume. Fold a length of aluminum foil into a triple thickness, making a 4-inch-wide band long enough to go around the dish and overlap by 2 inches. Butter and sprinkle the top half of the band with Parmesan, cornmeal or bread crumbs, just like the dish, and wrap it around the outside of the dish, making sure that it extends at least 2 inches above the top of the container. Tie in place with twine or secure with paper clips.

Don't peek! Position a rack in the center of the oven and preheat the oven to 400°F. When you put the soufflé into the oven, reduce the temperature to 375°F. Most soufflés bake in 25 to 35 minutes. Resist the temptation to open the oven door to check on the soufflé's progress for the first 20 minutes of baking, because the cool air might deflate it. If you like your soufflés fairly firm in the center rather than soft, bake for an extra 5 minutes.

Make a top hat for your soufflé: Before putting the soufflé into the oven, smooth the surface with a spatula and then make a circular indentation in the batter with your finger or the tip of a spoon, like a ditch or a moat, about 1 inch in from the edge of the dish and about 1 inch deep. The soufflé will rise inside this circle like a top hat.

Don't delay: When the soufflé is ready, serve it at once. A soufflé waits for no one.

Classic Cheddar Cheese Soufflé

Many variations later, this soufflé is still my favorite. Serve it with fresh tomato and basil salad in the summer and stewed tomatoes in the winter.

Fine dry bread crumbs for the soufflé dish

3 tablespoons unsalted butter

3 tablespoons all-purpose flour

1 cup milk

1 teaspoon Dijon mustard

½ teaspoon kosher salt

Freshly ground black pepper

3 large eggs, separated, at room temperature

1¼ cups grated cheddar cheese (about 5 ounces)

1 large egg white, at room temperature

¼ teaspoon cream of tartar

1. Position a rack in the center of the oven and preheat the oven to 400°F. Generously butter a 6-cup soufflé dish. Sprinkle lightly with bread crumbs, shaking the dish to coat evenly.

2. Melt the butter in a small saucepan over low heat. Add the flour and cook, stirring constantly, for 3 minutes. Gradually whisk in the milk and bring to a boil, stirring constantly. Cook, stirring constantly, for 3 minutes more. Stir in the mustard, salt and a grinding of pepper. Remove from the heat.

3. In a large bowl, whisk the egg yolks until blended. Whisk in a little of the white sauce to temper the eggs, then add the remaining sauce, whisking until blended. Stir in the cheese.

4. Place the 4 egg whites in a large bowl, add the cream of tartar and beat slowly with an electric mixer until soft peaks form. Increase the speed to high and beat until the peaks are stiff and smooth.

5. Using a rubber spatula, transfer about one-third of the egg whites to the cheese mixture and gently fold in until blended. Add the remaining whites to the cheese mixture and gently fold in until blended. Pour into the prepared dish.

6. Put the soufflé in the oven and reduce the temperature to 375°F. Bake until the soufflé is puffed and golden, 30 to 35 minutes. If you like your soufflé firm in the center, bake it for 5 minutes more. Serve at once.

Makes 4 servings

Spinach and Parmesan Cheese Soufflé

The classic spinach soufflé is often made with grated Swiss cheese, but freshly grated Parmigiano-Reggiano is even better, producing a lighter and more intensely flavored soufflé and complementing the spinach nicely. Serve for dinner or lunch, with a side dish of roasted tomatoes and basil.

Freshly grated Parmigiano-Reggiano or fine dry bread crumbs for the soufflé dish

1 10-ounce bag fresh spinach, stemmed and rinsed, or one 10-ounce package frozen chopped spinach

3 tablespoons unsalted butter

3 tablespoons all-purpose flour

1¼ cups milk

½ teaspoon kosher salt
   Freshly ground black pepper
   Freshly grated nutmeg

3 large eggs, separated, plus 1 large egg white, at room temperature

½ cup freshly grated Parmigiano-Reggiano cheese

¼ teaspoon cream of tartar

1. Position a rack in the center of the oven and preheat the oven to 400°F. Generously butter a 6-to-7-cup soufflé dish. Sprinkle lightly with cheese or bread crumbs, shaking the dish to coat evenly.

2. If using fresh spinach, steam it in a steamer basket set in a saucepan over 1 inch of boiling water until wilted, about 3 minutes. Drain and let cool, then drain in a strainer, squeeze out the liquid and finely chop the spinach. You should have about 1 cup. Or, if using frozen spinach, cook it according to the package directions, let cool and squeeze dry. Press the spinach between layers of paper towels to remove more moisture. If it is coarsely chopped, chop it fine. Set aside.

3. Melt the butter in a small saucepan over low heat. Add the flour and cook, stirring constantly, for 3 minutes. Gradually whisk in the milk and bring to a boil, stirring constantly. Cook, stirring constantly, for 3 minutes more. Add the salt, a grinding of pepper and nutmeg to taste. Remove from the heat.

4. In a large bowl, whisk the egg yolks until blended. Whisk in a little of the white sauce to temper the eggs, then add the remaining sauce, whisking until blended. Stir in the spinach and cheese.

5. Place the 4 egg whites in a large bowl, add the cream of tartar and beat slowly with an electric mixer until soft peaks form. Increase the speed to high and beat until the peaks are stiff and smooth.

6. Using a rubber spatula, transfer about one-third of the egg whites to the spinach mixture and gently fold in until blended. Add the remaining whites to the spinach mixture and gently fold in until blended. Pour into the prepared dish.

7. Put the soufflé in the oven and reduce the temperature to 375°F. Bake until the soufflé is puffed and golden, 30 to 35 minutes. If you like your soufflé firm in the center, bake it for 5 minutes more. Serve at once.

Makes 4 servings

Spinach, Dill and Feta Soufflé

Omit the nutmeg. Substitute ½ cup crumbled feta cheese for the Parmigiano-Reggiano and use bread crumbs to coat the soufflé dish. Add 2 tablespoons chopped fresh dill to the soufflé base along with the spinach.

Cheddar, Gruyère or another semihard cheese can be substituted for the Parmigiano-Reggiano.

Twice-Baked Soufflé in Tomato Cream Sauce

For those of us who would like to wow our friends and family with a soufflé but can't stand the thought of making one just before the guests arrive, this is the perfect solution. The soufflés are made up to one day ahead and left to cool. They will fall, but they are revived the next day when they are baked in a mixture of heavy cream and tomato. They emerge from the oven modestly puffed, soft and tender, topped with melted cheese and surrounded by lovely pink sauce.

1 recipe Spinach and Parmesan Cheese Soufflé (page 318) or Classic Cheddar Cheese Soufflé (page 316)

1 cup heavy cream

1 cup canned diced tomatoes, with their juices

1 fresh basil sprig

Kosher salt and freshly ground black pepper

½ cup grated Gruyère or fontina cheese

1. Place a rack in the lowest position in the oven and preheat the oven to 400°F. Generously butter six 5-ounce or four 8-ounce ramekins and arrange them in a roasting pan. Set a kettle of water on to boil.

2. Spoon the soufflé mixture into the ramekins, distributing it evenly. Run a fingertip around the inside of the rim of each ramekin so the soufflés will form a high hat.

3. Place the roasting pan in the oven and carefully add enough boiling water to come halfway up the sides of the ramekins. Bake until the soufflés are puffed and browned, 30 to 35 minutes. Remove from the oven and let stand in the water bath for 10 minutes. Transfer to a rack and let cool to room temperature; the soufflés will shrink.

4. Using a thin spatula, carefully loosen the sides of the soufflés from the ramekins. Lift the soufflés from the ramekins and place, browned side up, in individual approximately 1-x-4-inch gratin dishes or in a large baking dish. (If any of the soufflé remains stuck to a ramekin, loosen it with the spatula and stick it onto the side of the soufflé.) Cover and refrigerate until ready to bake. (The soufflés can be made to this point up to 1 day in advance.)

5. Position a rack in the center of the oven and preheat the oven to 350°F. Combine the cream and tomatoes and their juices in a medium saucepan and bring to a boil. Add the basil; reduce the heat and boil gently until reduced to about 1½ cups, about 10 minutes. Add salt to taste and a grinding of pepper; discard the basil. Spoon the mixture over the soufflés, dividing it evenly if they are in individual dishes. Sprinkle the tops with the cheese.

6. Bake until the soufflés are puffed and golden, 20 to 25 minutes. Serve at once.

Makes 4 main-course or 6 side-dish servings

Bake the soufflés the second time in individual gratin dishes or in one large baking dish.

Tomato and Basil Soufflé

Make this soufflé when garden tomatoes are at their height of flavor and your basil is dark green and bushy.

1 tablespoon freshly grated Parmigiano-Reggiano cheese, plus extra for the soufflé dish

1 pound ripe tomatoes, cored and quartered

¼ cup finely chopped onion

3 tablespoons chopped fresh basil

1 large garlic clove, minced

1 teaspoon kosher salt
Freshly ground black pepper

3 tablespoons unsalted butter

3 tablespoons all-purpose flour

4 large eggs, separated, plus 2 large egg whites, at room temperature

¼ teaspoon cream of tartar

1. Position a rack in the center of the oven and preheat the oven to 400°F. Generously butter a 2-quart soufflé dish. Sprinkle lightly with cheese, shaking the dish to coat evenly.

2. Combine the tomatoes, onion, 2 tablespoons of the basil and the garlic in a medium saucepan and bring to a boil, stirring. Reduce the heat to medium and cook until the tomatoes are softened, about 15 minutes. Let cool. Set a food mill over a medium bowl and puree the tomato mixture into it. (If you don't have a food mill, puree in a food processor and press through a strainer with a rubber spatula; discard the solids.) Return the puree to the saucepan; bring to a boil and boil gently until reduced to 1¼ cups, about 15 minutes. Stir in the remaining 1 tablespoon basil, the salt and a grinding of pepper.

3. Melt the butter in a small saucepan over low heat. Add the flour and cook, stirring constantly, for 3 minutes. Stir in the tomato puree just until blended. Remove from the heat.

4. In a large bowl, whisk the egg yolks until blended. Whisk in a little of the tomato mixture to temper the eggs, then add the remaining tomato mixture, whisking until blended. Set aside.

5. Place the 6 egg whites in a large bowl, add the cream of tartar and beat slowly with an electric mixer until soft peaks form. Increase the speed to high and beat until the peaks are stiff and smooth.

6. Using a rubber spatula, transfer about one-third of the egg whites to the tomato mixture and gently fold in until blended. Add the remaining whites to the tomato mixture and gently fold in until blended. Pour into the prepared dish. Sprinkle the top with the remaining 1 tablespoon cheese.

7. Put the soufflé in the oven and reduce the temperature to 375°F. Bake until the soufflé is puffed and golden, 30 to 35 minutes. If you like your soufflé firm in the center, bake it for 5 minutes more. Serve at once.

Makes 4 servings

Mushroom Soufflé with Pecorino Romano

The earthy essence of mushrooms permeates this soufflé. Serve with a side dish of roasted peppers.

½ cup freshly grated Pecorino Romano cheese, plus more for the soufflé dish

3 tablespoons extra-virgin olive oil

6 ounces cremini mushrooms, trimmed, wiped clean and finely chopped (about 1½ cups)

6 ounces shiitake mushrooms, stems removed, wiped clean and finely chopped (about 1½ cups)

¼ cup finely chopped fresh flat-leaf parsley

1 teaspoon minced fresh rosemary

1 teaspoon minced fresh thyme

1 garlic clove, minced

2 teaspoons kosher salt
Freshly ground black pepper

3 tablespoons unsalted butter

3 tablespoons all-purpose flour

1 cup milk

5 large eggs, separated, at room temperature
Pinch of cream of tartar

1. Position a rack in the center of the oven and preheat the oven to 400°F. Generously butter an 8-inch soufflé dish. Sprinkle lightly with cheese, shaking the dish to coat evenly.

2. Heat the oil in a large nonstick skillet over medium heat. Add the mushrooms and cook, stirring, until they begin to release their moisture. Increase the heat to medium-high and sauté until the moisture evaporates, about 5 minutes. Stir in the parsley, rosemary, thyme and garlic and sauté for 1 minute. Add 1 teaspoon of the salt and a generous grinding of pepper. Set aside to cool.

3. Melt the butter in a small saucepan over low heat. Add the flour and cook, stirring constantly, for 3 minutes. Gradually whisk in the milk and bring to a boil, stirring constantly. Cook, stirring constantly, for 3 minutes more. Add the remaining 1 teaspoon salt and a grinding of pepper. Remove from the heat.

4. In a large bowl, whisk the egg yolks until blended. Whisk in a little of the white sauce to temper the eggs, then add the remaining sauce, whisking until blended. Add the mushrooms and cheese.

5. Place the egg whites in a large bowl, add the cream of tartar and beat slowly with an electric mixer until soft peaks form. Increase the speed to high and beat until the peaks are stiff and smooth.

6. Using a rubber spatula, transfer about one-third of the egg whites to the mushroom sauce and gently fold in until blended. Add the remaining whites to the sauce and gently fold in until blended. Pour into the prepared dish.

7. Put the soufflé in the oven and reduce the temperature to 375°F. Bake until the soufflé is puffed and golden, 30 to 35 minutes. If you like your soufflé firm in the center, bake it for 5 minutes more. Serve at once.

Makes 4 servings

Goat Cheese and Sun-Dried Tomato Soufflé

The goat cheese adds the perfect tang and intensity of flavor to this soufflé, while the sun-dried tomatoes offer a counterpoint of sweetness.

Bread crumbs for sprinkling in the soufflé dish

3 tablespoons unsalted butter, plus more for the soufflé dish

3 tablespoons all-purpose flour

1 cup milk

½ teaspoon kosher salt

Freshly ground black pepper

5 large eggs, separated, at room temperature

8 ounces fresh goat cheese, crumbled

¼ cup oil-packed sun-dried tomatoes, rinsed and drained

2 tablespoons chopped fresh flat-leaf parsley

Pinch of cream of tartar

1. Position a rack in the center of the oven and preheat the oven to 400°F. Generously butter a 2-quart soufflé dish. Sprinkle lightly with bread crumbs, shaking the dish to coat evenly.

2. Melt the butter in a small saucepan over low heat. Add the flour and cook, stirring constantly, for 3 minutes. Gradually whisk in the milk and bring to a boil, stirring constantly. Cook, stirring constantly, for 3 minutes more. Add the salt and a grinding of pepper. Remove from the heat.

3. In a large bowl, whisk the egg yolks until blended. Whisk in a little of the white sauce to temper the eggs, then add the remaining sauce, whisking until blended. Stir in the goat cheese, sun-dried tomatoes and parsley.

4. Place the egg whites in a large bowl, add the cream of tartar and beat slowly with an electric mixer until soft peaks form. Increase the speed to high and beat until the peaks are stiff and smooth.

Round out the menu with a green salad, some salty black olives and a loaf of crusty bread.

5. Using a rubber spatula, transfer about one-third of the egg whites to the cheese mixture and gently fold in until blended. Add the remaining whites to the cheese mixture and gently fold in until blended. Pour into the prepared dish.

6. Put the soufflé in the oven and reduce the temperature to 375°F. Bake until the soufflé is puffed and golden, 30 to 35 minutes. If you like your soufflé firm in the center, bake it for 5 minutes more. Serve at once.

Makes 4 servings

Basic Roulade

This light roulade can be adapted to any number of fillings, from sautéed mushrooms to a mixture of chopped tomatoes and watercress.

4 tablespoons (½ stick) unsalted butter

5 tablespoons all-purpose flour

1½ cups milk, warmed

½ teaspoon kosher salt

Freshly ground white pepper

Pinch of cayenne pepper

6 large eggs, separated, at room temperature

½ cup grated Swiss, cheddar or Gruyère cheese (optional)

Pinch of cream of tartar

1. Position a rack in the center of the oven and preheat the oven to 350°F. Spray a 10-x-15-inch jelly-roll pan with nonstick cooking spray. Line the bottom and the sides of the pan with parchment paper trimmed to form neat edges and spray the parchment paper generously with nonstick spray.

2. Melt the butter in a medium saucepan over low heat. Add the flour and cook, stirring constantly, for 2 minutes. Gradually whisk in the milk and bring to a boil, stirring constantly. Cook, stirring constantly, for 3 minutes more. Add the salt, a grinding of white pepper and cayenne to taste. Remove from the heat.

3. In a medium bowl, whisk the egg yolks until blended. Whisk in about ½ cup of the white sauce to temper the eggs, then add the remaining sauce, whisking until blended. Stir in the cheese, if using.

4. Place the egg whites in a large bowl, add the cream of tartar and beat slowly with an electric mixer until soft peaks form. Increase the speed to high and beat until the peaks are stiff and smooth.

5. Using a rubber spatula, gently fold about one-quarter of the egg whites into the white sauce. Add the remaining whites to the white sauce and gently fold in until blended. Carefully spoon into the prepared pan (if you pour the mixture onto the pan, the whites will deflate) and spread evenly.

6. Bake until the roulade is puffed and golden, about 15 minutes. Remove from the oven and let stand for 2 minutes. Run a small spatula around the edges to make sure the paper is not sticking to the pan. Spray a 15-inch-long sheet of parchment paper generously with nonstick cooking spray and place on top of the roulade, sprayed side down. Invert onto a large rack and lift off the jelly-roll pan. Peel the parchment paper from the bottom of the roulade, gently releasing it with the edge of a spatula if it has stuck.

7. Fill the roulade while it is still warm, or let it cool to room temperature. If not using immediately, roll it up in parchment paper, wrap it in foil and refrigerate for up to 2 days. If you want to serve the roulade warm, you can reheat it, still wrapped in the foil, in a 300°F oven for about 10 minutes. (Don't worry if it cracks, as it will repair itself when the filling is spread inside.)

Makes 8 servings

Nonstick cooking spray works best here, and parchment paper is much easier to peel off than foil or waxed paper.

Avocado, Tomato and Fresh Corn Roulade
with Cilantro Mayonnaise

The filling for this roulade is like a chunky guacamole. Adjust the heat of the filling by adding more or less jalapeño.

Cilantro Mayonnaise

- ½ cup packed fresh cilantro leaves
- ½ teaspoon ground cumin
- ½ cup jarred or homemade mayonnaise (page 340)
- ½–1 teaspoon minced jalapeño, or to taste

- 1 cup fresh corn kernels (from 2 ears), finely chopped
- 1 cup diced avocado
- 1 tomato, cored, halved, seeded and finely chopped
- 1–2 tablespoons fresh lime juice
- 1 teaspoon minced seeded jalapeño
- ½ teaspoon minced garlic
- ½ teaspoon kosher salt, or to taste
  Freshly ground black pepper
- 1 Basic Roulade (page 328), made without the cheese, cooled
- 2 cups packed finely chopped curly leaf lettuce

1. **Make the cilantro mayonnaise:** Bring a small saucepan half-filled with water to a boil. Add the cilantro and blanch for 10 seconds; drain well. Cool and squeeze dry. Heat the cumin in a small dry skillet over medium heat until fragrant, about 10 seconds. Remove from the heat.

2. In a food processor, combine the cilantro, cumin, mayonnaise and jalapeño and process until pureed. Transfer to a small bowl, cover and refrigerate until ready to serve.

3. Combine the corn, avocado, tomato, lime juice, jalapeño, garlic, salt and a grinding of pepper in a medium bowl. Stir to blend. Spread over the roulade, leaving a ½-inch border around the edges. Sprinkle the lettuce over the filling.

4. Gently roll up the roulade from the long edge closest to you. If not serving immediately, wrap in plastic wrap and refrigerate for several hours or until ready to serve. Use a serrated knife to cut into thick slices. Serve with the cilantro mayonnaise on the side.

Makes 8 servings

Cheese Roulade with Spinach, Mushroom, Bacon and Gruyère

A thin layer of cheese melts deliciously into this roulade, melding with the warm mushroom-and-spinach mixture. Although the recipe calls for cremini mushrooms, almost any mushrooms, or a mixture, can be used. This roulade slices particularly neatly.

2 10- or 12-ounce bags fresh spinach, stemmed and rinsed

2 slices bacon, finely chopped

2 tablespoons extra-virgin olive oil

4 cups finely chopped mushrooms, preferably cremini or a mixture of cremini and white button

1 tablespoon chopped fresh flat-leaf parsley

1 teaspoon minced fresh thyme

1 garlic clove, minced
   Kosher salt and freshly ground black pepper

1 cup grated Gruyère cheese (about 4 ounces)

1 Basic Roulade (page 328), made with the cheese, warm or cooled

1. Place the spinach in a steamer basket set in a saucepan over 1 inch of boiling water and steam until wilted, about 3 minutes. Set aside to cool.

2. Transfer the spinach to a strainer and press down hard with the back of a spoon to extract as much liquid as possible, then squeeze in your hands to remove more. Turn the spinach out onto a doubled kitchen towel, fold the towel over the spinach and press down to extract more liquid. Finely chop the spinach. You should have about 1½ cups. Set aside.

3. Combine the bacon and oil in a large, heavy skillet and cook over low heat, stirring, until the bacon is golden brown, about 5 minutes. Increase the heat to medium, add the mushrooms and cook, stirring, until the liquid is evaporated and the mushrooms are golden, about 8 minutes. Add the herbs and garlic and cook, stirring, for 1 minute. Add the spinach and cook, stirring, until any remaining moisture has evaporated. The mixture should be fairly dry. Add salt to taste and a grinding of pepper.

4. Sprinkle the cheese evenly over the roulade. Distribute the spinach mixture evenly over the roulade, leaving a ½-inch border around the edges.

> **You can substitute two 10-ounce boxes of frozen chopped spinach for the fresh.**

5. Gently roll up the roulade from the long edge closest to you. If the roulade was still warm, serve at once. If it was made ahead and refrigerated, slide it onto a baking sheet, brush the top with a little melted butter and reheat in a preheated 350°F oven for 15 minutes. Use a serrated knife to cut into thick slices and serve.

Makes 8 servings

Smoked Salmon, Cream Cheese and Watercress Roulade

Cream cheese, chives and salmon show up on breakfast and brunch menus everywhere. Why not use the same combination to fill a roulade? The chopped watercress leaves add a nice peppery bite.

1 8-ounce package cream cheese, at room temperature

3 tablespoons minced fresh chives

1 tablespoon minced fresh dill

1 Basic Roulade (page 328), made without the cheese, cooled

2 cups coarsely chopped watercress

8 ounces smoked salmon, cut into ¼-inch dice

½ cup finely chopped seedless cucumber

2 tablespoons rinsed, drained and chopped capers

1. Combine the cream cheese, chives and dill in a medium bowl and beat with a wooden spoon until light. Spread the cream-cheese mixture over the roulade, leaving a ½-inch border around the edges. Sprinkle the watercress evenly over the cream cheese. Top with the salmon, cucumber and capers.

2. Gently roll up the roulade from the long edge closest to you. If not serving immediately, wrap in plastic wrap and refrigerate for several hours or until ready to serve. Use a serrated knife to cut into thick slices and serve.

Makes 8 servings

Dicing the salmon makes the roulade easier to slice.

CHAPTER 11   *Savory Sauces Made with Eggs*

"I sing the praise of Hollandaise
A sauce supreme in many ways
Not only is it a treat to us
When ladled on asparagus
But I would shudder to predict
A world without Eggs Benedict."
——OGDEN NASH

O f all the clever tricks that eggs can do, there's one that always amazes me. Whenever I whisk a cup of vegetable oil, a drop at a time, into a few spoonfuls of lemon juice or vinegar mixed with egg yolk, I feel a certain excitement —and tension. If I do it right, the two irreconcilable liquids will, somehow, miraculously meld and billow into an opaque ivory mound, thick enough to hold up a spoon. It's the same when I heat the yolks and lemon juice first and then beat in soft or melted butter: a golden mountain of airy thick foam rises before my eyes. I've done these things a zillion times, but every time it works, I hear myself say, "Wow!"

Making mayonnaise and hollandaise are two of the most magical and satisfying transformations that a home cook can accomplish. In actuality, though, the processes are not miraculous but scientific. Both mayonnaise and hollandaise are emulsion sauces, formed from two normally unmixable substances—water (in the form of lemon juice or vinegar) and fat (in the form of vegetable oil or butter). In both instances, the hero is egg yolk, which acts as an emulsifier, chemically bonding tiny particles of the two liquids to create a thick, smooth, stable suspension with a luxurious, light texture.

I have devoted most of this chapter to mayonnaise and hollandaise recipes and variations because they are two of the most delicious and versatile sauces you can serve. Both of these are so important, in culinary terms, that French cuisine classifies them as "mother" sauces—fundamental types from which a family of other sauces is derived. At one time, they were part of every good cook's repertoire, as well as every chef's, but today, unfortunately, most of us never enjoy their homemade goodness. Mayonnaise, of course, is primarily regarded as a sandwich spread, and it's so easy to open a jar of commercial mayo that most people never bother to try to make their own. And for most, hollandaise is only a restaurant indulgence, coating a brunch platter of eggs Benedict.

The taste and texture of homemade emulsion sauces and other egg-based sauces, though, are far superior to what you'll get from a jar or at a busy restaurant. There's no substitute when you want to dress a special salad or crown a fabulous piece of fish, a filet mignon or a homegrown vegetable. You can make these sauces by hand or in a blender or food processor. You can also choose between the traditional manner of preparation that uses raw yolks or the new methods that cook the eggs to eliminate any risk of illness. And you'll learn how to "rescue" sauces in the event that your emulsion should "break," or fall apart. Once you've found a method that's most comfortable, you will be able to whip up a favorite sauce in minutes.

Safe Sauces

Homemade mayonnaise, hollandaise and their many variations are traditionally made with uncooked or lightly cooked eggs. There is a slight risk of bacterial growth that may cause illness from some of these sauces, but it can be minimized if you observe safe handling practices and precautions. I have also given a version of cooked-egg mayonnaise on page 343, and the recipes for hollandaise cook the eggs sufficiently to kill any bacteria.

♦ **Use fresh eggs and handle them safely.** For sauces made with raw eggs, use the freshest eggs available—whether supermarket eggs or farm-fresh eggs. They should be free of cracks or dirt and should have been kept under refrigeration. Refrigerate them the minute you get them home.

♦ **Never serve a sauce made with raw eggs to anyone who is elderly, very young or pregnant or who has a weakened immune system.** Salmonella poisoning (page 430) can be fatal to such individuals. Choose sauces using cooked eggs, such as Cooked-Egg-Yolk Mayonnaise (page 343) and Classic Hollandaise (page 346). Using methods developed by food-science experts, the eggs in these recipes are cooked to 160°F (or 140°F and held there for 3 to 4 minutes), a temperature high enough to destroy any dangerous bacteria.

♦ **Store finished sauces safely.** All products containing eggs, either raw or cooked, should be kept refrigerated. Cooked-egg sauces such as hollandaise can be held over hot water for about 1 hour; if you will be using them later, refrigerate and reheat just before using. To reheat, place the cold hollandaise (it will be solid) in a double boiler over *almost* simmering water and allow it to warm for a few minutes, whisking gently to restore it to a creamy consistency. Hollandaise can be kept in the refrigerator, tightly covered, for up to 2 days. Mayonnaise made with raw eggs, as well as any foods containing raw-egg mayonnaise, should be used within 2 days.

Basic Mayonnaise

Basic mayonnaise made by hand is rich, thick and satiny smooth. Adding the salt and lemon juice or vinegar to the egg yolks before whisking in the oil gives the emulsion more stability.

Choose the type of oil according to how you plan to use the mayonnaise. For tomatoes or other full-flavored foods, mayonnaise made with a fruity extra-virgin olive oil is excellent. Mayonnaise made with unrefined extra-virgin olive oil will separate after 1 day. For a slightly unusual flavor, peanut oil can be used; for a distinctive nutty flavor, use walnut oil. For mayonnaise with a subtle flavor, a mild vegetable oil with no discernible flavor, such as canola oil, is preferable. Mayonnaise can be flavored with mustard, garlic, fresh herbs, curry powder, chipotle chiles in adobo sauce, minced anchovies, mashed avocado or myriad other flavorings.

2 **large egg yolks, at room temperature**

1½ **tablespoons strained fresh lemon juice or white wine vinegar**

¼ **teaspoon kosher salt, or more to taste**

Freshly ground white pepper

1 **cup vegetable or other oil**

1–2 **teaspoons Dijon mustard**

1. Combine the egg yolks, lemon juice or vinegar, salt and a grinding of white pepper in a large bowl. Whisk vigorously until smooth and light.

2. One drop at a time, whisk in about ⅓ cup of the oil. Once the mixture begins to thicken, whisk in the remaining ⅔ cup oil in a slow, steady stream, making sure each addition is blended before adding more. When thickened, whisk in the mustard and adjust the seasonings, if necessary. Keep refrigerated and use within 2 days.

Makes about 1½ cups

This recipe contains raw egg yolks. See Safe Sauces (page 338).

To make emulsified sauces that are not heated, the eggs should be at room temperature, never cold. To take the chill off the eggs, soak them (in their shells) in a bowl of very warm water for 10 to 15 minutes.

Rescuing Mayonnaise

As with hollandaise sauce, the emulsion that makes mayonnaise smooth and firm can "break," so it will appear curdled. This happens most often when the oil is added too quickly to the egg-yolk base.

To rescue the separated mayonnaise, start again: whisk an egg yolk in a clean bowl, then slowly drizzle in the broken mayonnaise while whisking constantly. Add water, fresh lemon juice or white wine vinegar (about 1 tablespoon) to thin the mayonnaise if it seems too thick.

Machine-Made Mayonnaise

Mayonnaise can be made quickly and easily in a food processor or a blender. This version has a lighter, fluffier consistency than handmade because it uses one whole egg and one egg yolk rather than two yolks and a little water. For a flavor variation, use lime juice or orange juice, rice vinegar or an herb- or berry-flavored vinegar instead of the lemon juice or white wine vinegar.

1	**large egg, at room temperature**
1	**large egg yolk, at room temperature**
1½	**tablespoons strained fresh lemon juice or white wine vinegar**
¼	**teaspoon kosher salt, or more to taste**
	Freshly ground white pepper
1	**cup vegetable or other oil**
1	**tablespoon hot water**
1–2	**teaspoons Dijon mustard**

1. Place the egg, egg yolk, 2¼ teaspoons of the lemon juice or vinegar, salt and a grinding of white pepper in a blender or food processor. Blend or process for 20 seconds.

2. With the motor running, slowly add about ¼ cup of the oil one drop at a time. Once the mixture begins to thicken, add the remaining ¾ cup oil in a thin, steady stream, alternating with the remaining 2¼ teaspoons lemon juice or vinegar and the hot water, blending until thickened. Scrape down the sides of the blender or work bowl as needed. Blend in the mustard to taste and more salt or pepper, if needed. Keep refrigerated and use within 2 days.

Makes about 1½ cups

This recipe contains raw egg yolks. See Safe Sauces (page 338).

Cooked-Egg-Yolk Mayonnaise

This recipe for homemade mayonnaise was developed by food scientists in response to concern over the possible contamination of raw eggs. The egg yolks are combined with lemon juice and water and cooked before the oil is added, ensuring that the eggs are bacteria-free. I have refined the technique with the help of Shirley Corriher, food scientist, colleague and author of *CookWise*.

2 **large egg yolks**

2 **tablespoons strained fresh lemon juice**

2 **tablespoons water**

½ **teaspoon sugar**

1 **teaspoon dry mustard**

½ **teaspoon kosher salt**

   Pinch of cayenne pepper (optional)

1 **cup vegetable or other oil**

1. Have ready a pie plate half-full of cold water and a few ice cubes, so you can cool the bottom of the hot skillet to prevent the warmed yolk mixture from curdling. Combine the egg yolks, lemon juice, water and sugar in a small skillet over very low heat and stir constantly with a heatproof rubber spatula until the mixture just begins to thicken. Immediately remove from the heat and set the pan briefly in the pie plate of water, then scrape the mixture into a blender and let stand until cooled, about 5 minutes.

2. Add the mustard, salt and cayenne, if using. With the motor running, add about ¼ cup of the oil one drop at a time. Once the mixture begins to thicken, add the remaining ¾ cup oil in a slow, steady stream. Transfer to a covered container and refrigerate. (The mayonnaise will keep for up to 1 week.)

Makes about 1½ cups

> *Any food that contains eggs, whether raw or cooked, must be kept refrigerated.*

Aïoli

Aïoli is the Provençal version of mayonnaise, made with garlic, eggs and olive oil. My favorite way to use aïoli is to spoon it over a plate of roasted peppers, chilled cooked green beans and halved hard-cooked eggs. Adjust the amount of garlic to your palate. Traditionally, aïoli contains 6 to 8 cloves of garlic per cup of oil. For a more subtle olive-oil taste, use half extra-virgin olive oil and half vegetable oil.

2 large egg yolks

3–6 garlic cloves, minced

½ teaspoon kosher salt, or more to taste

Freshly ground white pepper

1 cup extra-virgin olive oil

1 teaspoon strained fresh lemon juice

½ teaspoon cold water

1. Combine the egg yolks, garlic, salt and a grinding of white pepper in a food processor and blend well. With the motor running, slowly add about ⅓ cup of the oil, one drop at a time, until the mixture begins to thicken. Add the lemon juice and water in a slow trickle, then add the remaining oil in a slow, steady stream. Taste and add more salt or pepper, if needed.

2. Serve immediately, or refrigerate in a tightly covered container and use within 2 days.

Makes about 1 cup

This recipe contains raw egg yolks. See Safe Sauces (page 338).

Rouille

Rouille means rust in French, which best describes the color of this peppery Provençal sauce. It can be made with fresh or dried red chile peppers or cayenne. Rouille is traditionally stirred into bouillabaisse, a hearty fish soup. Because it can be fiery, rouille is used sparingly. Use more or less hot pepper, depending on your tolerance. Protect your hands with rubber gloves when handling chile peppers.

2 **large egg yolks**

4 **garlic cloves, chopped**

½ **fresh red chile pepper, seeded and chopped**

¼ **teaspoon kosher salt, or more to taste**

½ **cup pure or extra-virgin olive oil**

2 **teaspoons hot water**

1 **tablespoon tomato paste**

1. Combine the egg yolks, garlic, chile pepper and salt in a blender or food processor and process until pureed. With the motor running, slowly add about ¼ cup of the oil one drop at a time, until the mixture begins to thicken. Add the water in a slow trickle, then add the remaining ¼ cup oil in a slow, steady stream. Scrape into a small bowl and stir in the tomato paste. Taste and add more salt, if needed.

2. Serve immediately, or refrigerate in a tightly covered container and use within 2 days.

Makes about ⅔ cup

This recipe contains raw egg yolks. See Safe Sauces (page 338).

Classic Hollandaise

Hollandaise is an egg-yolk-thickened, lemony, rich butter sauce unequaled, in my opinion, in the world of sauces. The method below is virtually fail-safe. Hollandaise makes eggs Benedict scrumptious, naps a plate of pristinely cooked asparagus and cascades regally down the sides of tender poached salmon.

8 ounces (2 sticks) unsalted butter

3 large egg yolks

¼ cup boiling water

2 tablespoons strained fresh lemon juice, or more to taste

½ teaspoon kosher salt, or more to taste

¼ teaspoon freshly ground white pepper, or more to taste

The hollandaise can be made ahead and kept warm over hot water for about an hour or refrigerated for 1 day and reheated.

1. Place the butter in a small saucepan and melt over medium-low heat; keep hot.

2. Off the heat, whisk the egg yolks in the top of a double boiler (or in a heatproof bowl that will sit snugly over a larger pan) until blended. Slowly whisk in the boiling water and then the lemon juice.

3. Meanwhile, heat (do not boil) about 1 of inch water in the bottom of the double boiler (or a saucepan large enough to hold the heatproof bowl snugly).

4. Place the egg-yolk mixture over the hot water. Gradually dribble in the butter, whisking constantly. Continue whisking over hot — not boiling — water until the sauce is very thick and smooth. Remove from the heat. Add the salt and white pepper. Taste and add more salt, pepper or lemon juice, if necessary. Serve at once, or keep warm over hot water. To make sure that the water isn't too hot, bring it almost to a boil, then remove it from the heat. Set the pan or bowl with the hollandaise over the water and let stand off the heat until ready to serve. Gently reheat the water as it cools to hot, never boiling. Keep warm for up to 1 hour.

Makes about 2 cups

Rescuing Hollandaise

 When a hollandaise sauce "breaks," which means the butter and the egg-yolk base are no longer held in suspension together, it will look curdled. This can happen if the butter is added too quickly or if the sauce is kept over simmering water after you have made it and it gets too hot. In either case, you can "rescue" the sauce —that is, reconstitute the emulsion—by simply removing the pan from the double boiler (or the heatproof bowl from the pan of water) and whisking in 1 tablespoon of cold water. This will lower the temperature of the mixture, stop the curdling and smooth out the sauce. Set the pan back over hot (never boiling) water and whisk until thickened.

Blender Hollandaise

Hollandaise made in the blender has a fluffier, lighter consistency than hand-whisked hollandaise. Adding boiling water to the blended egg yolks and cooking the sauce in a double boiler ensure that the yolks are heated to a safe temperature. This sauce is delicious served over eggs Benedict or poached fish.

8 ounces (2 sticks) unsalted butter

3 large egg yolks

2 tablespoons strained fresh lemon juice

½ cup boiling water

½ teaspoon kosher salt

¼ teaspoon freshly ground white pepper

1. Heat the butter in a small saucepan until melted and very hot; keep hot.

2. Meanwhile, combine the egg yolks and lemon juice in the blender. With the motor running, drizzle in the boiling water.

3. With the motor running, add the butter to the egg yolks in a slow, steady stream, add the salt and white pepper.

4. Transfer to the top of a double boiler or to a heat-proof bowl that will sit snugly over a larger pan and whisk over very hot—not boiling—water until the sauce is hot. Remove from the heat. Serve at once, or keep warm over hot water until ready to serve, or for up to 1 hour. (The sauce can also be made ahead and refrigerated for 2 days; reheat before serving.)

Makes about 2 cups

VARIATION

Add 1 tablespoon Dijon mustard with the lemon juice.

Orange Hollandaise (Sauce Maltaise)

Classic Sauce Maltaise is hollandaise flavored with blood oranges. In this version, the juice of regular oranges is used. Boil ¼ cup fresh orange juice until reduced to 2 tablespoons and add 1 teaspoon fresh strained lemon juice. Substitute for the lemon juice in either of the hollandaise recipes. Stir in ½ teaspoon grated orange zest when you add the salt.

Chipotle Chile Hollandaise

Whisk 1 teaspoon minced canned chipotle chiles in adobo sauce into the Blender Hollandaise when you add the salt.

Béarnaise Sauce

Like hollandaise, béarnaise is an emulsified sauce, but it is made with a reduction of wine and vinegar cooked with shallots and herbs. The sauce is thickened with egg yolks and made velvety smooth with melted butter. Traditionally served with meat, fish, eggs and vegetables, béarnaise is a French classic.

½ **cup dry white wine**

½ **cup red wine vinegar**

2 **tablespoons minced shallots**

1 **sprig fresh flat-leaf parsley**

1 **sprig fresh tarragon or**
    ½ teaspoon dried

1 **sprig fresh chervil or**
    ½ teaspoon dried

½ **bay leaf**

8 **ounces (2 sticks) unsalted**
    butter

4 **large egg yolks**
    Kosher salt and freshly
    ground white pepper

1. Combine the wine, vinegar, shallots, parsley, tarragon, chervil and bay leaf in a small saucepan and bring to a boil. Reduce the heat and boil gently until reduced to a scant ¼ cup. Strain into the top of a double boiler or a heatproof bowl that will sit over a saucepan of water; press on the herbs with a rubber spatula to squeeze out all the flavor. Discard the solids.

2. Meanwhile, melt the butter in a small saucepan over medium-low heat; keep warm over very low heat.

3. Whisk the egg yolks into the wine reduction. Set the top of the double boiler or the heatproof bowl over 1 inch of hot—not boiling—water over low heat. Whisk constantly until the yolks begin to thicken, then immediately drizzle in the butter, whisking until the sauce is thick and smooth. Remove from the heat and add salt to taste and a grinding of white pepper. Serve at once, or keep warm in the double boiler or bowl set over hot (not boiling) water, off the heat.

Makes about 2 cups

Sauce Parisienne

I like this pretty pale pink sauce spooned over poached or coddled eggs served on steamed asparagus. You can also substitute the sauce for the hollandaise in eggs Benedict (page 113).

3 **large egg yolks**

¼ **cup heavy cream**

2 **tablespoons tomato puree**

3 **tablespoons unsalted butter, cut into small pieces, at room temperature**

1 **tablespoon strained fresh lemon juice**

¼ **teaspoon dry mustard**

½ **teaspoon kosher salt**

1. In the top of a double boiler or in a heatproof bowl set over a saucepan of 1 inch hot—not boiling—water, whisk together the egg yolks, cream and tomato puree, then whisk constantly until the mixture is thick and smooth. Whisk in the butter bit by bit until blended. Whisk in the lemon juice, mustard and salt. Keep the sauce warm over the hot water until ready to serve, or for up to 1 hour.

2. The sauce can also be made ahead and refrigerated for 2 days; reheat before serving.

Makes about ¾ cup

Salsa Verde

Salsa verde is a fresh green Italian sauce made with parsley. I especially like it served over slices of ripe tomato, tender boiled potatoes, steamed fresh asparagus or baby carrots and sliced roasted beets.

½ **cup finely chopped fresh flat-leaf parsley**

4 **anchovy fillets, drained, rinsed and patted dry with paper towels**

¼ **cup capers, drained, rinsed and finely chopped**

3 **tablespoons fresh lemon juice**

2 **tablespoons finely chopped sweet onion**

2 **tablespoons pine nuts, lightly toasted (page 271; optional)**

1 **garlic clove, minced**

¼ **teaspoon kosher salt, or to taste**

2 **large eggs, hard-cooked (page 162), peeled and halved lengthwise**

⅔ **cup extra-virgin olive oil**

1. Combine the parsley, anchovies, capers, lemon juice, onion, pine nuts, if using, garlic and salt in a medium bowl.

2. Remove the egg yolks from the egg whites. Finely chop the whites and add them to the parsley mixture. Press the yolks through a sieve onto a sheet of waxed paper or a small plate; set aside.

3. Gradually whisk ⅓ cup of the oil, one drop at a time, into the parsley mixture until blended, then gradually stir in the remaining ⅓ cup oil. Fold in half of the reserved yolks. Transfer to a serving bowl and sprinkle with the remaining yolks.

Makes about 1¼ cups

Egg, Lemon and Caper Sauce

Omit the anchovies and pine nuts. Substitute ¼ cup finely chopped mixed fresh flat-leaf parsley, dill or basil for the ½ cup parsley and add ½ teaspoon grated lemon or orange zest. Serve over poached, grilled or roasted fish as a perfect spring or summer meal.

CHAPTER 12   *Dessert Custards, Ice Creams and Nogs*

"Alas! My child, where is the Pen,
That can do justice to the Hen?
. . . Laying foundations every day,
Though not for public buildings, yet
For Custards, Cakes and Omelette.
. . . No wonder, Child, we prize the Hen,
Whose egg is mightier than the Pen."
—OLIVER HERFORD

As soon as my granddaughter, Seraphina, was big enough to stand safely on a stool next to me at the stove and grasp a big wooden spoon, we started to make custard together. It's become a ritual whenever I visit: I heat milk in a saucepan and then hold it as she stirs in chopped chocolate and sugar. We marvel at the ribbony swirls and chocolate smells and at how the white milk becomes smooth, dark and thick. Then we whisk eggs and egg yolks in a bowl, and she slowly stirs in the chocolate mixture, admiring the swirls of brown and gold. The hard part for her and me, too, comes next—waiting for the little cups of custard to bake. Of course we are excited to see that they are firm and set when we take them out of the oven—but then we have to wait again, until they are cool enough to eat. The joy we share at that moment is worth all the cleaning up—dishes and granddaughter both.

I have not yet confused Seraphina with the mature notion that there are many types of custard beyond our special chocolate kind. When she is old enough to read this book, she'll understand that almost any dish in which cream or milk (or another liquid) is cooked with eggs until thick and creamy can properly be called a custard. And from that broad perspective, all the desserts in this chapter are "custards," even though some are made in the oven and some on the stovetop.

Among these are a few of my own innovations as well as the classics. Custards comprise some of the most popular desserts in the world: the baked custard that's unmolded with its own caramel sauce, known as flan or crème caramel; the individual custards coated with a thin, crisp layer of caramelized sugar called crème brûlée; the delicate custards, baked and served in tiny lidded pots, called pots de crème; and a custard called Lemon

Curd, which is served as a spread or filling. There are custards that are sauces—vanilla-infused crème anglaise and its many flavorful variations. There's a custard that's turned into a beverage—my classic brandy eggnog—and a custard that's frozen into ice cream. And there's the classic foamy egg custard sauce known as zabaglione (or *sabayon*, in French), which is made with sweet wine rather than cream.

While all custards are essentially simple to prepare, they are not without their challenges. Egg yolks can easily be overheated and turn into scrambled curds in an instant. And caramelized sugar, which complements custard beautifully, can overcook quickly and become dark and bitter. Therefore, my recipes usually instruct you to bake custards in a water bath or cook them in a double boiler to shield them from direct heat. Frequently, too, you should strain custards to ensure that they will be glossy and smooth. And when caramelizing sugar, you'll want to pay careful attention, as the sugar mixture attains very high temperatures and can splatter dangerously.

Once you've mastered the basics, all kinds of variations are possible. Seraphina will be delighted to find that she can make custards with vanilla, caramel, hazelnut, coconut, orange, and Earl Grey tea and even sumptuous bread puddings, enveloped in a custard sauce and flavored with jam, nuts or dried cherries. For familiarity's sake, though, she'll be comforted to find her favorite Rich Chocolate Custards on page 367.

Classic Crème Caramel (Flan)

Crème caramel (in French) or flan (in Spanish) is a custard baked in a baking dish or other vessel lined with a thin layer of caramelized sugar. As the custard bakes, the crackling caramelized sugar melts, and when the cooked custard is thoroughly chilled, the caramel becomes a fragrant, bittersweet amber sauce that surrounds the custard when it is turned out. In Italy, this dessert is called *crema caramella*.

Caramel

- 1 cup sugar
- ¼ cup water
- 1 teaspoon fresh lemon juice

Custard

- 2 cups milk
- 1 cup heavy cream
- 1 vanilla bean, split lengthwise
- ¾ cup sugar
- 3 large eggs
- 6 large egg yolks

1. **Make the caramel:** Combine the sugar, water and lemon juice in a medium skillet and heat over medium heat, stirring, until the sugar is dissolved. Continue cooking, without stirring, until the syrup turns amber. Do not let it get too dark, or it will be bitter; also, keep in mind that once the caramel is removed from the heat, it will continue cooking for a few seconds. Immediately pour the caramel into a 9-inch glass or ceramic pie plate or round shallow baking dish, tilting it so that the caramel evenly coats the bottom. Set aside.

2. **Make the custard:** Heat the milk, cream and vanilla bean in a medium saucepan until small bubbles appear around the edges; do not boil. Remove from the heat, cover and let stand for 20 minutes.

3. Position a rack in the center of the oven and preheat the oven to 325°F. Set the caramel-coated pie plate or baking dish in a large baking pan. Set a kettle of water on to boil.

4. Remove the vanilla bean from the milk mixture and scrape the seeds into the milk mixture; discard the pod. Add the sugar, return to the heat and stir over low heat just until the sugar is dissolved.

Melted sugar is very hot, so be careful that it doesn't spatter on your skin. As soon as the sugar is caramelized to the degree you want, quickly pour it into the prepared dish(es); it will harden as it cools. Adding a little lemon juice along with the water keeps the caramel liquid. To further prevent crystallization of the caramel, do not stir but swirl the pan to distribute the sugar evenly before the sugar is melted.

5. Whisk the eggs and egg yolks in a large bowl until blended. Gradually stir in the warm milk mixture until blended; try to avoid making the mixture foamy. Place a strainer over a large glass measuring cup and strain the milk mixture into it. Let stand for a few minutes to allow any bubbles to subside.

6. Pour the custard into the pie plate or baking dish. Place the baking pan in the oven and add enough boiling water to the pan to come halfway up the sides of the pie plate or baking dish. Bake until a small sharp knife inserted in the center of the custard comes out clean, about 1 hour. (Be careful to insert the knife only halfway into the custard; you don't want to make any marks in the bottom of the flan, because it will become the top when it is turned out.) Remove the pan from the oven and, protecting your hands with oven mitts, lift the pie plate or baking dish from the water. Let cool to room temperature, then refrigerate until thoroughly chilled, at least 12 hours.

7. To serve, carefully run a knife around the edge of the crème caramel. Place a shallow bowl or deep platter over the top and invert the pie plate or baking dish. The flan will unmold onto the plate and the caramel sauce will surround the flan. Serve cold.

Makes 6 to 8 servings

Caramel Pots de Crème

This luxurious baked pudding is best when savored in small portions. I like to make it in little espresso cups or in small porcelain pots with lids, which are made especially for pots de crème.

1 cup sugar

¼ cup water

1 teaspoon fresh lemon juice

1 cup heavy cream

1 cup milk

1 vanilla bean, split lengthwise

8 large egg yolks

1. Combine the sugar, water and lemon juice in a medium skillet and heat over medium heat, stirring, until the sugar is dissolved. Continue cooking over medium-low heat, without stirring, until the syrup turns amber; do not let it get too dark or it will be bitter. Add the cream all at once. It will splatter a bit and the caramel will harden. Stir slowly with a wooden spoon to help dissolve the hardened caramel in the boiling cream. Remove from the heat and set aside. (Do not worry about small pieces of undissolved caramel; the mixture will be strained later.)

2. Meanwhile, heat the milk and vanilla bean in a small saucepan until small bubbles appear around the edges; do not boil. Remove from the heat, cover and let stand for 10 minutes.

3. Position a rack in the center of the oven and preheat the oven to 325°F. Arrange 6 to 8 small ramekins, espresso cups or little pots with lids in a shallow baking pan. Set a kettle of water on to boil.

4. Remove the vanilla bean from the milk and scrape the seeds from the pod and set aside; discard the pod.

5. Whisk the egg yolks in a medium bowl until blended. Add the caramel and milk and stir to blend. Strain into a large glass measuring cup, then stir in the vanilla seeds. Pour into the ramekins or other cups, distributing evenly. Let stand to allow the bubbles to subside.

6. Place the baking pan in the oven. Add enough boiling water to the baking pan to come halfway up the sides of the ramekins or cups. If using ramekins or espresso cups, cover with a baking sheet or a large sheet of foil. If using pots de crème cups, put the lids on the cups.

7. Bake until a small, sharp knife inserted in the center of a custard comes out clean, 25 to 30 minutes. Remove the pan from the oven and, using a spatula and protecting your hand with an oven mitt, remove the custards from the hot water. Cool on a rack. Refrigerate, covered, until chilled, then serve.

Makes 6 to 8 servings

Vanilla
An Investment in Flavor

The finest-quality vanilla comes from the islands of Madagascar, Réunion and the Comoros, in the Indian Ocean. Vanilla is expensive because it is the fruit of a tropical orchid whose blossoms must be hand-pollinated. You can get the most intense flavor by using a whole vanilla bean instead of vanilla extract; try it once, and you'll see what a difference it makes.

To use, soak the vanilla bean in the milk, cream, syrups or other liquid in the recipe. Once it is soft, split it and scrape out the tiny black seeds inside with the tip of a small spoon or knife and add them to the liquid. To substitute vanilla extract for one vanilla bean, add 2 to 3 teaspoons to the liquid after it is removed from the heat. Buy only pure vanilla extract, which is made from vanilla beans, sugar, water and alcohol.

Classic Vanilla Crème Brûlée with Raspberry Sauce

Because this crème brûlée is made in one large pan instead of small individual serving dishes, it can be served with a fruit puree on dessert plates. If you prefer individual dishes, follow the baking times in the recipe for Earl Grey Crème Brûlée (page 365) and omit the raspberry sauce.

3 cups heavy cream

1 vanilla bean, split lengthwise, or 2 teaspoons vanilla extract

8 large egg yolks

6 tablespoons sugar

½ cup superfine sugar

Raspberry Sauce (recipe follows)

You can also use a household propane torch or a small blowtorch made especially for cooking to caramelize the sugar. Follow the manufacturer's directions.

1. Combine the cream and vanilla bean (if using vanilla extract, don't add it until later) in a medium saucepan and heat until small bubbles appear around the edges; do not boil. Remove from the heat, cover and let stand for 30 minutes.

2. Position a rack in the center of the oven and preheat the oven to 325°F. Place a shallow 6-cup flameproof baking dish inside a larger baking pan. Set a kettle of water on to boil.

3. Remove the vanilla bean from the cream and scrape the seeds from the pod and set aside; discard the pod.

4. Whisk the yolks and sugar in a medium bowl until light in color. Gradually stir in the cream until the sugar is dissolved. Strain into a large glass measuring cup to remove any unbeaten egg; stir in the vanilla seeds or add the vanilla extract, if using.

5. Pour the custard into the baking dish. Transfer to the oven and add enough boiling water to the baking pan to come halfway up the sides of the baking dish. Bake until a toothpick inserted in the center comes out clean, 55 to 60 minutes. Let cool in the water bath, then refrigerate until very cold, at least 4 hours.

6. Up to 1 hour before serving, preheat the broiler. Carefully blot any moisture from the top of the custard with a paper towel. Sprinkle the custard evenly with the superfine sugar. Broil 3 inches from the heat, watching carefully and turning the pan as needed, until the sugar is melted and evenly caramelized, 1 to 2 minutes. Let stand for a few minutes to allow the sugar to harden. Serve at once or refrigerate until ready to serve. (The custard can be made 1 day ahead.)

7. To serve, spoon into dessert dishes and spoon the raspberry sauce over each serving.

Makes 8 servings

Raspberry Sauce

13 **10-ounce boxes frozen raspberries in light syrup, thawed**

1–2 **teaspoons fresh lemon juice**

1. Puree the raspberries in a food processor. Press through a strainer set over a bowl, pressing down on the puree with a wooden spoon to squeeze out all the juices. With a rubber spatula, scrape the puree from the outside of the strainer into the bowl. Cover and refrigerate the raspberry puree until ready to use. (The sauce will keep for 2 to 3 days.)

2. Before serving, add the lemon juice to taste.

Makes about 2 cups

Earl Grey Crème Brûlée

Earl Grey is a black tea flavored with bergamot, a small acidic orange. Its rich herbaceous flavor is the quintessential match for custard.

½ cup milk

1 tablespoon Earl Grey tea leaves (the contents of 2 tea bags)

1½ cups heavy cream

1 vanilla bean, split lengthwise

½ cup sugar

5 large egg yolks

¼ cup superfine sugar

1. Heat the milk and tea in a small saucepan over low heat until small bubbles appear around the edges; do not boil. Remove from the heat, cover and let stand for 20 minutes.

2. Meanwhile, combine the cream and vanilla bean in a small saucepan and heat until small bubbles appear around the edges; do not boil. Remove from the heat; stir in the sugar until dissolved. Cover and let stand for 10 minutes.

3. Position a rack in the center of the oven and preheat the oven to 325°F. Arrange six 5-ounce ramekins in a 13-x-9-inch baking pan or four 4-inch-wide fluted flan dishes in two 13-x-9-inch pans. Put a kettle of water on to boil.

4. Strain the milk into the cream mixture; discard the tea leaves. Remove the vanilla bean from the cream and scrape the seeds from the pod and set aside; discard the pod.

5. Whisk the egg yolks in a medium bowl until blended. Gently whisk in the warm cream mixture; do not whisk too vigorously, or small bubbles will form on top of the crème. Strain into a large glass measuring cup to remove any unbeaten egg; stir in the vanilla seeds.

You can also use a household propane torch or a small blowtorch made especially for cooking to caramelize the sugar. Follow the manufacturer's directions.

6. Divide the cream mixture evenly among the ramekins or flan dishes. Place the baking pan(s) in the oven and add enough boiling water to the pan(s) to come halfway up the sides of the ramekins or flan dishes. Bake until the custards are set in the centers when the pan is gently shaken, 30 to 35 minutes for the ramekins; 25 to 30 minutes for the flan dishes. Remove from the oven and, using a spatula and protecting your hand with an oven mitt, remove the custards from the hot water. Cool to room temperature on a rack, then cover and refrigerate until very cold, several hours or overnight.

7. Up to 1 hour before serving, preheat the broiler. Carefully blot any moisture from the tops of the custards with a paper towel. The results are better if you caramelize only two or three at a time. Place the ramekins or flan dishes on a baking sheet. Using a small spoon, sprinkle a thick layer of superfine sugar on top of each one. Broil about 4 inches from the heat, turning the baking sheet frequently, until the sugar is melted and evenly caramelized, 1 to 3 minutes, depending on the heat of the broiler. Repeat with the remaining custards. Let stand for a few minutes to allow the sugar to harden, then serve. Caramelize 1 hour or less before serving.

Makes 6 servings

Rich Chocolate Custards

Chocolate custard is a silky-textured version of good old-fashioned chocolate pudding. The luscious consistency comes from egg yolks; puddings, which taste slightly less rich, are generally thickened with cornstarch.

2 cups milk

3 ounces good-quality bittersweet or semisweet chocolate, finely chopped

⅓ cup sugar

2 large eggs

2 large egg yolks

1 teaspoon pure vanilla extract

Pinch of kosher salt

Softly whipped cream for topping (optional)

Experiment with different brands of chocolate. Scharffen Berger, made in California, is an especially deep, rich chocolate, with notes of dried fruit. But any good-quality bittersweet chocolate will do.

1. Position a rack in the center of the oven and preheat the oven to 350°F. Place six 5-ounce custard cups in a 13-x-9-inch baking pan. Set a kettle of water on to boil.

2. Heat the milk in a small saucepan over low heat until small bubbles appear around the edges; do not boil. Stir in the chocolate and sugar until the chocolate is melted and the sugar is dissolved. Remove from the heat.

3. In a medium bowl, whisk the eggs and egg yolks until blended. Stir in the milk mixture, vanilla and salt. Strain into a large glass measuring cup. Pour into the custard cups, distributing evenly.

4. Place the baking pan in the oven and add enough boiling water to come halfway up the sides of the custard cups. Bake until the custards are set in the centers when the pan is jiggled, 25 to 30 minutes. Remove from the oven and, using a spatula and protecting your hand with an oven mitt, transfer the cups to a rack to cool. Serve at room temperature, or refrigerate until chilled before serving.

5. Serve the custard in the custard cups, with a dollop of whipped cream, if desired.

Makes 6 servings

Baked Coconut Custards

The seductive taste of coconut is intensified when it is cooked into a custard. Though this is a rich dessert, made in small custard cups, it's a delightful finish to any meal.

⅔ cup sweetened flaked
   coconut

3 large eggs

1 large egg yolk

⅓ cup sugar

2 cups milk or 1 cup milk
   plus 1 cup heavy cream

1 teaspoon pure vanilla extract

1. Position a rack in the center of the oven and preheat the oven to 325°F. Place six 5-ounce custard cups in a 13-x-9-inch baking pan. Set a kettle of water on to boil.

2. Sprinkle the coconut into a small baking pan or pie plate and bake until golden, 5 to 6 minutes. Remove from the oven. Measure out ¼ cup of the toasted coconut and set aside. Divide the remaining coconut among the custard cups, using about 1 heaping tablespoon for each.

3. In a medium bowl, whisk the eggs, egg yolk and sugar until blended. Whisk in the milk or milk and cream and vanilla. Strain into a large glass measuring cup. Pour into the custard cups.

4. Place the baking pan in the oven and add enough boiling water to come halfway up the sides of the custard cups. Bake until the custards are set in the centers, 25 to 30 minutes. Remove from the oven and, using a spatula and protecting your hand with an oven mitt, transfer the cups to a rack. Cool slightly.

5. Sprinkle the tops of the custards with the reserved toasted coconut. Serve warm or chilled.

Makes 6 servings

Lemon Curd

Homemade lemon curd, a thick custard, is a multipurpose spread or filling. I like it on toasted cake or bread, as a filling for cookies, cakes and pies or folded into whipped cream as a topping for cakes or a filling for cream puffs.

5 **large egg yolks**

½ **cup sugar**

1 **tablespoon grated lemon zest**

½ **cup fresh lemon juice**

4 **tablespoons (½ stick) unsalted butter, cut into small pieces**

1. In a small, heavy saucepan, combine the egg yolks, sugar, lemon zest and lemon juice and cook, stirring, over medium-low heat until thickened. Do not boil. Reduce the heat to very low. Add the butter one piece at a time, stirring, until the butter is melted and the curd is very thick.

2. Pour the curd into a small bowl and cover with a piece of waxed paper or plastic wrap. Refrigerate until ready to use. (The curd can be stored for up to 1 week.)

Makes about 1 cup

VARIATION

Lime Curd

Substitute 2 teaspoons grated lime zest and ½ cup fresh lime juice for the lemon zest and juice.

Crème Anglaise

Crème anglaise is the French name for a rich, sweet custard sauce. It is used in many ways, from embellishing a simple fruit dessert to adorning an elaborate pudding. Once the technique is mastered, it will be indispensable to cooks who like to dress up their desserts.

2 cups milk

⅓ cup sugar

Pinch of kosher salt

4 large egg yolks

1 teaspoon pure vanilla extract

1. Combine the milk, sugar and salt in the top of a double boiler. Set the pan directly over low heat and cook, stirring, until the sugar is dissolved. Remove from the heat.

2. Place the egg yolks in a small bowl and whisk just until blended. Slowly stir some of the hot milk into the yolks to temper them, then add the yolk mixture to the milk and whisk until blended.

3. Meanwhile, heat about 1 inch of water in the bottom of the double boiler until simmering, not boiling.

4. Set the double boiler top over the bottom and cook, stirring constantly, until the custard coats the back of the spoon, 10 to 15 minutes. Remove from the heat, strain into a bowl and stir in the vanilla. The sauce can be served hot or cold. To cool it quickly, set the top of the double boiler in a pan of ice water and stir until cold.

Makes about 2 cups

♦ **Thin Custard Sauce:** Increase the milk to 2½ cups and the vanilla to 1¼ teaspoons.

♦ **Rich Custard Sauce:** Substitute 1 cup heavy cream for 1 cup of the milk and use 5 egg yolks.

♦ **Hazelnut Crème Anglaise:** Toast 1 cup hazelnuts (page 56) and finely grind in a food processor. Substitute 1 cup heavy cream for 1 cup of the milk in step 1, increase the sugar to ½ cup and omit the salt. Heat the nuts, cream and milk in a small saucepan until small bubbles appear. Remove from the heat; let stand, covered, for 1 hour. Strain the mixture through a sieve set over a bowl, pressing down hard on the nuts to extract as much flavor as possible. Discard the solids. Reheat the milk mixture and proceed with the recipe as directed in step 2.

♦ **Vanilla Bean Custard Sauce:** Add 1 vanilla bean, split, to the milk along with the sugar and salt in step 1. Let the hot milk steep off the heat, covered, for 10 minutes. With the tip of a knife or a teaspoon, scrape the softened seeds from the vanilla pod into the milk; discard the pod. Proceed with the recipe, omitting the vanilla extract.

♦ **Lemon Custard Sauce:** Stir 2 teaspoons finely grated lemon zest into the sauce in place of the vanilla extract in step 4.

♦ **Orange Custard Sauce:** Stir 2 teaspoons finely grated orange zest into the sauce in place of the vanilla extract in step 4.

♦ **Coffee Custard Sauce:** Stir 2 teaspoons of good-quality instant coffee crystals into the sauce with the vanilla extract in step 4. Or add 1 tablespoon of Kahlúa or other coffee liqueur.

Zabaglione

Zabaglione is a classic Italian wine custard, served warm or cold in wineglasses or dessert bowls. I like it best spooned over fresh orange segments, sliced strawberries or peaches, prunes soaked in Armagnac or a slice of pound cake, then garnished with fresh raspberries or blueberries.

4 **large egg yolks**

¼ **cup superfine sugar**

¼ **cup sweet Marsala wine**

1. Place the egg yolks in the top of a double boiler or in a heatproof bowl that will fit snugly over a larger pan. Place on a folded kitchen towel and beat with a whisk or a hand-held electric mixer until pale yellow. Beat in the sugar about ½ tablespoon at a time, beating well after each addition. Beat in the wine.

2. Pour about 1 inch of water in the bottom part of the double boiler and heat to simmering, not boiling. Reduce the heat to low. Set the top of the double boiler or the heatproof bowl over the simmering water and beat the zabaglione with a wire whisk until thick and foamy, at least 7 minutes. Pour into 4 wineglasses or dessert bowls. Serve at once.

Makes 4 servings

Coconut Macaroon Bread Pudding with Dried Cherries

An indulgent combination of coconut macaroons and dried cherries, this is a pudding to serve, like a birthday cake, for a special occasion.

4 tablespoons (½ stick) unsalted butter, melted

8 slices firm white bread

1 package (about 15 ounces) coconut macaroons or twelve 2-inch macaroons, crumbled

½ cup dried cherries

5 large eggs

⅓ cup sugar

2½ cups milk

½ teaspoon pure almond extract

1. Lightly brush a 9-inch square (2-quart) shallow baking dish with some of the melted butter. Brush the bread slices on one side with the remaining butter. Arrange 4 of the bread slices buttered side up in the bottom of the baking dish, cutting them as necessary so that they make a snug layer. Sprinkle half of the macaroons over the bread, then sprinkle with the dried cherries. Top with the remaining 4 bread slices, buttered side up, cutting them to fit snugly.

2. Whisk the eggs and sugar in a large bowl until blended. Gradually whisk in the milk. Add the almond extract. Pour over the bread in the baking dish, pressing down with a spatula to submerge the bread. Top with the remaining macaroons. Cover and refrigerate for at least 2 hours, or overnight.

3. Preheat the oven to 350°F. For a softer pudding, bake in a water bath: Set the baking dish in a larger baking pan, place in the oven and add enough boiling water to the baking pan to come halfway up the sides of the baking dish. If you choose not to bake the pudding in a water bath, the bottom and sides will be browner and the texture firmer. (The baking time will be the same either way.)

4. Bake until golden and puffy, about 45 minutes. Let stand for 15 minutes before serving.

Makes 6 to 8 servings

Strawberry Jam Bread Pudding with Almond Streusel Topping

This bread pudding combines the comforting quality of a jam sandwich with the sophisticated taste of toasted almonds and streusel topping. Of all puddings, I like bread puddings the most, perhaps because they are easily made from ingredients we all have on hand. This particular pudding is good served warm from the oven, cold from the refrigerator or at room temperature. Serve it for breakfast or as a dessert.

4 tablespoons (½ stick) unsalted butter, melted

8 slices firm white bread

½ cup strawberry jam

4 large eggs

⅓ cup sugar

2½ cups milk

1 teaspoon pure vanilla extract

¼ teaspoon pure almond extract

Almond Streusel Topping

½ cup all-purpose flour

½ cup packed light brown sugar

½ teaspoon ground cinnamon

5⅓ tablespoons (⅓ cup) cold unsalted butter, cut into small pieces

½ cup sliced natural almonds

1. Lightly brush a 9-inch square (2-quart) shallow baking dish with some of the melted butter. Place 4 slices of the bread on a work surface and spread with the jam. Top with the remaining 4 slices of bread. Brush with the remaining butter. Arrange the jam sandwiches in the baking dish, cutting them as necessary to fit snugly.

2. Whisk the eggs and sugar in a large bowl until blended. Gradually whisk in the milk. Add the vanilla and almond extracts. Pour over the bread in the baking dish, pressing down with a spatula to submerge the bread. Cover and refrigerate for at least 3 hours, or overnight.

3. **Make the streusel topping:** Combine the flour, brown sugar and cinnamon in a small bowl. Using a pastry blender or a fork, work the butter into the dry ingredients until crumbly. Add the almonds and gently stir to blend. Set aside.

4. Preheat the oven to 350°F. Sprinkle the streusel topping evenly over the pudding. For a softer pudding, bake in a water bath: Set the baking dish in a larger baking pan, place in the oven and add enough boiling water to the baking pan to come halfway up the sides

of the baking dish. If you choose not to bake the pudding in a water bath, the bottom and sides will be browner and the texture firmer. (The baking time will be the same either way.)

5. Bake until golden and puffy, about 45 minutes. Let stand for 15 minutes before serving.

Makes 6 to 8 servings

Vanilla Bean French Custard Ice Cream

Nothing is more satisfying than a scoop of creamy, rich vanilla-flecked homemade ice cream, a delicacy that I enjoy far too seldom. This tried-and-true recipe is one of my favorites. The chilling time (up to 24 hours) helps contribute to the smooth texture of the ice cream.

2 **cups heavy cream**

1 **cup milk**

1 **vanilla bean, split lengthwise, or 2 teaspoons pure vanilla extract**

2 **large eggs**

2 **large egg yolks**

⅓ **cup sugar**

For optimum smoothness, make the custard the day before you intend to freeze and serve the ice cream.

1. Combine the cream, milk and vanilla bean (if using vanilla extract, don't add it until later) in a medium saucepan and heat until small bubbles appear around the edges; do not boil. Cover and let stand off the heat for 30 minutes.

2. Lift the vanilla bean from the cream mixture and, using the tip of a spoon or a small knife, scrape the small seeds from the pod into the cream mixture; discard the pod.

3. Combine the eggs, yolks and sugar in a medium bowl and beat until light in color and thick. Whisk a little of the hot cream mixture into the eggs to temper them, then stir the egg mixture into the cream mixture.

4. Transfer to the top of a double boiler or a heatproof bowl and set over 1 inch of gently simmering water. Cook, stirring constantly, until the custard coats the back of the spoon, 15 to 20 minutes. Pour the custard into a large bowl. Add the vanilla extract, if using. Set the bowl in a larger bowl half-filled with ice. Refrigerate, covered, for at least 4 hours and up to 24 hours.

5. Transfer to an ice-cream maker and freeze according to the manufacturer's directions.

Makes about 1 quart

Rich Chocolate Ice Cream

Omit the vanilla bean. Prepare the custard as directed in step 4. While it is still hot, add 4 ounces of the best-quality bittersweet or semisweet chocolate, finely chopped, to the hot custard and stir over low heat until melted. Stir in 2 teaspoons vanilla extract.

French Custard Ice Cream

 With the following formula, you can create a base for many different flavors of ice cream:

♦ 3 cups heavy cream or half-and-half or 1½ cups heavy cream plus 1½ cups whole milk

♦ 2 large eggs

♦ 2 large egg yolks

♦ ⅓ to ½ cup sugar

Here's my basic method:

1. Heat the cream (or milk) until small bubbles appear around the edges.

2. If using a vanilla bean, let it soften in the heated milk for 30 minutes.

3. Beat the eggs and sugar until the sugar is dissolved and the mixture is light in color and thick.

4. Gradually stir the hot cream into the egg mixture.

5. Cook in a double boiler set over simmering, not boiling, water, stirring constantly, until the custard coats a spoon; this will take 15 to 20 minutes. To hasten the process, cook the sauce in a heavy-bottomed saucepan directly over low heat, stirring constantly with a heatproof rubber spatula. Be sure to reach all over the bottom and into the corners of the pan, and watch the custard carefully so that it doesn't boil. (If it does, it will

curdle and be ruined.) Properly done, this method will thicken the custard in half the time.

6. Once the custard is thick, strain it into a bowl. Cool slightly before adding vanilla or another extract, if using.

Flavor the cream (or milk) by heating it with:
♦ 1 cinnamon stick

♦ 1 vanilla bean, split lengthwise

♦ 2 strips orange or lemon zest

♦ cardamom seeds

For more flavor, depending on the other flavorings you have used, add to the custard:
♦ 2 teaspoons pure vanilla extract

♦ ½ teaspoon pure almond extract

♦ 1 teaspoon rum extract

♦ 4 ounces bittersweet chocolate, chopped

♦ 1 cup raspberry, strawberry, peach, cherry or other fruit puree. Use 1 cup less cream (or milk) and add the puree to the custard after it is cooked.

Rich Raspberry Ice Cream

Close your eyes when you taste this ice cream, and you'll think you are standing in the middle of a raspberry patch eating juicy, sweet, just-picked berries right off the bush. The flavors are clean and true, despite the fact that the ice cream is conveniently made from store-bought frozen berries. A bowl of this ice cream needs no adornment—just a spoon.

2 **10-ounce boxes frozen raspberries in light syrup, thawed**

2 **cups heavy cream**

4 **large egg yolks**

½ **cup sugar**

1. Puree the raspberries in a food processor. Press through a strainer set over a bowl, pressing down on the puree with a spoon to squeeze out all the juices. With a rubber spatula, scrape the puree from the outside of the strainer into the bowl.

2. Heat the cream in a small saucepan just until small bubbles appear around the edges; do not boil.

3. Meanwhile, combine the egg yolks and sugar in the top of a double boiler or a heatproof bowl that will sit over a saucepan of water and whisk, off the heat, until light in color and thick.

4. Gradually stir the hot cream into the yolks. Set the top of the double boiler or bowl over 1 inch of simmering water. Cook, stirring constantly, until the custard coats the back of the spoon, about 15 minutes. Remove from the heat; stir in the raspberry puree. Transfer to a large bowl. Set the bowl in a larger bowl half filled with ice. Refrigerate, covered, for at least 4 and up to 24 hours.

5. Transfer to an ice-cream maker and freeze according to the manufacturer's directions.

Makes about 1 quart

Classic Brandy Eggnog

Eggnog made from scratch is far superior to the supermarket variety. Many people, though, have never tasted the real thing and don't realize what they're missing. This recipe cooks the eggs in a custard, so it can safely be made a day ahead. The texture is silken and the flavor is rich, laced with just the right amount of brandy.

4 cups whole milk

6 large eggs

⅓ cup sugar

   Pinch of kosher salt

1 teaspoon pure vanilla extract

1 cup heavy cream

½ cup brandy, or more to taste

   Ground cinnamon

   Freshly grated nutmeg

1. Heat the milk in a small saucepan until small bubbles appear around the edges; do not boil. Remove from the heat.

2. In a large saucepan, combine the eggs, sugar and salt and whisk until very well blended. Gradually stir in 2 cups of the hot milk. Cook, stirring constantly, over low heat until the mixture is thick enough to coat the back of the spoon with a thin film (it should register 160°F on an instant-read thermometer), about 10 minutes.

3. Remove from the heat and stir in the remaining 2 cups milk and the vanilla. Place the pan in a bowl of cold water and stir until cooled. Cover and refrigerate until thoroughly chilled, at least several hours, or overnight.

4. Just before serving, beat the cream in a large bowl with an electric mixer until soft peaks form. Stir the brandy into the chilled milk mixture, then gently fold in the whipped cream.

5. Pour into a small punch bowl. Sprinkle with cinnamon and nutmeg and serve.

Makes twelve ½-cup servings

Mom's Eggnog Tonic

 I was a thin child, which, to my mother, could only mean that I wasn't healthy. Her solution was eggnog, not the boozy Christmas beverage but a delicious, fortifying 1950s version of a smoothie. It recalls that carefree time when no one worried about eating raw eggs.

Mom's eggnog recipe went like this: Place a whole egg, cold milk, a spoonful of sugar and a drop of vanilla extract in a large bowl with a pouring spout. Beat vigorously with a hand-held rotary beater. Pour into a tall glass and serve with a straw.

Although I remained a skinny kid, Mom was at least satisfied that I was properly nourished.

CHAPTER 13   *Elegant Meringues and Sweet Soufflés*

"This recipe is certainly silly. It says to separate the eggs, but it doesn't say how far to separate them."
—GRACIE ALLEN

As a teenage waitress in my Uncle Joe's diner, I thought I knew all about meringues: God knows how many pieces of lemon meringue and chocolate meringue pie I cut and served to our regular customers. But after I went to the "Big City" of Manhattan and became a pastry chef, I discovered a world of meringues—and other desserts based on whipped egg whites—far more intriguing than the thick, sweet layer of foam that topped the pies back home in Milton, New York. This chapter is a celebration of that airy realm in which egg whites are transformed into sweets of impossible lightness and luscious texture: melt-in-your-mouth cookies; elegant layered constructions of baked meringues, creams and fruits; and soufflés with dramatic height and dreamy consistency.

At the heart of these desserts is a physical transformation that is so simple, we often forget how amazing it is. With just a couple of minutes of whisking, we can turn a gloppy puddle of raw egg white into a glistening white tower of foam. What we're doing, of course, is incorporating air into the liquid whites, producing a mass of small bubbles. As we whip, the protein-rich (and fat-free) egg-white molecules coagulate to form stable, opaque walls around each tiny pocket of air.

Many of the techniques you will find in the following recipes are designed to preserve the lightness and loveliness of this foamy network. (You may want to review the tips for whipping egg whites on page 313.) To get the greatest volume of meringue, use room-temperature egg whites. A bit of acid—in the form of cream of tartar—helps to stabilize the foam and prevent it from becoming overbeaten and losing volume. Sugar beaten into the whites not only provides sweetness but helps specific proteins coagulate during cooking, forming a solid network as the moisture evaporates. And, for baked meringues, the oven is kept at a relatively low temperature so that the meringues dry slowly and thoroughly, resulting in a crisp texture and light color.

Baked meringues, plain or flavored with nuts, can be made into crunchy cookies, shaped into cups to hold ice cream or piped into the classic delicate circles called dacquoise and layered with whipped cream and fresh berries. In this chapter, you'll also find recipes for soft meringues floating on custard as well as one for an old-fashioned fluffy frosting made by beating sugar syrup into beaten whites.

Like meringues, the sweet soufflés in this chapter depend on the power of whipped egg whites to elevate a flavorful base into a high-rising treat. Unlike meringues, however, the expansion is rather fleeting, since the moist network of egg proteins and the starch in the base of the soufflé never become solid. The big rise takes place in the oven as the air pockets expand. Don't feel deflated when your soufflé sinks at the table: it has to collapse a bit as you open it up and it cools off. The trick for maximum drama and deliciousness is in the timing. Plan the mixing, baking and serving of a dessert soufflé to coordinate with the meal it accompanies—make sure that you're free to monitor its progress and that your guests are ready to eat the soufflé when it is perfectly risen.

Remember, a soufflé waits for no one. If you're in a rush, the Raspberry Soufflés (page 402) need only about 10 minutes in the oven. But even the ones that bake for a half-hour or more—banana, mocha and lemon—are worth the wait.

Yes, You Can Freeze Those Egg Whites

 Frozen leftover egg whites make excellent meringue. Freeze in a plastic container marked with the date and the number of whites. Or freeze the whites individually in an ice-cube tray and, when firm, transfer to tightly sealed freezer bags.

Chocolate Kisses

These crunchy little meringue cookies flavored with toasted hazelnuts, cocoa powder and ground cinnamon are known as *spumette* in Sicily. They're a favorite in Italian pastry shops in New York City's Little Italy. The late Richard Sax, beloved colleague and friend, shared this recipe with me many years ago.

1½ cups hazelnuts

1 cup plus 2 tablespoons confectioners' sugar

3 tablespoons unsweetened cocoa powder

¼ teaspoon ground cinnamon

3 large egg whites, at room temperature

Pinch of kosher salt

1. Preheat the oven to 350°F. Spread the hazelnuts in a shallow baking pan and lightly toast in the oven, 10 to 15 minutes. Spread a clean kitchen towel on the counter and empty the hot nuts onto the towel. Let stand until cool. Reduce the oven temperature to 300°F.

2. Rub the hazelnuts with the towel to remove the loosened skins. Coarsely chop the nuts and set aside.

3. Butter and flour three baking sheets. Sift together the confectioners' sugar, cocoa powder and cinnamon. Set aside.

4. Beat the egg whites and salt in a large bowl with an electric mixer until the whites form stiff but not dry peaks. In three additions, sprinkle the sugar mixture over the whites and fold in gently. Sprinkle with the hazelnuts and gently fold to combine.

5. Drop the batter by level tablespoons about 2 inches apart onto the prepared baking sheets. Bake until dry to the touch but still soft, 14 to 15 minutes. Using a thin spatula, transfer the still warm cookies to a rack to cool.

Makes 36 cookies

Hazelnut Meringue Cookies

These crisp, delicate meringues melt in your mouth. They are similar to the Italian meringue cookie called *ossi di morto*, or "bones of the dead." Serve the cookies with coffee after dinner or with a fruity sorbet or another light dessert.

2 **large egg whites, at room temperature**

⅛ **teaspoon cream of tartar**

⅓ **cup sugar**

½ **teaspoon pure vanilla extract**

⅓ **cup hazelnuts, toasted and coarsely chopped**

1. Preheat the oven to 250°F. Lightly butter a large baking sheet and line it with parchment paper.

2. Place the egg whites and cream of tartar in a large bowl and beat with an electric mixer until the whites form soft peaks. Add the sugar, 1 tablespoon at a time, beating until the whites form stiff, smooth peaks. Sprinkle the vanilla and hazelnuts over the meringue and gently fold in with a rubber spatula to blend.

3. Drop the meringue by rounded tablespoons about 2 inches apart onto the prepared baking sheet. Flatten each blob of meringue with the back of the spoon or a flat spatula, spreading it into a flat 1½-inch disk and making sure there is at least one piece of hazelnut in the center.

4. Bake for 1½ to 2 hours until dry but still slightly soft. Cool the cookies on the pan set on a rack. The meringues will turn crisp as they cool. Remove with a spatula when cool. Store in an airtight container. (If the cookies become sticky, place them on a baking sheet and crisp in a 300°F oven for 10 minutes.)

Makes about 30 cookies

TO TOAST HAZELNUTS:
Preheat the oven to 350°F. Spread the hazelnuts in a shallow baking pan. Bake until lightly toasted, 10 to 15 minutes. Spread on a clean kitchen towel and let cool. Rub briskly with the towel to remove the skins. Or place the cooled nuts in a large strainer and rub briskly until the skins are loosened.

Meringue Cups

Meringues shaped into cups or small bowls make a lovely dessert when filled with ice cream and topped with fresh berries or other fruit. Try these with ice cream or sorbet and sliced peaches and blueberries, fresh figs and raspberries or a mixture of red currants, raspberries, blueberries and blackberries. The fruits should be sweetened with a very light hand, if at all.

6 **large egg whites, at room temperature**

¼ **teaspoon cream of tartar**

¼ **teaspoon kosher salt**

¾ **cup sugar**

¾ **cup superfine sugar**

1 **teaspoon pure vanilla extract**

1. Preheat the oven to 250°F. Line two large baking sheets with parchment paper or foil. Using a 2-to-2½-inch template (no larger, or the meringues won't bake properly), draw 12 circles on the parchment paper or foil. (Use a glass or a cookie cutter as a template.)

2. In a large bowl, combine the egg whites, cream of tartar and salt and beat with an electric mixer until soft peaks form. Combine the sugars and add them 1 table-spoon at a time to the whites, beating, until the whites are glossy and very stiff and the sugar has dissolved. (A small amount of meringue rubbed between your fingers should feel smooth.) Beat in the vanilla.

3. Fill a large pastry bag fitted with a large plain or star tip and pipe the meringue in a tight coil within each outline on the baking sheets. If you want, you can pipe an extra circle on top of the outermost circle of each to form a shallow meringue cup. Or, using the back of a tablespoon, spread the meringues within the circles. If using a tablespoon, make a hollow in the center of each meringue.

4. Bake for 1 hour, or until the meringues are creamy white and firm to the touch. Turn off the oven and let the meringues sit in the oven for at least 2 hours, or overnight, to dry out.

Raspberry Sauce (page 364) and Chocolate Brandy Sauce (page 414) are good toppings for the ice cream or sorbet, instead of or in addition to the fruit.

5. Store in a large airtight container. (If, for some reason, the meringues soften, place them on a baking sheet in a 300°F oven for 10 to 15 minutes. They will dry out and become crisp again.)

Makes 24 cups

Dacquoise with Lemon Curd and Strawberries

Dacquoise (also called *broyage*) refers to any meringue that has ground nuts added to it. In this rendition, the meringue is flavored with finely ground almonds. Dacquoise uses less sugar than other hard meringues, making it more compatible with other ingredients when you're creating new desserts. Here I layer it with a tangy lemon curd, stiffly whipped cream and sliced strawberries. This is a special dessert, but it's also easy, because the lemon curd and meringues can be made ahead and then assembled just before serving.

Dacquoise

- 4 **large egg whites, at room temperature**
- ⅛ **teaspoon cream of tartar**
- **Pinch of kosher salt**
- 1 **teaspoon pure vanilla extract**
- 1 **cup sugar**
- ⅓ **cup blanched almonds, finely ground**
- ⅓ **cup sifted cornstarch**

- **Lemon Curd (page 369)**
- 2 **cups heavy cream**
- ½ **teaspoon pure vanilla extract**
- 2 **pints fresh strawberries, rinsed**

1. **Make the dacquoise:** Preheat the oven to 325°F. Line two large baking sheets with parchment paper and, using a 9-inch round cake pan as a guide, trace a total of 3 circles on the paper with a pencil.

2. In a large bowl, combine the egg whites, cream of tartar, salt and vanilla and beat with an electric mixer until the whites form soft peaks. Beat in ¾ cup of the sugar 1 tablespoon at a time, until the whites are glossy and very stiff and dull and the sugar has dissolved. (A small amount of meringue rubbed between your fingers should feel smooth.)

3. In a small bowl, combine the remaining ¼ cup sugar, the almonds and cornstarch. Sprinkle over the meringue and gently fold in until blended.

4. Using a small spatula, spread the meringue within the circles. Or spoon the meringue into a large pastry bag fitted with a ½-inch plain tip. Starting in the center of each circle and holding the tip about 1 inch above the baking sheet, pipe a long, tight coil of meringue to fill the circle and make a solid round.

5. Bake for 35 to 40 minutes, or until dried to the touch but not colored. Cool in the pan on racks. Using the tip of a spatula, release the 3 rounds from the parchment paper. The meringues can be stored, wrapped in plastic or aluminum foil, for several days.

6. Make the lemon curd; set aside.

7. To assemble the dessert, reserve 8 whole berries with hulls for the garnish, then slice the remaining berries. Combine the cream and vanilla in a medium bowl and beat into stiff peaks. Place one round of dacquoise on a serving plate smooth side down. Spread with half the lemon curd and one-third of the whipped cream. Arrange one-half of the sliced strawberries randomly on top of the cream. Add the second round of dacquoise smooth side down. Spread with the remaining lemon curd, one-third of the whipped cream and the remaining sliced strawberries and top with the remaining dacquoise. Spread with the remaining whipped cream and the whole strawberries. Serve at once, or refrigerate until ready to serve. The meringues will become less crisp if they are refrigerated, but actually, I prefer them that way.

Makes 6 to 8 servings

> **The dacquoise can be made into either 3 large rounds or small individual rounds. It will make 30 small (3-inch) meringues for 10 servings. If making individual meringues, double the recipe for lemon curd and use 3 cups heavy cream and 3 pints strawberries.**

Individual Hazelnut Dacquoises with Whipped Cream and Raspberries

Layered with puffs of whipped cream, topped with raspberries and covered with sieved confectioners' sugar, these crunchy little meringues are ethereal in both looks and taste.

Dacquoise

- 4 **large egg whites, at room temperature**
- 2 **teaspoons pure vanilla extract**
- ½ **teaspoon cream of tartar**
- 1 **cup superfine sugar**
- 1 **cup hazelnuts, toasted (page 388) and coarsely ground**

- 1½ **cups heavy cream**
- 3 **tablespoons confectioners' sugar, plus more for sprinkling**
- 1 **teaspoon pure vanilla extract**
- 1½ **pints raspberries**

1. **Make the dacquoise:** Preheat the oven to 250°F. Line a large baking sheet with parchment paper and, using a 3-inch round cookie cutter as a guide, trace 24 circles on the paper with a pencil.

2. In a large bowl, combine the egg whites, vanilla and cream of tartar and beat with an electric mixer until the whites form soft peaks. Beat in ½ cup of the superfine sugar 1 tablespoon at a time, until the whites are very stiff and dull and the sugar has dissolved. (A small amount of meringue rubbed between your fingers should feel smooth.) Combine the remaining ½ cup sugar and the nuts in a small bowl and add to the meringue. Gently fold in until blended.

3. Using a small spatula, spread the meringue within the circles. Or spoon the meringue into a large pastry bag fitted with a ½-inch plain tip. Starting in the center of each circle and holding the tip about 1 inch above the baking sheet, pipe a tight coil of meringue to fill the circle and make a solid round.

4. Bake until dry to the touch and a pale cream color, about 1 hour. Turn off the oven and let the meringues sit in the oven for at least 1 hour, or overnight, to dry out. When the meringues are cool, store in an airtight container until ready to use. (The meringues will keep for about 1 week.)

If your meringues become soft when stored, dry them out again in a 300°F oven for 10 to 15 minutes, or until crisp.

5. To assemble the dessert, whip the cream with the confectioners' sugar and vanilla until stiff. Place 1 meringue on each of eight plates. Spread each meringue with a thin layer of whipped cream. Top with one-half of the raspberries. Place another meringue on top of each and repeat the layers of whipped cream and raspberries. Top with the remaining meringues and sprinkle generously with confectioners' sugar. Serve at once, or refrigerate until ready to serve, up to several hours.

Makes 8 servings

Floating Island (Oeufs à la Neige)

This dish is a triumph of contrasting textures: cloudlike meringue "eggs" (*oeufs* in French) floating in a rich custard sauce, topped with tasty, brittle threads of caramelized sugar.

3 cups milk

1 vanilla bean, split lengthwise

1 cinnamon stick

4 large egg whites, at room temperature

1 cup sugar

About 1 cup heavy cream or half-and-half

8 large egg yolks

Caramelized Sugar Threads (page 397; optional)

1. Combine the milk, vanilla bean and cinnamon stick in a large skillet. Heat just until small bubbles appear around the edges; do not boil. Remove from the heat, cover and steep for 15 minutes.

2. Meanwhile, to make the meringues, beat the egg whites in a large bowl until foamy. Beat in ½ cup of the sugar ½ tablespoon at a time, until the egg whites are thick and glossy.

3. Reheat the milk mixture over low heat until it is barely simmering. Using a large spoon, add 4 rounded spoonfuls of meringue to the simmering milk. Poach, uncovered, for 2 minutes. Gently turn each meringue and poach for 2 minutes more. Place a double thickness of paper towels on a large plate and, using a slotted spoon, transfer the meringues to the plate. Repeat with the remaining meringue, making 4 more meringues. Cover and refrigerate until ready to serve.

4. Remove the vanilla bean and the cinnamon stick from the milk and pour the milk into a large glass measuring cup. Add enough cream or half-and-half to measure 3½ cups. With the tip of a teaspoon, scrape the seeds from the vanilla pod and set aside. Discard the pod and the cinnamon stick.

5. Heat the milk mixture in the top of a double boiler directly over low heat. In another large bowl, combine the egg yolks and the remaining ½ cup sugar and whisk to blend. Gradually whisk the hot milk mixture into the yolks until blended. Return to the top of the double boiler.

6. Pour 1 inch of water into the bottom of the double boiler and bring to a boil; reduce the heat to a gentle simmer. Set the top of the double boiler over the bottom and cook the custard mixture, stirring constantly, until thickened enough to lightly coat the back of a spoon, 15 to 20 minutes. Remove from the heat; strain; stir in the vanilla seeds. Chill by setting the bowl into a larger bowl half-full of ice water. Stir until the custard is lukewarm. Refrigerate until cold, about 2 hours.

7. To serve, ladle the custard sauce into 8 deep bowls and top each with a meringue. Or, for a grander presentation, pour the sauce into a large, shallow serving bowl and float the meringues in the sauce. Serve with Caramelized Sugar Threads, if desired.

Makes 8 servings

Both the meringues and the custard sauce can be made several hours ahead and refrigerated, making this a great dessert for a large group.

Caramelized Sugar Threads

½ cup sugar

1 tablespoon water

1 teaspoon fresh lemon juice

Before you begin, top the custard sauce with the meringues, ready to serve. In a small, heavy skillet, combine the sugar, water and lemon juice. Heat over medium-low heat, without stirring, until the sugar dissolves and turns amber. Remove from the heat and carefully but quickly drizzle the syrup over the custard and meringues, moving the skillet back and forth to make thin "threads" of sugar. The caramel will turn hard and brittle almost instantly.

Meringue Frosting

This type of cooked meringue is sometimes called Italian meringue. Its stark white color makes a stunning contrast to a dark chocolate cake, and its sweetness is the perfect foil for the dense bitter chocolate notes. It's a recipe that seems to have a place in everybody's childhood memories. When I was a kid, we called it fluffy white frosting. Prepare this frosting just before you plan to use it.

½ **cup plus 2 tablespoons sugar**

½ **cup hot water**

3 **large egg whites, at room temperature**

½ **teaspoon pure vanilla extract**

1. In a medium saucepan, combine ½ cup of the sugar and the water (do not stir). Heat, without stirring, over medium-high heat until the sugar is dissolved. Bring to a boil, brushing down the sides of the pan with a pastry brush dipped in water to dissolve any sugar crystals clinging to the pan, and boil until the temperature reaches 240°F on a candy thermometer, 6 to 8 minutes. (This is called the "soft ball" stage: a small bit of the syrup dropped into ice water will form a soft ball.)

2. Meanwhile, beat the egg whites in a large bowl with an electric mixer on medium speed until soft peaks form. Increase the speed to high and beat in the remaining 2 tablespoons sugar 1 teaspoon at a time, until the whites are stiff and glossy.

3. While beating the whites, add the boiling syrup in a slow, steady stream near the sides of the bowl so it doesn't get into the beaters and spatter. Continue beating until the meringue has cooled completely, about 5 minutes. Beat in the vanilla. Frost the cake with the meringue immediately.

Makes enough frosting for one 13-x-9-inch cake or two 8-to-9-inch layer cakes

Alice Medrich's Cooked Meringue

This recipe is based on a technique developed by cookbook author and pastry chef extraordinaire Alice Medrich. The soft meringues traditionally used to top pies and other desserts are not baked long enough for the interior temperature to destroy any harmful bacteria that might be (although rarely is) present in the whites. With this method, however, the egg whites are cooked to 160°F before they are baked, ensuring their safety.

2 **tablespoons water**

½ **teaspoon cream of tartar**

4 **large egg whites**

½ **cup sugar**

1. Bring 1 inch of water to a gentle simmer in a large skillet. Combine the 2 tablespoons water and the cream of tartar in a medium stainless steel bowl. Add the egg whites and sugar and whisk briskly to combine thoroughly and break up any clots of egg white (which have a tendency to scramble). Place an instant-read thermometer in a cup of very hot water near the stove.

2. Set the bowl in the skillet. Stir the egg-white mixture briskly and constantly with a rubber spatula, scraping the bottom and sides of the bowl often to avoid scrambling the whites. After 1 minute, remove the bowl from the skillet. Quickly insert the thermometer, tilting the bowl to cover the stem by at least 2 inches. If the temperature is less than 160°F, rinse the stem of the thermometer in the hot water in the skillet and return to the cup of hot water. Put the bowl back in the skillet and stir as before until the temperature reaches 160°F when the bowl is removed.

3. Using an electric mixer, beat the egg whites on high speed until cool and stiff.

4. Swirl over the top of a pie or tart, being careful that the meringue seals the edges of the crust, before baking.

Makes enough to cover a 9-to-10-inch pie or tart

To make this recipe, you will need an instant-read thermometer.

Lemon Soufflés with Lemon Sauce

Lemon soufflé is sturdiest when a basic vanilla soufflé base is used and lemon zest is added for flavor. To reinforce the lemon flavor, I pour a sweet-tart lemon sauce over each serving or ladle it into the center of individual soufflés.

3 tablespoons unsalted butter, plus more for the dishes

¼ cup sugar, plus more for the dishes

2 tablespoons all-purpose flour

¾ cup milk, heated

4 large eggs, separated, plus 1 large egg white, at room temperature

1 tablespoon finely grated lemon zest

1 tablespoon fresh lemon juice

½ teaspoon pure vanilla extract

¼ teaspoon cream of tartar

Lemon Sauce (recipe follows)

1. Place a rack in the center of the oven and preheat the oven to 400°F. Generously butter five 4-to-5-ounce ramekins; sprinkle with sugar, shaking out the excess. Refrigerate the dishes until ready to fill and bake.

2. In a large saucepan, melt the butter over low heat. Stir in the flour and cook, stirring, for 2 to 3 minutes. Remove from the heat and whisk in the milk and the ¼ cup sugar until smooth. Return to the heat and cook over medium heat until the mixture comes to a boil and thickens, about 5 minutes. Remove from the heat and let stand, stirring occasionally, until lukewarm. Transfer to a large bowl.

3. Beat the egg yolks one at a time into the milk mixture. Stir in the lemon zest and juice and the vanilla.

4. Place the egg whites and cream of tartar in a large bowl and beat with an electric mixer until stiff peaks form. With a large spatula, fold about one-third of the egg whites into the yolk mixture, then add the remaining whites, folding very gently but thoroughly.

5. Pour into the prepared ramekins. Arrange on a baking sheet and place in the oven; immediately reduce the oven temperature to 375°F. Bake for 12 to 15 minutes, or until puffed and set. Serve immediately, with the lemon sauce.

Makes 5 servings

Lemon Sauce

½ cup sugar

1 tablespoon cornstarch

1 cup cold water

2 teaspoons grated
   lemon zest

⅓ cup strained fresh
   lemon juice

2 tablespoons unsalted
   butter

In a small saucepan, stir the sugar and corn-starch until blended. Slowly stir in the water until smooth. Cook over medium-low heat, stirring gently, until the mixture boils. Add the lemon zest and juice, then stir in the butter until melted. Serve warm. The sauce can be made ahead and refrigerated for 2 days and reheated.

Makes about 1½ cups

Raspberry Soufflés

In the 1970s, an innovative Swiss chef named Fredy Girardet introduced a lighter, more delicate soufflé made without the flour-and-milk base.

5   half-pints raspberries or two 10-ounce boxes frozen raspberries in juice, thawed

⅓   cup plus 2 tablespoons sugar, plus more for the dishes

1   teaspoon fresh lemon juice, or more to taste

3   large eggs, separated, plus 1 large egg white, at room temperature

¼   teaspoon cream of tartar

   Confectioners' sugar for sprinkling

I find that these soufflés bake more evenly and hold up longer if they are prepared in individual dishes. Pour a spoonful of the thick raspberry sauce into each soufflé before serving.

1. Puree the raspberries in a food processor and press through a strainer into a bowl. Discard the solids. Set aside 1 cup puree for the soufflé. To make the raspberry sauce, stir 2 tablespoons of the sugar into the remaining puree until dissolved and add the lemon juice. Refrigerate until ready to serve.

2. Place a rack in the center of the oven and preheat the oven to 375°F. Generously butter six 4-to-5-ounce ramekins. Sprinkle the dishes with sugar and shake out the excess. Refrigerate the dishes until ready to fill and bake.

3. In a large bowl, beat the egg whites and cream of tartar with an electric mixer until foamy. Gradually add the remaining ⅓ cup sugar 1 tablespoon at a time, and beat until stiff peaks form.

4. Whisk the egg yolks in a large bowl, then whisk in the reserved 1 cup puree until blended. Gently fold in half of the egg whites until blended. Add the remaining egg whites and fold until blended

5. Spoon into the prepared ramekins. Place on a baking sheet and bake until the soufflés rise 1 inch over the rims of the dishes, 12 to 14 minutes.

6. Immediately sprinkle the top of each soufflé lightly with confectioners' sugar. With a large spoon, make a slit in the top of each soufflé and spoon in some raspberry sauce. Serve at once.

Makes 6 servings

Mocha Soufflé with Hazelnut Crème Anglaise

This soufflé contains both semisweet chocolate and cocoa powder and is flavored with instant espresso powder. The top is chewy, the inside soft and airy. You could also serve it with Caramel Pecan Sauce (page 405).

½ **cup sugar, plus more for the soufflé dish**

6 **ounces semisweet chocolate**

6 **large eggs, separated, at room temperature**

2 **tablespoons instant espresso powder**

1 **tablespoon boiling water**

½ **teaspoon pure vanilla extract**

2 **tablespoons unsweetened cocoa powder**

Pinch of kosher salt

½ **teaspoon cream of tartar**

Confectioners' sugar for sprinkling (optional)

Hazelnut Crème Anglaise (page 371) or softly whipped heavy cream

1. Place a rack in the center of the oven and preheat the oven to 450°F. Generously butter a 6-cup soufflé dish; sprinkle with sugar and shake out the excess.

2. Place the chocolate in the top of a double boiler or in a metal bowl set over a saucepan of simmering water and heat, without stirring, until melted; then stir until smooth. Remove from the heat.

3. In a large bowl, whisk the egg yolks and ¼ cup of the sugar until blended. In a small bowl, combine the espresso powder and boiling water. Add the melted chocolate and the espresso to the yolk mixture and stir until blended and the sugar is dissolved. Stir in the vanilla and set aside.

4. Sift the remaining ¼ cup sugar, the cocoa powder and salt onto a sheet of waxed paper. Place the egg whites in a large bowl and beat with an electric mixer on medium-low speed until foamy. Add the cream of tartar and continue beating on medium speed until the whites are just beginning to make soft mounds. Beat in the cocoa mixture 1 tablespoon at a time, gradually increasing the speed. Beat until the whites form smooth, glossy stiff peaks.

5. Carefully fold a spoonful of the egg-white mixture into the yolk mixture until thoroughly blended. Add the remaining egg-white mixture and fold in gently, leaving a few streaks of whites in the chocolate base.

6. Spoon into the prepared soufflé dish, smoothing the top. Bake for 10 minutes. Reduce the oven temperature to 350°F and bake until puffed, about 20 minutes more.

7. Remove the soufflé from the oven and immediately sprinkle with confectioners' sugar, if desired. Spoon the soufflé onto dessert plates, including some of the outer crust and the soft center in each serving. Serve topped with the Hazelnut Crème Anglaise or whipped cream.

Makes 4 to 6 servings

Banana Soufflés with Caramel Pecan Sauce

Light as air but with the familiar flavor of ripe banana, these little soufflés are perfect topped with a drizzle of caramel sauce dotted with chopped toasted pecans. For intense banana flavor, use a banana that is very ripe.

Caramel Pecan Sauce

- 1 **cup packed light brown sugar**
- 8 **tablespoons (1 stick) unsalted butter, cut into small pieces**
- ½ **cup heavy cream**
- ½ **cup pecans, toasted (page 56) and coarsely chopped**

Banana Soufflés

- ¼ **cup sugar, plus more for the soufflé dishes**
- 3 **tablespoons unsalted butter**
- 2 **tablespoons all-purpose flour**
- ¾ **cup milk, heated**
- 1 **large ripe banana, peeled**
- 1 **tablespoon fresh lemon juice**
- 4 **large eggs, separated, plus 1 large egg white, at room temperature**
- 2 **teaspoons pure vanilla extract**
- ¼ **teaspoon cream of tartar**

1. **Make the caramel pecan sauce:** Combine the brown sugar, butter and cream in a small, heavy saucepan and bring to a boil, stirring constantly. Simmer over medium-low heat until thickened, about 8 minutes. Remove from the heat and fold in the pecans. Serve warm or at room temperature. Reheat just before serving.

2. **Make the soufflés:** Place a rack in the center of the oven and preheat the oven to 400°F. Generously butter six 4-to-5-ounce soufflé dishes; sprinkle with sugar and shake out the excess.

3. In a large saucepan, melt the butter over low heat. Stir in the flour and cook, stirring, for 2 to 3 minutes. Remove from the heat and whisk in the milk and ¼ cup sugar until smooth. Return to the heat and cook, stirring, until thickened, about 3 minutes. Remove from the heat and let stand, stirring occasionally, until lukewarm. Transfer to a large bowl.

4. Mash the banana with the lemon juice in a small bowl. Beat the egg yolks one at a time into the milk mixture. Stir in the banana mixture and the vanilla.

5. Place the egg whites and cream of tartar in a large bowl and beat with an electric mixer until stiff peaks form. With a large spatula, fold about one-third of the egg whites into the yolk mixture, then add the remaining whites and fold in very gently but thoroughly.

Make the sauce 1 or 2 days in advance. Reheat, stirring, over low heat just before serving.

6. Pour into the prepared ramekins. Arrange on a baking sheet and place in the oven; immediately reduce the oven temperature to 375°F. Bake for 12 to 15 minutes, or until the soufflés are puffed and set to the desired doneness. Serve immediately, passing the caramel pecan sauce for drizzling over the tops.

Makes 6 servings

CHAPTER 14   *Cookies, Cakes, Pies and Tarts*

"The egg is to cuisine what the article is to speech."
—ANONYMOUS

My love of baking began with the heavenly Saturdays I spent as a child in the kitchen with Nana—my maternal grandmother, Antoinette Abbruzzese—learning to mix and roll pie dough, crack and separate eggs and whip up cake batters and icings.

These long afternoons did not seem like cooking lessons but playtime full of magical transformations. As I watched Nana create sweets of all sorts from eggs, flour, butter and sugar—nimbly freeing egg yolks from their cloak of white, creaming butter and sugar and heaping meringues on top of pies—I was impressed with her ease and intuitiveness in the kitchen and the heartfelt happiness with which she baked. And it thrilled me when she approved of what I did, when she told me I had "little hands of gold."

I'm also happy to offer these recipes as a grand finale to the "eggsploration" throughout this book. Although the role of eggs in cakes and pies is not as obvious as it is in custards, meringues and soufflés, almost every type of cake and most pies and tarts depend on egg power for fine taste and texture.

In some of the recipes here, eggs contribute in rather subtle ways. My favorite tart dough, for instance, owes its incredible richness to the single egg yolk that binds the flour and butter together. A multitextured treat like Mocha Meringue Pie in Cookie Crust uses eggs in both the creamy mocha layer and the shimmering crown of whipped meringue that tops it.

I've created desserts with several types of cake, and in each of them, eggs are handled in a different way to provide leavening and distinctive texture. The heavenly lightness (and whiteness) of Lemon Angel Food Cake comes exclusively from a great volume of beaten egg whites. Spiced Sponge Roll with Maple Cream Filling and Walnut Praline, on the other hand, incorporates separately beaten egg yolks as well as whipped whites to give a richer flavor and a golden cast to the cake crumb. The French version of sponge cake, called génoise, whips up warmed whole eggs to achieve a marvelously high froth, into which clarified butter and a small amount of flour are folded. My version adds cocoa powder, too, for a luscious Chocolate Génoise with Meringue Frosting.

For us dedicated home bakers, these desserts are a good lesson that our "hands of gold" owe a great deal to the magical effects that eggs lend to almost all our creations.

Tender Egg Yolk Cookies

Jim Concannon, the grandson of the founder of the Concannon Winery, in Livermore, California, which is celebrating 116 years of continuous production, tells the story of these egg yolk cookies: "My father would buy large quantities of eggs from local chicken ranchers. The whites were used to clarify the wine and the yolks went to the kitchen, where my mother, Nina, was creative in finding uses for them. My fondest memories are of her egg yolk cookies." I have adapted the recipe slightly, using butter instead of shortening or margarine. The cookies are so delicate, buttery and sweet that they literally melt in your mouth.

2¾ cups all-purpose flour

1 teaspoon baking soda

1 teaspoon cream of tartar

5 large egg yolks

1 teaspoon pure vanilla extract

8 tablespoons (1 stick) unsalted butter, at room temperature

1½ cups sugar

1. Position a rack in the center of the oven and preheat the oven to 350°F. Lightly butter two baking sheets, preferably heavyweight, line with parchment paper and lightly butter the parchment.

2. Sift the flour, baking soda and cream of tartar into a medium bowl. Set aside.

3. Beat the egg yolks in a medium bowl with an electric mixer until thick and pale yellow, 2 to 3 minutes. Add the vanilla and set aside.

4. In a large bowl, beat the butter and sugar until light and fluffy. Add the egg yolks and gently beat until blended. Gently stir in the flour mixture with a wooden spoon until well blended. Do not overmix — the dough should be firm, not sticky.

5. Form the dough into small balls, about ¾ inch in diameter, and place about 1 inch apart on the prepared baking sheets. Bake, one sheet at a time, until golden, 12 to 15 minutes. Cool on the pans on racks, then remove the cookies with a wide spatula.

Makes about 70 cookies

Profiteroles with Chocolate Brandy Sauce

Profiteroles are small cream puffs made from pâte à choux, the same eggy pastry used to make Gougère (page 157). They can be filled with savory or sweet mixtures. These are filled with ice cream and smothered in chocolate sauce.

4 tablespoons (½ stick) unsalted butter, cut into small pieces

1 cup water

2 teaspoons sugar

Pinch of kosher salt

1 cup sifted all-purpose flour

4 large eggs, at room temperature

1 large egg yolk mixed with 1 teaspoon water for egg wash

2 pints Vanilla Bean French Custard Ice Cream (page 376) or best-quality store-bought vanilla ice cream

Chocolate Brandy Sauce (page 414), still warm

1. Position a rack in the center of the oven and preheat the oven to 400°F. Lightly butter two large baking sheets; dust with flour and shake off the excess.

2. Combine the butter, water, sugar and salt in a medium saucepan. Bring to a boil, stirring to melt the butter; remove from the heat. Immediately add the flour and stir vigorously to make a thick paste that cleans the sides of the pan and forms a ball. Transfer to a large bowl. Using a large spoon, break the dough into sections to hasten the cooling. Cool for 5 minutes.

3. Meanwhile, stir the eggs in a bowl until blended. With an electric mixer, gradually beat the eggs into the dough, about 1 tablespoon at a time, beating until thoroughly incorporated. Stop the mixer occasionally and scrape down the sides of the bowl. The paste should be smooth, with a dull satiny sheen, and very thick.

4. Drop the paste by rounded tablespoonfuls onto the prepared baking sheets, about 6 on each sheet, placing them about 2 inches apart. Or, if you prefer, spoon the paste into a large pastry bag fitted with a ½-inch plain round tip and, holding the tip about 1 inch above the baking sheet, pipe out mounds of the paste about 1½ inches in diameter. Lightly brush the egg wash evenly over the tops of the puffs.

5. Bake until the puffs are dark golden brown, 22 to 25 minutes. Open the oven door and stick the point of a small, sharp knife into the side of each puff to release some of the steam. Turn off the oven and close the door; let the puffs dry out in the oven for 10 minutes. Transfer to a rack to cool.

6. To fill the puffs, carefully cut each one in half. Place a rounded scoop of ice cream in the bottom half of each one, reassembling the puffs and placing them on a cookie sheet in the freezer as you fill them. Cover with foil until ready to serve. (The puffs can be assembled up to 1 day ahead.) Or, if you prefer, assemble the puffs just before serving so that the pastry isn't chilled or frozen.

7. Arrange the puffs in shallow dessert bowls. Pass the warm chocolate sauce on the side.

Makes about 12 puffs, or 4 to 6 servings (2 or 3 per serving)

You can fill these cream puffs with Lemon Curd (page 369), a mixture of Lemon Curd and whipped cream, plain vanilla-flavored whipped cream, Vanilla Bean French Custard Ice Cream (page 376), Rich Chocolate Ice Cream (page 377), French Custard Ice Cream (page 378) or Rich Raspberry Ice Cream (page 380).

Chocolate Brandy Sauce

¾ cup packed light brown sugar

6 tablespoons unsweetened cocoa powder

1 cup heavy cream

3 tablespoons unsalted butter

3 ounces bittersweet or semisweet chocolate, chopped

2 tablespoons brandy

¾ teaspoon pure vanilla extract

1. In a small saucepan, combine the brown sugar and cocoa powder. Add the cream and butter and whisk until blended. Cook, whisking, over medium-low heat until the mixture is very hot. Add the chocolate and stir until it is melted and the sauce is smooth. Remove from the heat. Pour through a strainer into a bowl.

2. Cool slightly. Stir in the brandy and vanilla. The sauce can be made ahead, refrigerated for 1 week and reheated.

Makes about 2 cups

Lemon Angel Food Cake

Featherlight angel food cake is the perfect sponge for fresh fruit juices, which is why I like to make it in the summer, when fruit is at its juiciest and most flavorful. Prepare a mélange of berries and sliced peaches and plums. If the fruit is perfect, it won't need another thing, but you could add a sprinkling of superfine sugar or a squirt or two of lemon juice. This cake is perfumed with lemon zest, a perfect match for any fruit topping.

¾ cup sugar

¾ cup confectioners' sugar

12 large egg whites, at room temperature

1½ teaspoons cream of tartar

½ teaspoon kosher salt

2 teaspoons pure vanilla extract

1 cup cake flour, sifted

1 tablespoon finely grated lemon zest

1. Preheat the oven to 325°F. Sift the sugars onto a sheet of waxed paper and set aside.

2. Combine the egg whites, cream of tartar and salt in a large bowl. Beat with an electric mixer until soft peaks form, then beat in the vanilla. Gradually fold in the sugars and then the flour, sprinkling about ¼ cup at a time over the beaten whites and very gently folding in. Fold in the lemon zest.

3. Pour the batter into an ungreased 10-inch tube pan. Bake, without opening the oven door, until the cake is golden and pulls away from the sides of the pan, about 1 hour and 15 minutes. Remove from the oven, invert the tube pan (over a bottle if the pan doesn't have little "legs" around the rim) and let cool thoroughly.

4. Using a knife, loosen the cake from the sides of the pan and the center tube and invert on a serving dish.

5. With a serrated knife, cut the cake in a slow, easy motion.

Makes 10 servings

Serve the cake plain or with a fresh-fruit topping, or frost with whipped cream flavored with vanilla or almond extract.

Fallen Chocolate Soufflé Cake

Made without flour or butter, this moist, tender cake has a pure chocolate flavor. It cuts into neat wedges and makes a lovely dessert served with a mound of softly whipped cream.

8 ounces good-quality semisweet or bittersweet chocolate, coarsely chopped

6 large eggs, separated, at room temperature

½ cup sugar

1 teaspoon pure vanilla extract

⅛ teaspoon cream of tartar

1 cup heavy cream, softly whipped

1. Position a rack in the center of the oven and preheat the oven to 325°F. Lightly butter an 8-inch springform pan.

2. Melt the chocolate in the top of a double boiler over hot water; set aside to cool to room temperature. (Or melt in the microwave for 3 minutes, stirring every 30 seconds, until smooth.)

3. Beat the egg yolks in a large bowl with an electric mixer until thick and light in color. Beat in 6 tablespoons of the sugar 1 tablespoon at a time, until thick and light. Add the chocolate and vanilla and stir until blended. The mixture will be thick.

4. Beat the egg whites in a large bowl with an electric mixer until foamy. Add the cream of tartar. Gradually beat in the remaining 2 tablespoons of the sugar, until the whites form shiny soft peaks. Add one-quarter of the whites to the yolk mixture and fold in until blended. Spoon the remaining whites over the yolk mixture and gently fold in until incorporated.

5. Pour the batter into the prepared pan, smoothing the top. Bake until the top has puffed and is firm to the touch, 35 to 40 minutes. Remove from the oven and cool on a rack. The cake will fall and the edges will crack slightly.

Because the flavor and texture of this cake improve upon standing, I like to make it a day ahead.

6. When the cake is cool, loosen the outside rim of the pan and remove. Wrap the cake loosely with plastic wrap and refrigerate until ready to serve.

7. To serve, cut into wedges and top each with a spoonful of whipped cream.

Makes 8 servings

Chocolate Génoise with Meringue Frosting

Génoise is a lush cake made with whole eggs whipped to a great volume and clarified butter. The contrast of the densely flavored chocolate cake and the stark white frosting is stunning.

8 tablespoons (1 stick) unsalted butter

½ cup all-purpose flour

½ cup unsweetened Dutch-process cocoa powder

6 large eggs, at room temperature

1 cup sugar

1 teaspoon pure vanilla extract
   Meringue Frosting (page 398)

1. **Clarify the butter:** Melt the butter in a small saucepan over low heat and cook until the foam disappears and there is a light brown sediment on the bottom, 4 to 5 minutes. Remove from the heat. Skim any crust from the top and discard. Pour the clear liquid into a small bowl, leaving the sediment in the bottom of the pan; discard the sediment. Set aside to cool to room temperature.

2. Preheat the oven to 350°F. Butter two 9-inch round cake pans. Line the bottoms with parchment paper and lightly flour the sides.

3. Sift together the flour and cocoa powder; set aside.

4. Combine the eggs and sugar in a large metal mixing bowl. Place 1 inch of water in a saucepan large enough to hold the bowl. Heat the water in the saucepan until hot but not boiling. Place the bowl over the hot water and heat the egg mixture, stirring gently to prevent the eggs from cooking on the bottom, until lukewarm, about 3 minutes. Remove from the heat.

5. Beat the egg mixture with an electric mixer on high speed until light, fluffy and almost tripled in volume, 10 to 12 minutes. Sprinkle about one-third of the flour mixture at a time over the beaten-egg mixture and fold in very gently, being careful not to deflate the egg mixture, alternating the flour with the cooled clarified butter and the vanilla. Do not overmix.

6. Pour the batter into the prepared pans. Bake until the cake pulls away from the sides of the pans, about 25 minutes. Cool on a rack.

7. When the layers are cool, loosen each one from the sides of the pan and turn it out onto a clean kitchen towel. Remove the parchment paper. Cool completely before frosting.

8. Place one cake layer on a serving plate and spread 1½ cups of the frosting over it. Place the second layer on top and frost the sides and top with the remaining frosting. Slice into wedges and serve.

Makes 8 to 10 servings

Spiced Sponge Roll
with Maple Cream Filling and Walnut Praline

Sponge cakes are incredibly versatile, and for that reason I make them often. Baked into a sheet and rolled up around whipped cream, lemon curd, chopped fruit or buttercream, they make an impressive, easily assembled dessert. This sponge cake is flavored with ground spices and filled with a maple whipped cream.

Spiced Sponge Cake

- ½ cup sifted all-purpose flour
- ½ cup sifted cornstarch, plus more for dusting the towel
- 1¼ teaspoons ground cinnamon
- ½ teaspoon freshly grated nutmeg
- ¼ teaspoon ground cloves
- 8 large eggs, separated, at room temperature
- ⅛ teaspoon kosher salt
- ½ cup sugar
- 1 teaspoon pure vanilla extract
- ¼ teaspoon pure almond extract

Maple Cream Filling (page 422)

About 6 tablespoons Walnut Praline (page 423)

1. **Make the sponge cake:** Preheat the oven to 375°F. Lightly butter an 18-x-12-inch baking sheet. Line with waxed paper or parchment paper and lightly butter the paper. Sprinkle the paper and sides of the pan with flour. Shake out the excess.

2. Sift the flour, cornstarch, cinnamon, nutmeg and cloves onto a sheet of waxed paper; set aside.

3. In a large bowl, beat the egg whites and salt with an electric mixer on medium speed until soft peaks begin to form. On high speed, beat in the sugar 1 tablespoon at a time, until the egg whites form stiff, glossy peaks.

4. In a medium bowl, whisk the egg yolks and the vanilla and almond extracts until thick and light in color. Fold one-quarter of the beaten egg whites into the yolks until blended. Gradually fold the lightened yolk mixture into the whites. Sift half of the flour mixture over the whites and gently fold to blend. Repeat with the remaining flour mixture, folding gently until blended.

5. Pour the batter into the prepared pan, spreading it to the edges and smoothing the surface with a large spatula. Bake until the cake is golden on top and begins to pull away from the sides of the pan, 10 to 12 minutes; do not overbake.

6. Remove the pan from the oven and immediately loosen the cake from the sides of the pan with a small spatula. Lightly dust a clean towel with cornstarch. Place the towel on the cake, cornstarch side down, and place a rack over the towel. Invert and remove the pan. Let cool.

7. When the cake is cool, peel off the paper. If not filling the cake immediately, roll it up in the towel (from the long side) to keep it moist until you are ready to fill it. (The sponge cake can baked up to 1 day ahead. Wrap the towel-covered roll tightly in foil; store at room temperature.)

8. **To fill and frost the sponge roll:** Unroll the cake (if it was rolled) and spread half of the cream filling over it, leaving a ½-inch border around the edges of the cake. Sprinkle with ¼ cup of the praline. Roll up loosely, so as not to squeeze out the cream, and transfer to a rectangular or oval platter, seam side down. Spread the remaining cream over the roll, leaving the ends exposed. Serve at once, or refrigerate until ready to serve. (The sponge roll can be refrigerated for up to 3 hours before serving.) Sprinkle with a light dusting (about 2 tablespoons) of the praline just before serving.

Makes 10 to 12 servings

Maple Cream Filling

2½ cups heavy cream,
  very cold

¼ cup confectioners'
  sugar

¼ cup maple syrup

1 teaspoon pure vanilla
  extract

½ teaspoon maple
  flavoring (optional)

Whip the cream in a large bowl until soft peaks form. Add the confectioners' sugar and beat until stiff peaks form. Slowly beat in the maple syrup, vanilla and maple flavoring, if using. Cover and refrigerate until ready to use. (The filling can be refrigerated for up to 1 hour before using.)

Makes enough to fill and frost 1 sponge roll

Walnut Praline

This recipe makes more than you need for the sponge roll, but it is easier to make in a larger batch and keeps very well. I like walnuts with the maple cream, but if you prefer, you can use pecans or almonds. Sprinkle the extra praline over ice cream, fruit, cakes or puddings.

1 **cup sugar**

1 **tablespoon fresh lemon juice**

½ **cup coarsely chopped walnuts**

1. Generously butter a 13-x-9-inch baking pan.

2. Combine the sugar and lemon juice in a heavy skillet and stir gently over medium-low heat until the sugar dissolves and turns golden, about 12 minutes. Remove the skillet from the heat; quickly stir in the walnuts and immediately pour into the buttered pan. Let cool thoroughly.

3. Turn the praline out onto a cutting board. Break into small pieces by hitting it hard with the back of a heavy knife or a mallet. Place half of the praline at a time in a food processor and process until powdered. Store in an airtight container at room temperature. (The praline can be stored for up to 2 months.)

Makes about 1½ cups

Lemon Curd Tart with Berries

This pretty fresh-fruit tart is perfect for flavorful summer berries. The pastry and the lemon curd can be made in advance; then all you need do is assemble the tart.

½ cup red currant jelly

1 9-inch Favorite Egg Yolk Pastry shell (opposite page), baked and cooled

Lemon Curd (page 369)

2 cups fresh berries (raspberries, blueberries or thinly sliced strawberries or a mixture)

Confectioners' sugar for sprinkling

1. Place the jelly in a small saucepan and heat, stirring, until melted.

2. Spread a thin layer of the liquefied jelly on the bottom of the cooled pastry crust. Reserve the remaining jelly. Spread the Lemon Curd evenly in the crust.

3. Arrange the berries on top of the lemon curd: whole raspberries and/or blueberries should be placed close to one another, sliced strawberries should be arranged in tight, overlapping rings.

4. Reheat the reserved jelly, then lightly brush the tops of the berries with it. Just before serving, sprinkle the tart lightly with sieved confectioners' sugar.

Makes 6 servings

Favorite Egg Yolk Pastry

There are several reasons this is my favorite pastry. The first is that it is buttery and delicious, like the best homemade butter cookie. It is, in fact, called *pâte sucrée* in France and is used to make cookies as well as tart shells. Another reason I love it is that it can be quickly made in a food processor. And it won't suffer if it is put in the tart pan, covered with plastic and refrigerated for a day or two before baking.

1¼ cups all-purpose flour

2 tablespoons sugar

   Pinch of kosher salt

8 tablespoons (1 stick) unsalted butter, chilled and cut into small pieces

1 large egg yolk

1 teaspoon pure vanilla extract

1. Combine the flour, sugar and salt in a food processor and process to blend. Add the butter bit by bit, pulsing until the mixture forms fine crumbs.

2. In a small bowl, whisk the egg yolk and vanilla together. With the motor running, drizzle the yolk mixture through the feed tube of the food processor just until the pastry forms a ball.

3. Turn the dough out onto a work surface and, with floured hands, lightly gather it together. Flatten into a disk with the palm of your hand and place in a 9-inch tart pan with a removable bottom. With floured fingertips, spread and pat the pastry over the bottom and up the sides of the tart pan. Cover with plastic wrap and refrigerate for at least 1 hour or up to 24 hours.

4. To bake, preheat the oven to 400°F. Cut a round of parchment paper or waxed paper large enough to line the pastry crust and fit it into the pan. Add about 1 cup dried beans or rice to weight the paper down. Bake for 10 minutes. Remove the paper and beans or rice. Reduce the oven temperature to 350°F and continue baking until the bottom is golden, about 15 minutes. Cool completely, then fill as desired.

Makes one 9- or 10-inch tart shell

In this crust, it pays to use the best-quality unsalted butter, for its flavor will truly be appreciated.

Mocha Meringue Pie in Cookie Crust

You get a double dose of chocolate in this creamy pie: a chocolate-cookie crust and a smooth chocolate-custard filling. A splash of espresso and a dash of cinnamon add a sophisticated touch.

Crust

24 **Nabisco Famous chocolate wafers, each broken into about 4 pieces**

2 **tablespoons sugar**

½ **teaspoon ground cinnamon**

4 **tablespoons (½ stick) unsalted butter, melted**

Filling

½ **cup sugar**

¼ **cup unsweetened cocoa powder**

¼ **cup cornstarch**

¼ **teaspoon ground cinnamon**

1 **cup milk**

½ **cup heavy cream**

½ **cup strong brewed espresso**

2 **ounces semisweet chocolate, chopped**

3 **large egg yolks**

1 **teaspoon pure vanilla extract**

1. **Make the crust:** Preheat the oven to 350°F. Place the cookies in a food processor and process to fine crumbs. Combine the cookie crumbs, sugar and cinnamon in a medium bowl; add the butter and stir until well blended. Press over the bottom and up the sides of a 9-inch pie plate, making sure the edges are even. Refrigerate for 20 minutes, or until cold.

2. Bake the crust for 8 minutes. Remove from the oven and let cool.

3. **Make the filling:** In a medium saucepan, combine the sugar, cocoa powder, cornstarch and cinnamon; stir until blended. Gradually stir in the milk, cream, espresso and chocolate. Cook, stirring gently, over medium heat until the mixture boils and thickens.

4. Meanwhile, in a small bowl, whisk the egg yolks until blended. Stir a spoonful of the hot chocolate mixture into the eggs to temper them, then add the yolks to the saucepan. Cook over low heat, stirring, until very thick, about 3 minutes; do not boil. Remove from the heat and let cool slightly, then stir in the vanilla.

5. Scrape the filling into the cooled pie crust. Smooth the surface with a spatula. Refrigerate for about 3 hours, until well chilled.

Meringue
(or substitute Alice Medrich's
Cooked Meringue, page 399)

   3 large egg whites, at room
      temperature

  ¼ teaspoon cream of tartar

   6 tablespoons sugar

6. **Just before serving, make the meringue:** Preheat the oven to 350°F. In a large bowl, beat the egg whites and cream of tartar with an electric mixer until foamy. Gradually beat in the sugar 1 tablespoon at a time, until the whites form stiff, glossy peaks.

7. With a thin spatula, spread half of the meringue over the pie filling, spreading it to the edges. Then add the remaining meringue, mounding it by the spoonful to make soft billowy clouds on top of the pie.

8. Bake until the meringue is lightly browned and heated through, 15 to 20 minutes. If using Alice Medrich's Cooked Meringue, bake for only 8 to 10 minutes, until lightly browned. Let cool. Serve at room temperature.

Makes 6 servings

Lemon Chiffon Tart

Folding lemon curd and meringue together creates a light chiffon effect. The delicate filling is nicely offset by the crisp, buttery crust.

4   **large egg whites, at room temperature**

   Pinch of kosher salt

¼   **cup sugar**

1   **cup Lemon Curd (page 369)**

1   **9-inch Favorite Egg Yolk Pastry shell (page 425), baked and cooled**

1. Preheat the oven to 350°F. Beat the egg whites and salt in a large bowl with an electric mixer until soft peaks form. Beat in the sugar 1 tablespoon at a time, until the whites are stiff and smooth, not grainy. Add the Lemon Curd and gently fold to combine.

2. Spread the lemon filling in the baked shell, mounding it in the center. Bake until the filling is lightly browned, about 15 minutes. Cool on a rack. Serve at room temperature.

Makes 6 servings

The Lemon Curd can be prepared up to 1 week ahead. The unbaked crust can be made a day ahead and refrigerated. The crust is most tender and tasty when baked an hour or two before it is filled with the meringue.

"Un oeuf
is enough."

—Ray Eisenberg

The Last Word on Egg Safety

 Very few eggs are ever infected internally with bacteria. But in the process of handling and cooking, eggs may become contaminated and a potential source for the spread of infection. The bacteria of concern today is *Salmonella enteritidis,* which can cause gastrointestinal illness. It can survive in the hen's internal organs and be transmitted to the egg. Although rare—only 1 in 20,000 eggs is affected—salmonella in eggs is not to be treated lightly. While the symptoms usually last only 24 to 48 hours, they can lead to serious complications in the very young, the elderly, pregnant women and anyone with an immune-system disorder.

Since eggs at room temperature—in fact, anywhere between 40°F and 140°F—provide fertile ground for the rapid multiplication of bacteria, raw eggs and raw-egg products should never be left out of the refrigerator any longer than necessary. Kitchen sanitation will reduce the risk of cross-contamination. *Most important, cooking eggs to a final temperature of 160°F or holding them at a temperature of 140°F for 3½ minutes will destroy any bacteria.* Cooked egg dishes should also be refrigerated if you are making them more than 2 hours ahead. Keep the following basic food-safety precautions in mind:

♦ Wash hands, utensils and work surfaces carefully with hot, soapy water after contact with raw eggs.

♦ Unless you are absolutely sure of the safety and freshness of the eggs you are using, do not serve raw eggs.

♦ Do not serve raw eggs in any form to the very young, the elderly, pregnant women or anyone with a compromised immune system.

♦ To make sure that soft-cooked, poached, basted, fried or coddled eggs are safe, bring them to 140°F for 3½ minutes. At that point, the yolk will be thickened (not hard) and the white will have changed from transparent to solid white.

♦ In general, raw egg whites do not support bacterial growth and are considered safer than raw yolks. But if in doubt, avoid them.

Index